ISBN 978-1-330-85878-3
PIBN 10114783

This book is a reproduction of an important historical work. Forgotten Books uses
state-of-the-art technology to digitally reconstruct the work, preserving the original format
whilst repairing imperfections present in the aged copy. In rare cases, an imperfection in
the original, such as a blemish or missing page, may be replicated in our edition. We do,
however, repair the vast majority of imperfections successfully; any imperfections that
remain are intentionally left to preserve the state of such historical works.

1 MONTH OF FREE READING

at

www.ForgottenBooks.com

By purchasing this book you are eligible for one month membership to ForgottenBooks.com, giving you unlimited access to our entire collection of over 700,000 titles via our web site and mobile apps.

To claim your free month visit:

www.forgottenbooks.com/free114783

English
Français
Deutsche
Italiano
Español
Português

www.forgottenbooks.com

Mythology Photography **Fiction**
Fishing Christianity **Art** Cooking
Essays Buddhism Freemasonry
Medicine **Biology** Music **Ancient**
Egypt Evolution Carpentry Physics
Dance Geology **Mathematics** Fitness
Shakespeare **Folklore** Yoga Marketing
Confidence Immortality Biographies
Poetry **Psychology** Witchcraft
Electronics Chemistry History **Law**
Accounting **Philosophy** Anthropology
Alchemy Drama Quantum Mechanics
Atheism Sexual Health **Ancient History**
Entrepreneurship Languages Sport
Paleontology Needlework Islam
Metaphysics Investment Archaeology
Parenting Statistics Criminology
Motivational

GERMANY UNDER THREE EMPERORS

EMPEROR WILLIAM II AND THE EMPRESS AUGUSTA VICTORIA

GERMANY UNDER THREE EMPERORS

BY

PRINCESS CATHERINE RADZIWILL

(CATHERINE KOLB-DANVIN)

With Eight Photogravure Plates

CASSELL AND COMPANY, LTD
London, New York, Toronto and Melbourne
1917

CONTENTS

PAGE

INTRODUCTION ix

Part I

Before the Empire

CHAPTER

1. THE DAWN OF IMPERIALISM 1

2. BISMARCK'S POLITICAL DÉBUT . . . .

3. PRUSSIA AND RUSSIA . . . . . .

4. AUSTRIA AND PRUSSIA . . . . . .

5. GENIUS AT THE HELM . . . . . .

6. FREDERICK III. AND HIS FATHER . . . .

7. PLAYING WITH AUSTRIA . . . . .

8. AUSTRIA BECOMES A PAWN . . . . .

Part II

The Process of Union

9. FIRST STEPS TO EMPIRE . . . . .

10. WELDING THE SOUTHERN STATES . . . .

11. THE PROCESS CONTINUES . . . . .

12. NEW LIGHT ON THE EMS DISPATCH . . .

13. SEDAN AND PARIS . . . . . .

14. INAUGURATION OF THE SPY SYSTEM . . .

15. A KING BECOMES EMPEROR . . . .

Contents

Part III

Development of Militarism

CHAPTER   PAGE

16. BISMARCK AND THE EMPRESS   209

17. JUGGLING WITH WAR   221

18. BALKAN INTRIGUES   232

19. FEARS OF ISOLATION   243

20. THE DUAL ALLIANCE   .   .   .   .   .   .

21. SOME MISSING DOCUMENTS   .   .   .   .   .

22. BULGARIAN MATTERS   .   .   .   .   .   .

23. BEHIND THE VEIL OF INTRIGUE   .   .   .   .

Part IV

William II. in Power

24. LAST DAYS AND FIRST DAYS   .   .   .   .

25. WILLIAM II. AND BISMARCK   .   .   .   .

26. AFTER THE CRASH   .   .   .   .   .   .

27. THE OUTCOME   .   .   .   .

INDEX   369

ILLUSTRATIONS

EMPEROR WILLIAM II. AND THE EMPRESS AUGUSTA
   VICTORIA . . . . . . *Frontispiece*

PAGE

PRINCE VON BISMARCK . . . . . .

MARSHAL VON MOLTKE . . . . . .

EMPEROR WILLIAM I. IN 1871 . . . . .

WILLIAM II. IN 1884 . . . .

EMPEROR WILLIAM I. IN 1884 . . . . .

EMPEROR FREDERICK III. . . . . . .

EMPEROR WILLIAM II. IN 1899 . . . . .

EMPEROR WILLIAM II. IN 1905 338

INTRODUCTION

AMID all the grave preoccupations that have absorbed the world during the last three years and prevented it from thinking about the past I experienced a strong feeling of hesitation before deciding to relate the incidents of which I write. And yet, according to the eloquent remark of Catherine the Great, it is only in reading the past that one can foresee the future, so far, at least, as the historical development of nations is concerned.

Perhaps, indeed, Europe would have fared better had it studied with closer attention the events that gradually transformed Prussia into the powerful war machine the great European conflict has proved her to be.

The processes of Militarism spread over three reigns. In the development of these processes is embodied practically all the history which Germany has made under William I., Frederick III., and, so far, William II. 'Any account of Germany under these three Emperors, therefore, must perforce make that predominance the thread of the narrative, and particularly must this be so with the present volume, which deals with the political evolution of Germany in its relations with the rest of Europe.

From this same cause, too, it is inevitable that, even to the limits of iteration, one name should recur. For who but Bismarck was mostly responsible, through the three reigns, for the international political situation?

ix

Yes; one always attributes to Prince von Bismarck the creation of the German Empire such as it became in 1914.

In reality, however, Bismarck, with all his genius, was a consequence of Prussian development; Prussian development was not the consequence of his presence at the head of affairs. He was not like Richelieu, a man of wide conceptions which he carried through in defiance of every obstacle. Bismarck did not create, he only built. As a worker he was, undoubtedly, one of the most gigantic figures the world has ever seen. The future alone can prove whether the edifice to which he placed the topmost stone will continue to stand after passes the tempest which is sweeping round the world in unabated fury. Yet the past may help us to an intelligent anticipation.

One cannot foresee the storms of the morrow. The only thing which is within human power is to examine the past with care. To do so is the aim of this book. To the task I bring some material it has been within my discretion to divulge, and which has long been within my knowledge. At this distant date no great harm can be done by thus bringing to light personal experiences and private documents which may help to a clearer view of the path the Prussian has trod during the three reigns.

CATHERINE RADZIWILL

Part I

Before the Empire

GERMANY UNDER THREE EMPERORS

I

The Dawn of Imperialism

MANY people who have not taken the trouble to study closely the history of Prussia in particular, and of Germany in general, when speaking about the events which raised the Hohenzollerns to an Imperial Throne, do so under the impression that the war of 1870 with France was the great lever. But twenty-two years before the disaster of Sedan a Parliament assembled at Frankfurt had offered the crown of the Hohenstaufens and of the Habsburgs to King Frederick William IV., King of Prussia.

Had there been at his side a Minister possessing the undoubted and unscrupulous genius of Prince von Bismarck, he might have been persuaded into accepting the diadem. But Frederick William, whose mind was as timid as his nature was tortuous, could not agree to what he conceived would be a revolt against tradition— the degradation of the Austrian dynasty to the position of a vassal of another German Power.

When thinking of those years between the Revolution of 1848 and the Franco-German War, one must always remember that there existed in Germany two different countries, as it were—Monarchical Germany

B

and Democratic Germany.   The former was represented by the King of Prussia, whilst the majority of
his advisers held Democratic opinions.   Both parties
wanted union, for the very fact that the Parliament
assembled at Frankfurt had been called into being was
owing to the unacknowledged yearning after German
unity under the supremacy of one or other of the
German Princes.   That Parliament had met in order
to bring some kind of order out of the chaos that had
existed ever since 1815 and the Congress of Vienna.
It had met also for another purpose, of which every
one of its members was aware though he would never
have owned to it: to exclude Austria from the new
Germany.   Herein lay the divergence between the
Monarchical and the Democratic attitudes.

We may say, therefore, that the national passion
for unity which has become so overbearing in the
present Germany already existed in 1848, but it had
not yet gathered sufficient courage or power or vanity
to assert itself.   It was as a means of transition from
a system of government which was weakening Germany, and threatening it with impotence, that this
Frankfurt Parliament, at whose decisions King Frederick William IV. was afterwards so terribly indignant, proceeded almost immediately upon its election
to create a Central Power from among the members of
one of the reigning German dynasties.   The name of
the Archduke John of Austria obtained almost all the
votes of the Assembly, which elected him to this
supreme dignity on the 29th of May, 1848.

The Archduke, as Imperial Vicar, immediately
called together a responsible Ministry, and assumed
the attitude of a Constitutional Sovereign.   Unfortu-

nately for him, and for the success of an attempt that was doomed to failure almost before it had been entered upon, the new ruler had not to deal only with a nation; his task was also to exercise supreme authority over one Emperor, five Kings, Grand Dukes and Dukes without number, and free towns like Hamburg and Bremen. How could he possibly bring them all to act according to his instructions without wounding their extremely sensitive consciousness of their own authority?

The Ministry believed that it could reconcile all the interests at stake by deciding that the armies of the different German States were to swear allegiance to the Imperial Vicar, with one common flag—the red, black and gold colours of Germany—as the symbol of the new unity.

This pretension, the significance of which lay in dispossessing the German independent Princes of the command of their own troops—the foremost of their rights—instead of smoothing matters, caused a storm of indignation all over the country. In Prussia especially it gave rise to an opposition which no persuasion could allay. The army hastened to protest against a humiliating decision which would have been contrary to all the traditions associated with the name of Frederick the Great. The King, who was the first to cry out, declared that nothing in the world would ever make him agree to what he characterised as a monstrous proposal, the result of which would have been to make him surrender his authority over his troops to a power that owed its existence to revolution.

What infuriated Frederick William especially, though he did not openly acknowledge it, was the fact that the representative of this revolutionary power was a Prince belonging to the House of Habsburg, which had always been beaten in battle wherever they had encountered the Hohenzollerns. He declared that he would resist to the last the decrees of the Imperial Vicar. All the other German Princes followed his example, so that, though the Central Ministry of Frankfurt went so far as to fix a day upon which the oath of allegiance to the Archduke John was to be sworn, no such oath was ever taken. The Prussian army remained under the command of the King of Prussia, whilst the Hanoverian, Saxon, Bavarian, and Würtemberg troops still recognised their respective Sovereigns as supreme military chiefs.

Remembering all that took place at that time, one cannot help discovering food for thought in the fact that the Frankfurt programme was carried out almost to the letter twenty-two years later. But this time it was for the benefit of Prussia. Even at the time of Archduke John's brief span of power people in every part of Germany whispered to each other that the ferocious opposition of Prussia to the scheme of one large German army might vanish altogether in the then improbable case of the King of Prussia being offered its command. And the prophets were right.

This idea of unity, which was already gaining ground, was assiduously cultivated by partisans of the then Prussian Kingdom, who proceeded with alacrity to encourage the Frankfurt Parliament to vote the constitution of a new German Empire, from which Austria was to be excluded. This, however, was fated only to take place after the decisive battle of Sadowa had ratified the decisions of an Assembly no one had ever taken seriously into account, but which, nevertheless, laid the foundations of the work that Bismarck was to accomplish with such success later on. For when this separation of Austrian from the German community became an accomplished fact in 1866, after the Treaty of Nikolsburg, it had been already voted some seventeen years earlier by the National Assembly of Frankfurt.

It is not inopportune, perhaps, here to remind ourselves that it is chronicled in the Memoirs of Baron von Bunsen that this idea of ousting Austria from her place in the German Confederation had been viewed with considerable sympathy by several English statesmen. Lord Palmerston, Lord John Russell, Sir Robert Peel and others said to Bunsen that the Parliament of Frankfurt, in taking the initiative of such a resolution, had shown proof of real political intuition.

It must be remembered, in order to explain why these clever politicians had been led to take such a point of view of a situation that could not but engross their attention on account of the complications that were bound to follow upon its development, that at the time to which I am referring the Austrian Government was in the hands of an intelligent, daring and inexorable man, whose ambitions constituted a perpetual threat to the safety of Europe. Prince Felix Schwarzenberg had replied to the votes of the Frankfurt Assembly, which had excluded the realm of the Habsburgs from the common German Fatherland, by declaring his intention to oblige the new Empire to accept all the Austrian provinces that had not hitherto been included in the German Confederation, e.g. Hungary, Bohemia, Galicia, etc. This mass of foreign peoples, once they had been merged into the Empire, almost inevitably would have obliged it to submit to the policy of reaction pre-conceived by Austria. Thereby Prince Schwarzenberg, the precursor of Bismarck, would have created a Central European Empire of over seventy millions of inhabitants which would have swallowed Prussia and quashed her pretensions for ever. It would also have constituted a permanent uncertain factor in European politics; hence the opposition it produced.

In proof of the opinion I have already ventured to express, I reproduce in its entirety a curious letter from the then well-known Donoso Cortès. It will be seen that it emphasises the point that Bismarck was not the originator of the revival of a German Empire for the profit of the Hohenzollerns, as so many people think. He simply took up with unusual ability, much unscrupulousness, and a certain degree of recklessness, an idea that had already appeared before a few minds gifted with more perspicacity than others, as being the inevitable result of the development of a situation that had been carefully prepared from the days of Frederick the Great. The disaster of Jena merely caused the matter to be relegated to the background for a season; it certainly never induced any thought of abandonment.

Donoso Cortès wrote on May 23rd, 1849, from Berlin to a friend : " The Austrian, Bavarian and Hanoverian Plenipotentiaries have assembled here to discuss, in the name of the respective Sovereigns, a new German Constitution, and, in accord with Prussia, they have elaborated one which will shortly be promulgated.

" This Constitution is nearly the same as the one of the Frankfurt demagogues, except for a few modifications. For instance, the Imperial veto will not be a suspensive, but an absolute one; whilst the vote of

the citizens will not be universal, but restricted and subject to certain conditions determined beforehand.

"Germany is to become a military State that will
be designated an Empire. This Empire will be ruled
by the King of Prussia, who, however, will not be
called Emperor, but bear a name which in German will
mean 'Guardian of the Empire.' No other German
State will be allowed to maintain at foreign Courts its
independent diplomatic agents, nor accredit any. This
right will only belong to the Guardian of the Empire,
and the King of Prussia himself will only be able to
avail himself of it in virtue of his quality as such.

"Austria is to remain outside the Union, forming
a separate Empire.

"As you can see for yourself, this means the
mediatisation of all the independent German Princes,
who, finding themselves placed between the revolution
that weighs upon their future and Prussia that crushes
them with her protection, have no other choice left to
them than that of the way in which they are to die.
They have been called together not to hear whether they
wish to live, but to learn whether they desire to perish
from the hand of a king or of a peasant. At present
the future of that immense and mighty German Empire
which is itself as yet unformed is uncertain : will it be
democracy or Monarchy; ruled by an obscure, glib-
tongued demagogue, or the King of Prussia?"

That a statesman of long experience and superior intelligence should have been compelled to ask such a
question in 1849 must necessarily require the presump-
tion that already certain people whose political acumen
allowed them to guess the probable march of events
considered that Prussia becoming supreme in Germany

was only a matter of time. In reality it was even more a question of form. Prussia was preparing her own aggrandisement without leaving those spheres of the divine right so dear to the pious heart of its King; she was advancing with discretion, noiselessly, slowly, but she was advancing all the same, and things had already gone so far that sagacious spectators of her conduct like Donoso Cortès could see whither they led. I have only quoted his letter because it is but one among the many proofs that could be advanced in favour of the theory that in May, 1849, Prussia was already making ready to grasp Imperial dignity as her legitimate possession, and that according to the best judges nothing would be able to stop her.

Donoso Cortès, however, had been absolutely mistaken in his prophecy that the independent German Sovereigns would be forced into the dilemma of having to perish either at the hand of a king or by the demand of the populace. They resigned themselves to nothing of the kind, but tried to play a double game. Outwardly they seemed to be in perfect accord with Frederick William IV., but in the secret of their hearts they were still expecting that Austria would be able to recover sufficient strength to deliver them from Prussia.

This was clearly proved when a little later Austria, having really recovered the full liberty of her movements, Hanover and Saxony denounced the Treaty which they had accepted on May 26th. Frederick William IV., who believed he had coerced them to his policy, had been in reality their dupe. The Kings of Hanover and Saxony had found in the Treaty an excellent pretext to gain time, which was the only thing they wanted. Indeed, on the very day after he had agreed to the

arrangement proposed by Prussia in regard to the
Treaty which had bound it with its neighbours, the
King of Hanover had written to the Duke of Wellington
to consult him as to the conduct which he ought to follow
in such a grave juncture. "Would he not do better,"
he asked, "to keep his liberty in spite of the Treaty
he had been compelled to conclude by trying to delay
things as long as possible, so as to allow to Austria
sufficient time to reconstitute her strength and her
army?" In spite of the indignation of the Iron Duke,
the King persisted in his opinion. This, too, was shared
by Saxony. The Government there made no secret of
its intentions to break the Treaty, and Herr von Beust,
questioned on the point, had replied: "We have reserved ourselves a door to escape from the obligations
we have entered upon. We have let the Bavarian
Government know that, unless it and the Vienna Cabinet
consent to join the Alliance, we should not consider
ourselves as bound by it. This declaration has produced
in Munich the impression which we had expected it to
make. Bavaria will refuse to accept the Treaty of
May 26th, and we shall thus be free to disengage ourselves from its terms whenever we like."

Some Prussian statesmen have tried to represent
Prussian policy at that time as a model of disinterestedness and chivalry. We who look at things by the light
of subsequent events do not feel quite so ready to award
it such praise, but find reason for the attitude of Prince
Schwarzenberg, who attributed the hesitations which
at the last moment kept back Frederick William IV.
from adding to the embarrassments of his neighbours,
and especially to the distress of Austria, to the feeling
that the time had not yet come when Prussia might,

without danger for her future prestige, assert herself as the one great Power in Germany.

Prince Felix Schwarzenberg, the Emperor Francis Joseph's Prime Minister, was one of Prussia's most dangerous foes. This great nobleman was an exception among the ignorant Austrian aristocracy. He was certainly a great man, even if not a great statesman, and he at least had a carefully elaborated programme that he followed all the time that he remained in office—that is, until his death, because he expired in harness. He hated Prussia with one of those ferocious hatreds which knows no bounds, and even when he had to fight against internal difficulties that very nearly wrecked the Austrian Monarchy he was thinking of the moment when he would be enabled to crush Prussia, in whom he already saw the foe of the morrow—the one enemy to whom Austria was to owe its final humiliation.

The Prince had understood very well, if others had not, the real significance of that Treaty of May 26th, 1849, which the King of Prussia had compelled the Sovereigns of Hanover and Saxony to sign, and which associated them with him in one political existence. It was the beginning of that future unity of which Prussia was to become the centre. This state of things he meant to destroy. By a stroke of genius he persuaded Prussia to conclude another Treaty, this time with Austria, a Treaty which put an end to the power of the Imperial Vicar, and which constituted an interim authority exercised by Prussia and Austria in turns, in the name of the German Confederation; its term was to extend until May 1st, 1850. It was opening the door to all kind of discussions, and it was directed straight against Prussia and her ambitions. One can but wonder how the latter was induced to accept such a revolution, because it was nothing else, in the government of the German States. King Frederick William IV. evidently did not realise its importance, because he immediately proposed to call together another Parliament at Erfurt—that is, the Parliament which, according to the Treaty of May 26th, had, with the help and co-operation of the rulers of the German independent States, to remodel the Constitution of Frankfurt. As soon, however, as he had declared this intention, Hanover said that Prussia did not interpret correctly the sense of the Treaty of May 26th, and that the King of Hanover had only allied himself with the King of Prussia in order to fight the democracy, but not at all to transform Germany into one vast and united State. The people having been crushed, the Treaty of May 26th had become null, and Hanover consequently repudiated it altogether. Thanks to the intrigues—for it is impossible to call his conduct by another name—of Prince Felix Schwarzenberg, the famous Alliance of the three Kings, which went in Germany by the name of "*Dreikönigsbündniss*," remained nothing but a dead letter, devoid of every sense.

At the same time, also by reason of the influence which directly or indirectly he succeeded in exercising over the minds of certain Sovereigns and Ministers in Germany, the Prince caused indignant protestations without number against the supremacy which Prussia had claimed as a right, to shake the whole of the Southern German States. They began to awaken to the fact that their independence was being seriously threatened. On February 27th, 1850, Bavaria, Saxony and Würtemberg signed a Convention which had for its object the preservation of the sovereign rights of the small States in that future German Constitution about which everybody was talking, but which no one cared to see become a fact, with the exception, of course, of Prussia. A fortnight later the King of Würtemberg, in opening the Chambers at Stuttgart, uttered words which caused undescribable emotion all over Germany.

' Gentlemen," said the King of Würtemberg, " the dream of a united great German State is the most dangerous of all dreams, not only from the point of view of Germany, but also from that of Europe. Every violent fusion of the German races, every complete subordination of one of these races to the other, would carry in itself the danger of our own inner dissolution, and would be the death of our national existence. It is only the maintenance of the old fidelity to historical traditions, and of the rights of each of us, that can assure us strength and salvation amidst the storms of the present day. I, together with the Governments allied with me, desire that each nation should remain in possession of its undoubted right to be represented in a German Assembly. We do not wish to raise a new political edifice upon the ruins of our old rights and privileges, we desire only to give to the former Confederation a new shape more in harmony with the spirit and the needs of the present time. We wish to see the just pretensions of Prussia allied with the general interests of Germany, and if we consent to sacrifice our own particular and personal rights, it is not in favour of this or that Power that we do so, but for the general welfare, for the good of the Fatherland. We do not care to be Austrians or Prussians, we wish with Würtemberg, and with the help of Würtemberg, to remain Germans."

The impression produced by this speech was so immense that the Berlin Cabinet went so far as to break diplomatic relations with Stuttgart. But beyond this platonic expression of an anger which was natural under the circumstances, Prussia abstained from any manifestations that might have compromised her policy, which was trying to shape itself in the minds of certain people.

In those years some personalities, who were to play an important part in the reconstitution of that new Germany to which three successful wars were to give birth, were beginning to interest themselves in Prussian politics. There were in Berlin at that moment some persons who were already looking towards the then Prince of Prussia, and to hope that he might repair some of the mistakes into which his brother had been led or had allowed himself to drift. Among these persons was the man who was to destroy all the work of Prince Schwarzenberg, the man who for a quarter of a century was to become the leading political power in Europe, as well as one of the most imposing figures of his time, and who was to die at Friedrichsruhe as Prince Bismarck of Schönhausen.

CHAPTER II

Bismarck's Political Début

ON February 5th Bismarck, who had already begun to attract public attention, was elected to the Prussian Second Chamber. In his early speeches he defended extreme Conservative principles with such energy that he had very quickly acquired the reputation of being a ferocious reactionary. He had openly declared that he would not hesitate at anything which would strengthen Royal authority. To his Monarchical convictions Bismarck added a decided conviction that to Prussia alone belonged the future of Germany. And this he maintained in spite of the arrogance of Prince Schwarzenberg, who just at that time was starting the campaign which was to end with the Convention concluded at Olmütz between Austria and Prussia. The result of this achievement in diplomacy was that Prussia had to give way on every side to her rival under circumstances that constituted one of the most shameful humiliations to which an independent Power had ever been driven.

Though unavowed, this Convention of Olmütz was really one of the reasons of Prussia's aggression against Austria in 1866. By the war they hoped to wipe out the indignity of Olmütz. To explain this in detail would take too long, and, moreover, the thing has now lost significance, unless as an introduction to the work which Bismarck was to complete at Sadowa. The Convention arose out of the insurrection in Hesse, the Elector of which had appealed to the German Diet of Frankfurt for help in subduing his rebellious subjects, whilst the latter, thinking that they had good reason to complain of their Sovereign, had claimed the succour of Prussia. For the first time, in consequence, Frederick William IV. found himself in a dilemma. Either he had to fight against Austria, the representative of that Holy Empire whose shadow he still worshipped, or to place himself resolutely as the protector of those whom Austria oppressed.

The position was a terrible one for a mind like his, in which, in spite of everything, mysticism remained the dominating factor. Ignoring the representations which were made to him by his Ministers, that even in the latter case it was indispensable to make some display of military force, he tried to negotiate. The King resisted even the entreaties of his personal friend, General von Radowitz, the Minister of Foreign Affairs, to show some energy in presence of the haughty insolence of Schwarzenberg. For once Prussia found that she had to do with an adversary whom no concessions would disarm. Prince Schwarzenberg had not only secured for Austria the co-operation of Bavaria and of Würtemberg, but also had succeeded in putting himself into accord with the Emperor Nicholas of Russia, who, during an interview with Francis Joseph at Warsaw, had encouraged him to crush the idea of a United Germany.

When all this came to the ears of Frederick William IV. he was more than ever encouraged in his opinion that every kind of sacrifice ought to be made by Prussia rather than accept the alternative of an armed conflict with Austria. Radowitz resigned, and his successor, von Manteuffel, by order of his Sovereign, wrote to Prince Schwarzenberg that the Prussian Government did not oppose the decisions of the Diet in regard to Hesse. Schwarzenberg did not wish for anything better, but he was far too clever and experienced a diplomat to show at once the satisfaction which this communication of Manteuffel had been to him, and he delayed replying to it. This dallying with fate, however, was fatal. A few days brought a sudden change in the decisions of the King of Prussia, who at last gave way to the clamours of public opinion and authorised General von Radowitz to mobilise his army, obliged von Manteuffel to give his consent, and thus brought a little more confusion into a situation which was already chaotic.

As a military measure this mobilisation came much too late. As a political demonstration it was devoid of importance, because the commanders of the Prussian troops received orders which practically took away any freedom of action. The whole conduct of the Berlin Cabinet had been characterised by a foolishness which verged almost on the criminal, and of which Schwarzenberg had at once seen the weakness. Von Manteuffel's dispatch had been dated November 3rd, and it was only on the 9th of the same month that he received a reply. This reply was more an ultimatum than anything else, because, before consenting to negotiate with Prussia and to disarm her own troops, Austria required guarantees upon three points:

1. The dissolution of the Treaty with Hanover and Saxony.

2. The formal recognition of the authority of the Frankfurt Diet.

3. The evacuation of the Electorate of Hesse.

Under these conditions she was willing to take part in a conference, but reserved to herself the right to submit any decisions this conference might take to the ratification of the Diet. In case Prussia did not immediately signify its acquiescence to these demands the Austrian Minister in Berlin, von Prokesch, had orders to ask for his passports.

The demands caused von Manteuffel much consternation. He offered to grant some part of what was demanded, but Prokesch showed himself inflexible, and asked the same day for his passports. After the personal intervention of the King, von Prokesch consented to a delay of two days, which he declared he was doing entirely on his personal responsibility, and for which he expected that he would be most severely censured by his Government.

At last, after a repeated exchange of letters and of notes, which Schwarzenberg made as offensive in tone as possible, Manteuffel—who saw that nothing could avail against the determination of the Vienna Cabinet—wrote asking his formidable opponent for an interview, and without even waiting for a reply, started for Olmütz, where, with insolent leisure, Schwarzenberg at last joined him. The outcome of that interview was the famous Convention by which Prussia accepted all the conditions dictated to her, and humbly reassumed its earlier position as a vassal of the Habsburgs. The comedy ended : drama followed, in which Austria was not to have the most glorious nor the principal part.

The impression which the immoderate victory of Prince Schwarzenberg excited in Germany can best be interpreted in the words of a foreigner who happened to be in Berlin at that time. This personage wrote to one of his friends in France a letter to which subsequent events were to give significance : "You ask me for my opinion as to what has taken place at Olmütz," says this man, who was none other than my own father. "Neither is Prussia so weak as one believes, nor Austria so strong as one thinks, or as one could suppose, judging by the light of the events which have just taken place. Austria has abused the momentary advantage which circumstances of which she has not realised the real causes have given to her; whilst the so-called defeat of Prussia has left her military strength intact, it has embittered her national resentment against the people who—intentionally, perhaps—allowed her to be humiliated in order to excite hatreds which, without the Convention of Olmütz, would have died a natural death. After this no one in Prussia will allow their anger to cool."

That public opinion was most bitter, and that Olmütz really laid the foundation of the idea of revenge, which was cemented by Sadowa, can be appreciated nowhere with more intensity than in a letter addressed to Baron von Bunsen by one of his intimate friends, Count Albert Pourtalès, then Prussian Minister at Constantinople, who, on learning the details of the arrangement at Olmütz, expressed his indignation in a fiery epistle which deserves to be quoted, because it lays bare all that inexorable programme which every Prussian carried written in his heart since the signing of this ill-fated convention, but which Bismarck alone proved strong enough to bring through and to execute

"*Constantinople, January 18th*, 1851.

"If you think me full of bitterness against Radowitz, my dear friend, you must not wonder that I cannot find words to express my indignation against Manteuffel, because, in spite of Haugwitz, in spite of George William, in spite of Tilsit, our history offers nothing, in my opinion, that can be compared to the defeat of Olmütz. To think that we have called together the Chambers and the Army in order to receive a box on the ear during a State ceremony! To think that we have jested with all the remembrances of 1813; and in what a way! How does one dare to mention the concessions that Austria has made to us, because next to the executioner Rechberg we have been allowed to place another; because we have been allowed to drag ourselves secretly towards Holstein, as if we were thieves or receivers of stolen goods.

"All this is so painful that I cannot find expressions capable of describing all that I feel. But in my sorrow I remember the French proverb, '*Aide-toi, le ciel t'aidera.*' We cannot expect others to do anything for us if we do nothing ourselves. Never mind how bad, how shameful our position is to-day, there is one fact that neither cowardice nor treason can destroy, and this fact is, that Germany still has a future, and that in Germany it is Prussia who will be called to take the lead. The history of the last few years proves that Fate continually gives us back this hegemony which we have refused so often and in such a miserable way. The blind party of the *Kreuzzeitung* can talk as much as it likes of its so-called historical system; Rochow, Gerlach, Stahl can continue as much as they like to speak and to act against the interests of Prussia, and in the sense of the ones dear to Austria and to Russia. They will fail in their attempts to pervert public opinion, because it is God and not Manteuffel who rules the world. The

Dresden conferences will lead to nothing; the best they can achieve will be but a weak reproduction of the Constitution elaborated by the Diet, and this the least breath of wind will carry away.

"In the meantime, my dear friend, we must work without interruption against our good friends Nicholas and Francis Joseph; we must encourage the Turks; we must advise the Italians to rally round the house of Savoy; we must make the national revolutionary party throughout Europe understand and realise that the Piedmont and Prussia are the only two European States whose existence and future are closely linked with the success of the nationalist idea on a reasonable basis. We must come to an understanding with the Liberal party in Sweden —which the other day obtained a great triumph in the Parliament of Stockholm—because, sooner or later, the Swedish Liberals will feel and act as should real Scandinavians. We must prevent, no matter at what cost, the smaller German States from becoming stronger than is now the case; we must strangle at its birth this diabolical idea that could only have been conceived by the Habsburgs of a Hanoverian-Saxon-Oldenburg Sonderburg, and then   we must wait for the moment when Austria, in trying to regulate her financial condition and organise her political system, makes a tremendous fiasco of both, as she is bound to do when this moment arrives, then, as one says in French, 'chacun son tour.' Then we shall return to this abominable Schwarzenberg, with full interest, all the harm that he has done to us."

Whether this cry of hatred had been a spontaneous outburst on the part of Count Pourtalès or whether he had simply repeated what he had heard from others is immaterial. The point of his letter is, that it forevisions with accuracy the story of what was to happen sixteen years later—it can be considered as a prophecy of Sadowa. It is impossible exactly to understand the events which occurred in 1866 if one did not look upon them as a consequence of Olmütz in 1850.

In all this we find a great example of the final justice which history deals out to all. Though Frederick William IV. had refused to accept the Imperial Crown which was offered to him by the votes of a Parliament which he persisted in considering as the product of a revolution, he had nevertheless tried to exclude Austria from the German circle, in order one day to become himself absolute master in Germany. The progress of this idea, that Germany must be confiscated for the profit of Prussia, was a kind of evolution; the crowned mystic of Berlin who had refused to agree with the Council on the question of Federation eventually came to the same conclusion as the German democracy. Was it a coincidence only that this agreement was not reached until it seemed possible to the King that Prussia could dictate?

Prince Schwarzenberg, thinking that the weak and dreamy character of King Frederick William IV. would make Austria's enterprise easier, attempted to exclude Prussia from the German Confederation, or at least to paralyse her movements by relegating her to the position of a second-rate Power, something like Bavaria or Saxony. He temporarily achieved this by the Olmütz Convention.

Sixteen years later the Battle of Sadowa destroyed what Olmütz had created, and the Treaty of Nikolsburg finally ejected out of Germany the ancient monarchy of the Habsburgs. Prince Schwarzenberg had died almost on the morrow of this victory, of which he had made use without regard to equity or to moderation. Thereafter another of the Schwarzenberg type arose in Germany, but this time in Prussia. He had the same genius, perhaps even more, the same character, the same audacity, the same disdain for justice, the same confidence in the brutal strength represented by big guns. It is he who finally triumphed.

And what was his opinion on this Olmütz Convention? The majority of Germans saw in it one of the bitterest humiliations which had ever fallen to the lot of Prussia. Austria considered it to be one of the greatest diplomatic triumphs she had ever obtained. In this man's eyes, however, it had no importance whatever, except for the manner in which it could be used to excite public opinion against Austria. This man was Bismarck, and in his Memoirs, when reviewing the events of those critical days for the Prussian Monarchy, he writes the following significant phrase · "The great error of our Prussian diplomacy during that time was to believe that others would do for us what we did not dare to do ourselves." Bismarck's worst enemies can never accuse him of having fallen into this error; on the contrary, he rather dared more than he ought to have done. This made him a great man, but it also prevented him from becoming great in the abstract sense which we attach to a word susceptible of many different interpretations. His nature was far too calloused for him to resent the humiliation of any temporary failure provided it only retarded but did not endanger the security of a future which he was beginning to see quite clearly. But Olmütz furnished him with a pretext for his hatred against Austria, which was more assumed than real; because it was only individuals he hated; nations he simply despised. He was always willing to make friends with the political enemy of the day before. He was not at all an opportunist; but he never neglected an opportunity, especially when it meant the destruction of something which he found in his way. He always liked to wipe out old scores, but was very careful that in doing so any projects he entertained in regard to a third party should not be erased.

In 1900 a book, published in Vienna, immediately upon its appearance was bought in and destroyed by the Prussian Government because of certain facts which it disclosed and which they could not allow to become public property. This book was called "A Kienast's Monograph." Among other interesting things which it contained was a conversation which Count Scherr Thoss, a Hungarian refugee who had been compromised during the mutiny of 1848 and taken refuge in Paris, had had with Bismarck in the year 1862, when the latter, after his appointment as Prussian Minister President, had returned for a few days to France to present his letters of recall to Napoleon III. The Count had begged the new Minister to grant him an audience, at which it turned out that the Hungarian nobleman wanted to offer to Prussia the services of his countrymen against Austria should Austria become entangled in a war with Prussia. This eventuality, the Count said, appeared to be within the limits of probability. If we are to believe his Memoirs, which were written in 1881 and never printed, Bismarck heard him with great attention, and then replied to him with a frankness that surprised him, not having been used to meet the like in a diplomat :

"You are quite right; my aim is to take revenge for the shame inflicted upon my country at Olmütz. I will destroy Austria. I mean to get for Prussia the place which belongs to her by right in Germany as a pure-blooded German State. I realise quite well of what importance the help of Hungary would be to us, and I also know that, already, Frederick the Great has had negotiations with dissatisfied Hungarian Magnates as to an alliance between Hungary and Prussia. If we are victorious in the war which will break out before long, then you may feel quite sure that Hungary also will recover her freedom."

When the Count in the course of further conversation touched on the necessity of securing the neutrality of France by offering some inducement for her abstention from intervention, Bismarck owned to him that he had already secured the consent of Napoleon III., and that it had cost him nothing to obtain. It was true that the Emperor had spoken of his desire for the cession of the Saarbruck coal fields, but he had bluntly refused, and prided himself on his firmness.

What, however, Bismarck did not mention to Seherr Thoss was what else had transpired during his momentous interview with the French Sovereign. The interview had taken place in the latter's study after Bismarck had presented his letters of recall and at which no one else had been present, not even the Empress. The Prussian Minister mentioned the burning question of an eventual cession of Luxemburg to Prussia in exchange for annexing Belgium to France. So persuasive, indeed, was Bismarck in his explanations as to the manner in which this monstrous infraction of treaties that had been solemnly accepted was to be effected, that at last Napoleon had been induced to reply that he would think about it, and then give his views on the subject. At this promise Bismarck had eagerly caught, understanding the importance it would be for him to have in his possession indisputable documentary evidence that such an idea had been entertained by the Emperor.

Bismarck may have thought his secret safe. And so it was for the moment; but Scherr Thoss was far too clever to believe that such a shrewd mind as Napoleon III.'s would have given a promise of neutrality to Prussia without some definite advantageous condition being understood between them. This is demonstrated by a remark the clever Hungarian makes in his Memoirs to the effect that he would not feel surprised if the policy which Bismarck meant to inaugurate after becoming Prussian Prime Minister did not bring many surprises along with it not only for his countrymen, but for the world at large. To this the Count adds, not without melancholy, "It is always a matter for regret when fate brings one into contact with men about whose sincerity and veracity one cannot help entertaining doubts."

Count Scherr Thoss was to meet Bismarck again seven years later, in January, 1869, after the war of 1866 had revenged Prussia for the humiliation of Olmütz. Another result of the conflict was the reconciliation between Hungary and the dynasty of the Habsburgs, by which Hungarian exiles were free to return to their native land. This time the conversation was conducted in different terms. The future Chancellor of the future German Empire had already formed intentions toward Austria. He was foreseeing the hour when he would call upon the Dual Monarchy to contract a close alliance with its conqueror of the day before. There was no longer any question of sympathising with the cause of the Hungarian rebels, or even with any aspirations of Hungary toward

separation from the Austrian Empire, whose supremacy
it had refused to accept, and with whom it had only
submitted to collaborate in politics when driven to that
course by political necessity. In relating this second interview with Bismarck the Count makes one short but significant comment as to its sense and purpose. "His
words would have surprised me had I not known that
everything could be expected from this extraordinary
man whose principles were wholly Prussian." And this
is what these principles induced Bismarck to say :

"Prussia has absolutely no necessity to favour strife
between Austria and Hungary   On the contrary,
it is to our greatest interest to see the Austro-Hungarian
Monarchy become stronger and enter into close relations of friendship with us. The sincerity of this wish
is founded on the present development of Austro-
Hungary. One consequence of this Dual development
is that it does away with any fear of our being in danger
of an aggression from that side. Another consideration
is that it is of immense importance for us to become the
ally of Austro-Hungary. They have not yet forgiven
us in Vienna for 1866, but this will come in time, when
it is realised there what strength will accrue to Austro-
Hungary from an alliance with us. . . . As regards
France, we shall soon be at war with her because she
has not forgiven us for Sadowa, which she considers as
a personal defeat. We shall win this war. . . . And
then a long period of peace will follow, during which
we shall be obliged always to keep an attentive eye on
France and on her doings. Perhaps we shall require
another war to prove to France that we are not to be
beaten. When Frenchmen realise this fact there will
exist no reason why France and Germany should not

entertain good and neighbourly relations with one another. The real enemy of civilised Europe will then be only Russia. When the Tsar has built the railways he needs and reorganised his army, Russia will be able to march against us with two millions of soldiers. In those days Europe will be forced to unite itself in a strong coalition in order to be able to resist this Power."

It seems strange to read this to-day, but at the same time it must be recognised that the man who had uttered these words judged well of a political situation, for the creation of which he was chiefly responsible. One cannot help feeling a sincere regret that this massive intelligence had only "Prussian principles," and that he did not place his genius at the service of a better cause than to secure the triumph of sheer brutal force.

According to the terms of this Olmütz Convention, Prussia had engaged herself to take part in a Congress to be held at Dresden to regularise the German Confederation. This Congress re-established the rights of the former Frankfurt Diet. King Frederick William IV., who by that time had heard a good deal about Bismarck, and who had been struck by the energy with which the latter had defended the cause of the Monarchy in the Prussian Chamber, sent for him, and offered him the post of King's Delegate at the Diet. Bismarck accepted without hesitation. He afterwards remarked that at that moment he had had the intuition to realise that it was the opportunity of his life, and that he would be a fool to refuse it.

King Frederick William, surprised at his immediate acquiescence, told him that he " must be very courageous to take upon himself duties with which, after all, he was not familiar."

" If I find that I cannot fulfil them I shall be the first one to ask to be relieved of them," proudly replied Bismarck. " I have the courage to obey if your Majesty has the courage to give me orders."

" In that case we can try," said Frederick William IV.

The experience was more successful than could have been foreseen. The new Prussian Delegate, however, soon made himself felt among his colleagues by a dignified insolence, which left no doubt in their minds as to his determination not to allow either himself or his country to be crushed by the importance either of Austria or of any other Power which considered itself if not superior, at least equal to Prussia. It is useless to remind the reader of the anecdote of the cigar which he lighted, during the debates of the Diet, in response to the one which Count Thun was smoking. It is too well known to be repeated in detail, but this was but one of the small things with which he contrived to assert his personality, and little by little to force all the other members of the Bundestage to take his opinions into consideration. One day Thun lost his patience, and allowed the exclamation to escape, " Manteuffel was not so insolent as you at Olmütz " To which Bismarck replied instantly, " We are not at Olmütz, and we shall never return there, and I . . ." He waited a few seconds, then slowly added, " I am not Manteuffel."

These years which he spent in Frankfurt proved of the greatest use to him. It was then that he learnt diplomacy in handling big affairs of world-import, and the experience which he amassed during this stage of his public life helped him considerably later on, when he had to give his main attention to foreign politics. Then, again, he used the time he had at his disposal to make several journeys abroad, and during a visit which he paid to Paris at the time of the Great Exhibition, while he was the guest of his colleague, Count Maximilian Hatzfeldt, at the Prussian Legation, he had the opportunity of being presented to Queen Victoria and to the Prince Consort.

The Crimean War was raging at the time referred to, and Bismarck had done his best to prevent Prussia taking part in it, as he did not think it opportune for his country to enter into a quarrel with which it had nothing to do. Moreover, a conflict with Russia would have interfered for the time being with his dream of revenge against Austria for the Olmütz humiliation. His decision to abstain was further accentuated by the fact that during the Congress of Paris, which he had attended as Prussian Plenipotentiary, his Austrian colleague had treated him with a disdain he was the last man in the world to forgive. About this time he wrote to his friend, General von Gerlach, a letter in which he expressed his conviction that the time had come when Prussia ought no longer to submit to be considered as a negligible quantity by her neighbours. Owing to an indiscretion the contents of this epistle were divulged. It came to the knowledge of the Austrian Foreign Office, and thereafter the relations between the two countries became even more strained than ever. Perhaps it had been written with that intention. With Bismarck one never knows.

Concerning this visit to Paris, it is interesting to read in the Memoirs of the Chancellor his appreciation of Napoleon III., whom he then met for the first time, and with whom he had opportunity to converse on more than one occasion. Among other things he says:

"The Emperor gave me to understand in general terms that he wished for a close alliance between France and Prussia. He told me that these two neighbouring States, who were both at the head of European civilisation, ought to help each other." It had evidently been reported in Berlin that Bismarck had tried to win the good graces of Napoleon III., because the next time that he visited the Prussian capital the King asked him one day, in rather ironical terms, what he thought of the Emperor, to which Bismarck answered, that though he considered him "an intelligent and amiable man, he did not think him so clever as he was generally thought to be."

Frankfurt had been a stage in the career of the future German Chancellor, an initial stage, one may almost say. His attitude whilst there had been a surprise for his friends and a bitter disappointment for his enemies, who had hoped that he would render himself guilty of so many blunders that he would never more be employed in any official capacity after this experience.

As for Bismarck himself, he had fully meant to make his period in the Confederation Parliament a stepping-stone to much higher things. It is difficult to say whether he was already at that time dreaming of the Foreign Office, but that some idea of the kind was crossing his brain can be inferred from the fact that he tried to avoid being sent to Vienna as Minister. He knew very well that the reign of Frederick William IV. was drawing to a close, and he wanted to remain in the vicinity of his future master, in whom he had discerned, as he expressed it himself in his picturesque and rough language, "the soul of a King."

At the time when the state of health of the Sovereign

was giving rise to the gravest apprehensions, and when it was already evident that a Regency would have to be instituted, Bismarck came again to Berlin and had a long conversation with the Prince of Prussia, the future William I., during a walk which they took together in the park at Potsdam. The Prince discussed with Bismarck whether, on ascending the throne, he ought to accept the Constitution as it was, or if he had better insist on some modifications being introduced into it. The reply which he obtained is sufficiently characteristic to deserve being reproduced in the words of the man who framed it:

" I told him," says the Chancellor in his Reminiscences, " that as a point of right he could reject the Constitution, because though a son is bound by dispositions taken by his father this does not apply to the brother of a Monarch, but I advised him for political reasons not to provoke in the country a feeling of political insecurity which would follow on the rejection of the Constitution, even if this were done from excellent motives. ' One must not,' I added, ' every time a new Sovereign ascends the throne, cause national apprehension that it may mean a change in the whole political system.' The prestige of Prussia in Germany, and the efficacy of its influence in Europe, would be diminished by dissensions between the Crown and the Landtag, and the whole of Liberal Germany would protest against the projected measure. I further insisted on the point that all constitutional questions must be subordinated to the needs of the country and to its political situation in regard to the rest of Germany. Moreover, there was no need at the present moment, I added, to touch our Constitution; the question of internal peace was by far the more important matter with which the Prince could concern himself on his accession."

In the meanwhile one began to get uneasy in Berlin at the presence of one so generally disliked as Bismarck, and especially at the conversations which he was having with the future Sovereign. People even asked him why he did not return to Frankfurt. He replied that he thought his presence was more useful and necessary in Berlin. In reality he wanted to see the turn events would take, and to be present when the Royal authority passed into other and stronger hands than Frederick William IV. He was, however, to wait for a considerable time before being called upon to take in his own hands the reins of Prussian government, because, though the Prince of Prussia, owing to the mental illness of his brother, was appointed Regent in 1858, he did not ask Bismarck to enter the Cabinet. On the contrary, he appointed him Minister in Petersburg, which, in the opinion of his opponents, was a method of getting him out of the way of people whom his presence irritated. Among others, the Regent's Consort, the Princess Augusta, had never "taken" to the talented statesman who was, in the years to come, to pursue her so mercilessly with his enmity and to thwart her with such persistence, even after she had become Empress.

CHAPTER III

Prussia and Russia

AT the Russian Court Bismarck for the first time really came into active touch with international politics from other points of view than those of Prussia and Germany. That visit widened his outlook and helped him to lay his plans for the future, particularly in regard to Austria. Before he left Petersburg he had learnt that though Russia would not help him to wipe out the shame of Olmütz, it would look with a certain satisfaction on the abasement of the Habsburg Monarchy—the Tsar had not forgiven the treachery of Austria at the time of the Crimean War.

Bismarck had always sympathised with the Romanoffs, the autocratic character of whose government appealed to his own authoritative individuality, and he very quickly came to the conclusion that Prussia could not rise unaided to the position which she coveted. The Hohenzollerns were bound by family ties to the Russian reigning dynasty, and no opportunity of persuading the latter to enter into closer relations with their relatives in Berlin ought to be neglected. At least that was Bismarck's opinion, and he therefore decided, even though he knew it was against the will of those above him in State affairs, to employ his best efforts to draw Russia into the inner circle of Prussian politics. He was well aware that he would encounter opposition in Court circles, especially on the part of the Princess of

Prussia, whose decidedly anti-Russian feelings were very well known.

Bismarck did not at that time hate the Princess Augusta with the same intensity he was to display later on, but he did not like her, and feared her influence over the Prince Regent. He therefore adopted a line of conduct all his own, and proceeded to act as if he had received no instructions from home at all. Indeed, if we are to believe all that we have heard concerning his early days in Petersburg, he made no little stir in diplomatic circles. He told Count de Nesselrode, the Russian Chancellor, on the first occasion of speaking to him on matters of State and in reply to a question on the point of his authority · "I have brought no instructions, but I mean on my return to instruct others as to what ought to be our future relations with your country." Nesselrode was far too wise a statesman to allow himself to be surprised by this *boutade*, and he ironically remarked that it was impossible to use the word "ought" in politics; his own experience had taught him that "it is never the things which one ought, but those which one can, that events allow one to do."

In Austria Bismarck's appointment to Petersburg was viewed with dismay. The Austrian Ministry, which was just as clumsy at that time as it is to-day, imagined that it would be advantageous to make an attempt to bribe him. The anecdote becomes the more interesting when one remembers that this system of "oiling" the people whose help one wants, which he denounced with much indignation, was put into practice by himself when he was in office on a hitherto quite unknown and unprecedented scale.

In his Reminiscences the Prince records: "In

March, 1859, when I was staying in Berlin previous to my departure for Russia, I received, on the very morning that I was to start for my new post, a letter from a certain Levinstein, a Jewish banker who, as I was aware, was in touch with the leading men in foreign political circles. This letter was couched in the following terms:

" ' I take the liberty to wish most humbly a safe journey and a successful mission to your Excellency, and I hope that we shall soon be able to present to you again our duty in this capital, because the services which you can render in your own country will be far more useful here than abroad.

" ' I have made to-day a Stock Exchange operation which, as I hope, will bear productive fruits. I shall have, later on, the honour to speak to you about it.

" ' In Vienna your mission in Petersburg causes some uneasiness, because one considers you as an adversary of Austria.

" ' It would be very useful for us if your Excellency would consent to write me *a few lines* saying that *personally* you are not badly disposed in regard to Austria; these lines might be of incalculable value. It is a pleasure to me to offer to you my services for the time of your absence, and if you desire it I shall watch over your interests either here or anywhere else you may be pleased to say. You would never be served with more disinterestedness and loyalty than by me.

" ' In expressing to you my sincere feelings of consideration, I remain

" ' Your Excellency's must humble servant,

" ' LEVINSTEIN.

" ' *Berlin, March 23rd, 1859.*'

"I did not reply to this letter," writes Bismarck, "but received in the course of the day, just before starting for the railway station, a visit from Mr. Levinstein. He brought me an autograph letter from Count Buol, then Austrian Foreign Minister, and he proposed that I should take part in a financial operation which would 'bring me a yearly income of 20,000 thalers without any risk whatever.' I replied to him that I had no money to invest; but the banker observed that no funds whatever would be required for this transaction, and that all I should have to do would be to champion, at the Russian Court, the policy followed in Vienna, because the financial business in question could only be successful if relations between Russia and Austria remained good.

"It would have been most important for me," continnes Bismarck, "in view of the future, to have in my hands some document proving that I had been right in telling the Regent that I strongly doubted the sincerity of the policy of Count Buol. I therefore said to Levinstein that in such a serious matter I required a better guarantee than verbal assertions, with nothing behind them except a few lines from Count Buol, which he had not even handed over to me. He refused to give me anything in writing, but raised his offer to 30,000 thalers a year. After that I told Levinstein he had better retire, and myself prepared to leave the room. He followed me on the stairs, saying that I had better beware, because it was not a pleasant thing to have the Austrian Government for an enemy. It was only after I had bade him observe that the stairs were very steep and that I was a stronger man than he that he left me in a hurry.

"This so-called negotiator was personally known to

me on account of the confidence which our Foreign
Office reposed in him. He had been several times sent to
me on special missions by Manteuffel, but when I became
Minister for Foreign Affairs I immediately suppressed
all intercourse with Levinstein. Many years later I took
opportunity to relate the whole incident to King
William I., and at the same time to enlighten him as
to the corruption which had formerly existed in our
Foreign Office.''

The curious thing in all this passage, in the glaring
absence of scruples on the same point in his own
diplomacy, is the indignation of Bismarck. No one in
the world manipulated the Secret Service funds with
more dexterity than the Iron Chancellor during the years
he ruled at the Wilhelmstrasse. He certainly beat
Austrian statesmen in that respect, for not only did he
succeed in obtaining, for a handsome consideration,
people in high position in Petersburg to serve him, but
much later, after the War of 1870, he entertained similar
relations with certain eminent French political men.

The real memoirs of the Iron Chancellor have not
yet seen the light of the day. They exist, nevertheless,
carefully preserved in a bank—not a German one—and
his instructions to his heirs were to allow half a century
to elapse after his death before publishing them. In
these one may expect far more intimate revelations as
to his work in Russia than at present extant. His
Reminiscences are devoid of certain curious details of vital
interest. Nevertheless the few pages of this volume in
which Bismarck describes his sojourn in Russia contain
one or two comments worthy of notice. Rather bitterly
he remarks that already, in 1859, Russian society had
begun to shake off German influence. At one time

it had been strong and powerful at the Court of the Romanoffs, through the sympathies of the Empress Alexandra Feodorovna, the consort of Nicholas I., who was the sister of the King of Prussia and the daughter of the famous Queen Louise whose memory is to this day dear to every German heart.

As an instance of the change, the younger Russian officers and officials would always make a point, when addressed in German, to reply in French or not to reply at all. The older generation of the time of Nicholas I. and Alexander I., Bismarck considered, were much better educated and far more cultivated than their children; and mainly to this declension among young people can be ascribed, says Bismarck, the weakening of German influence over the Russian higher classes.

At that time the German "Kultur" had not yet asserted itself, but in this estimate one can already see it appearing on the European horizon, with all its insufferable pretensions to infallibility, which reached their culminating point with the outbreak of the present war. This same super-vanity is seen in the way the Prussian Colossus referred to Prince Gortschakov. Whilst Bismarck had been Envoy in Petersburg he had flattered and cultivated the Prince, but on becoming head of the Prussian Foreign Office he proceeded to make the Russian statesman aware that he considered himself his superior in personal magnetism as well as in political acumen. With serene complacency Bismarck diagnoses the natural reserve with which such conduct was met: "As soon as I showed myself on the scene as a German, as a Prussian, or rather as his rival in European opinion and in the esteem of historians, his former kindness for me changed into bitter jealousy."

The sojourn of Bismarck in Russia did not last a long time, but long enough for him to consider Russia as a country "in regard to whom nothing can give us reason to foresee a conflict arising out of clashing political interests. We shall never be at peace with France," is his dictum, " but a war with Russia will never become necessary for us unless the mistakes of Liberalism or the awkwardness of the dynasty produce a false situation." The friends the Chancellor made in Petersburg and certain agents he secured proved of considerable use in keeping him informed as to what was going on in Petersburg, and especially of the sentiment of the Court in regard to the idea of a German union under the protectorate of Prussia, about which he managed to convey some hints in conversation with different Russian political personalities of the day. No one in Russia at the time gave any thought to the possibility of Prussia rising to the rank and importance of a first-rate Power. Austria, on the other hand, they watched with constant and unfailing interest. Prussia's future, they considered, might be one of honest mediocrity; as for a Prussia healthy, strong and ambitious, the idea was ludicrous.

A few persons, more observant than others, had gauged with some accuracy the character of this man who went about quietly, but who at the same time took great care to assert himself with an almost stubborn determination every time the interests of his country came into question. One of those who, from the first moment that he had met him, had been struck by the personality of Bismarck was my own father, Rzewuski, who in his diary left long chapters concerning the future creator of the modern German Empire, passages that I am going to reproduce because they afford a valuable contribution to modern history and present quite a different valuation of the Iron Chancellor from that arrived at by his contemporaries.

"I met last night at dinner," writes my father on April 12th, 1859, "the new Prussian Envoy, Herr von Bismarck. I had heard all kinds of stories about him, some people pronouncing him an insolent, disagreeable, overbearing man, whilst others declared him to be only a dull fool, very much taken up with an exaggerated idea of his own importance. Bloudov was the only person who had a good word for him, whilst Antoinette[1] had told me that she did not in the least share the general opinion of our superficial society concerning this 'Prussian,' as Marie Stolypin had named him and everyone, thereafter, called him. All these different appreciations put together had made me rather curious in regard to this paragon, and I was very glad when Adlerberg introduced me to him. We had not much time to talk before dinner, but during the meal I took occasion to observe Bismarck. I was struck by the strength of individuality denoted by the shape of the head of this much-discussed personage. His physiognomy gave one the impression of great power, combined with considerable self-control and inexorable will. When he becomes old he will look like a bulldog, eager to attack and to fight, and already now there is at times when something annoys him—which I fancy was the case once or twice during the meal—an expression in his eyes which is singularly ferocious. Combined with it, and in curious contrast to it, is an excessive, almost too great, politeness and courtesy. Altogether, he is a strange individual, and

---

[1] Countess Antoinette Bloudov, one of the personal friends of the Empress Marie Alexandrovna, known for her Slavophil sentiments.

one almost regrets that fate did not put him into another
position than the one which he occupies; he would have
made a splendid Prime Minister in a constitutional
country, but his force seems sadly wasted there where
his destiny has put him.

"After dinner I approached him, and we began
smoking together in our host's study. I asked him how
he liked Russia, to which he replied that so far what
he had seen of it had pleased him very much. His only
regret was that he did not speak the language, because
this ignorance prevented him from journeying to the
interior which, he was sure, must be most interesting.
'Petersburg is too much European,' he added. 'One
only sees in it the civilised side of your country; it is
the other one I would like to know.'

"I told him that in Moscow and in Kiev, for instance, he could easily travel without speaking Russian,
but he made a gesture of impatience at my remark,
which seemed to indicate a distaste for contradiction that
rather amused me.

"I asked him how he had fared at his reception by
the Emperor, to whom he had presented his credentials
a few days before. 'I suppose that I ought to make
the conventional reply to you that I was delighted,
and that the Emperor showed himself unusually kind
and amiable to me. I cannot do so, however. The
reception was like all receptions of this kind ought to
be. Every new Minister, when he makes his debut at
a Court, is warmly welcomed. How can it be otherwise? In my career it is the last step, the retiring before
the fall of the curtain, which is the important thing.'

"I could not help smiling, and remarked that he was
a cynic. 'Perhaps I am,' was the blunt reply.

' Humanity is not such a beautiful thing that one should nurse illusions in regard to it. In my whole life I have met but one person on whom I could absolutely rely and of whom I could be absolutely sure; it is my wife. The rest do not count.'

" He then changed the conversation, asking me whether I had been in Germany often and when I had visited it the last time. I replied that I had spent some months in Frankfurt after my marriage, which had taken place at Schwalbach, and that I might have had the opportunity to meet him there.

" ' When was that? ' he immediately asked.

" ' In September, 1853.'

" ' I was not at Frankfurt at the time,' he quickly remarked; 'I was at Norderney. I thought I had not seen you, I would have remembered your face; every new arrival of some importance was noticed there at the time.'

" I excused myself by saying that I was not a personage of importance.

" ' You were already a general aide-de-camp to the Emperor of Russia,' he said. ' Surely you will not deny that this is considered as important in our good Fatherland? '

" He smiled, and I laughed, too; then we began discussing Frankfurt. I expressed my curiosity as to whether he regretted the time he had spent there.

" ' Certainly not; it was a most interesting time, and I think that I did some good too. Some people wanted to be put in their places, and I fancy I succeeded in doing so.'

" He smiled again, a broad smile which was a kind of noiseless laugh that impressed me unpleasantly. The

man began to interest me tremendously, and I could
see that he realised such was the case. He then started
to question me in a quick, resolute way that savoured
of imperativeness concerning the impressions which my
different journeys in Germany had produced upon my
mind, and he seemed particularly pleased when I told him
that, so far as I could judge, the national feeling was
developing itself with an astonishing rapidity in Prussia,
whilst Southern Germany seemed, on the contrary, to
be growing more insular than had been the case ten years
before.

" ' You have observed this? ' he exclaimed. ' My dear
Count, you are the first foreigner I have met who has
made such a remark.'

" I then related to him some of my personal experiences during my last journey abroad, and this led us to
talk about Paris, which he called ' a most pleasant place,'
but he confessed he would not care to live there, at least
not in any official capacity. He spoke of the Emperor
Napoleon and of the Empress, whom he characterised
as ' *une bien jolie femme, qui se creit des aptitudes poli-
tiques.*' I asked him whether this was a defect in his
eyes, and he said, ' Yes, in a certain sense, because the
consort of a Sovereign is always badly advised when she
tries to keep herself informed as to affairs of the State.'
However,' he added, ' in France it is not quite the same
thing as in other countries, and I can understand the
weakness of Napoleon in presence of his beautiful wife.
At all events, she has one great quality, she does not
intrigue, and any political influence she chooses to exercise is done quite openly; she does not care for back
doors, and that is a thing that everyone cannot say ! '

" I fancied that there was a covert allusion in the

remark and that he would have liked me to ask for an explanation, but I did not care to do so, and so changed the conversation. Adlerberg then came up to us and put an end to our *tête-à-tête*. But before I took leave of our hosts, Herr von Bismarck asked me to call upon him, expressing in a few polite words the pleasure he had had in making my acquaintance. I shall certainly not allow his to drop ; he interests me immensely, and we have got so very few men of real value here at present that it is a pleasure to be able to talk with one who, whatever may be his shortcomings, is certainly an intelligent and even, in certain respects, a remarkable fellow. This opinion of mine, however, does not seem to be shared by others, because the next day I was asked at my step-daughter's what I had found to talk about with the new Prussian Minister, and when I said that I had extremely enjoyed the conversation we had had together, someone remarked that this was affectation on my part, because anyone more dull than ' this Prussian ' could seldom be found."

Three days later my father wrote again in his diary concerning his acquaintance with Bismarck :

' This morning I called upon the Prussian Minister. He received me with great cordiality, and the conversation at once turned on politics. Someone had told him that I had been violently opposed to the intervention of Russia in the Hungarian insurrection, and that I had even expressed this opinion to Nicholas I. ; he asked me whether such had really been the case. I replied in the affirmative, adding that, having studied history, and especially the history of Poland, I had formed the opinion that Austria and the Habsburgs could never be honest in their dealings with anyone. Bismarck assented with an alacrity the later remembrance of which gave me considerable thought. I quoted the remark of the Emperor Nicholas that he had not rushed to Hungary from a desire to crush a revolution, as he had been accused of doing, but because he had seen a brother Sovereign in distress and had thought it was his duty to rescue him.

" 'Yes,' said Bismarck, 'but this is not sufficient when one is responsible for the welfare of an Empire. Politics must also be concerned with the necessities not only of the moment, but also of the future.'

" The words struck me immensely, and I could not help telling him so, adding that so very few people had realised this fact.

" 'People seldom give themselves the trouble to think,' was the disdainful retort.

" 'This is a reproach it will not be possible to hurl at you,' I said.

" ' Oh, I do not count,' he said negligently. ' People do not mind what I say, and yet I feel quite sure that the day will come when I shall make myself listened to. However, the time has not come for that. For the present I am quite content with watching all that is going on in the world; I do not, though, fall into the error so common to men in public life of forming opinions—mine being all ready a long time since—yet I will confess that for some time to come I shall not attempt to enter the Prussian Cabinet, as some people say I am aspiring to do. The political situation is too unsettled there for the possibility of pushing through any important reforms just now. And then, after all, a Regent is not quite the same thing as a King, though he carries all the responsibilities of a Sovereign. To do certain things one must have the uncontested right to be addressed as " Your

Majesty" by those upon whom the act works to detriment.'

"I remarked that he was a staunch Monarchist.

"'Yes,' he said, 'I have always been one, and I mean to end my days as such. Republics have not yet made good, "*n'ont pas encore fait leurs preuves.*" Our country as yet is still a small and poor one, poorer and smaller in the opinions of those who do not know her well than she is in reality. She can only develop herself and rise to some importance under the protection of a Monarchical form of government. Besides, I doubt the possibility of Prussia becoming great and strong without the Hohenzollerns being there to help her.'

"'It is a pity,' I said, 'that your diplomacy has shown itself so weak in presence of the demands of Austria.'

"'Do not say our diplomacy,' he quickly interrupted; 'say rather our policy, which has always been inspired by feelings of absolute condescension in regard to Austria. Austria is the great danger, though, mind, I would never advocate a perpetual enmity with her on our side. She may be very useful to us in the future, only she must be crushed into the conviction that without Prussia she cannot do anything. If it would be possible for us to establish our supremacy in Germany without quarrelling with Austria none would rejoice more than myself, but it is entirely out of the question, unfortunately, because they will never hear reason in Vienna (*On ne sera jamais raisonnable à Vienne*) until events have persuaded Count Buol, with all his valets (*avec tous ses laquais*), that we are not at all afraid of war, because we can fight with even chances. Now, as concerns Russia, it is a very different thing, and what I

have come here for is to persuade your Government, if
I can, that its friendship is something for which we care
a good deal, and that we should not hesitate for one
moment to sacrifice Austria and put ourselves against
her with you if this were the price you asked for your
alliance with us.'

"'Excuse my asking you the question,' I said, 'but
have you come here to offer us any such alliance?'

"'Offer it, no; but to persuade you that it is worth
having, yes,' he instantly retorted.

"'I am not a diplomat,' I replied, 'and I am not
a public man. I am a soldier who, owing to circumstances, is compelled to remain strictly within the limits
of his military activity; therefore, all that I can tell you
can only have an academic interest for you; but, considering the fact that in Prussia you cannot feel any
sympathy for us in view of our attitude in 1850, when it
was only our encouragement which decided Austria to
insist on the most painful conditions of the Convention
which you signed with her at Olmütz, you cannot feel
any affection for us. What can therefore induce you
suddenly to exhibit such a desire for our alliance? This
is entirely inconsistent with Prussian traditions.'

"'But it is not Prussia who is anxious for the
friendship of Russia,' said von Bismarck, 'it is only I
who desire it, and who mean to win it.'

"There was such an assurance in the words of this
extraordinary man, such a conviction of his own, not
importance—he would have been incapable of such
pettishness—but of his own superiority, that he struck
me in that moment as being really, if not a great man,
at least one inspired with great thoughts, and I could
not help expressing to him my admiration for his clear

outlook. He received my compliments with an indifference that also struck me as something quite out of the common. Herr von Bismarck lit a big cigar, offered me one, and settled down in his chair, as if about to begin a long conversation. Unfortunately, we were interrupted by a visitor, and I had perforce to take my leave. But at dinner I spoke about my visit of the afternoon to my mother-in-law, and expressed to her the interest which my conversation with the Prussian Minister had excited in my mind, and I told her that I certainly meant to see as much of him as possible during the few days that remained to me in Petersburg.''[1]

[1] My father was at the time in command of an army corps stationed at Niegine, in the government of Poltawa, and had come to Petersburg for a few weeks' leave

CHAPTER IV

Austria and Prussia

AFTER the remarks in his diary related in the previous chapter my father mentions that several times he had interviews with Bismarck, but without entering into particulars concerning the conversations. On May 17th, however, I find the following references to the great statesman, which may be read with a certain interest, as in many of the judgments expressed traits of Bismarckian character can be discovered that at the time they were observed by the clever man who consigned them to his diary had not yet developed with the energy which burst forth later on.

"I went yesterday to take leave of Herr von Bismarck, and to express to him the great pleasure which his acquaintance had afforded me. He received me with his usual graciousness, and remarked that he hoped I would not forget him, which I could with all sincerity assure him was not likely to be the case. He is indeed a most interesting man.

"Whether the high opinion which he entertained in regard to the future of his own country is justified it is difficult to say, especially in view of the very poor opinion which is entertained abroad concerning Prussia and Prussian diplomats. The remark which he made to me once, that a land which had given birth to a Frederick the Great was not to be despised, may be quite true as regards the past, but one could have replied to him that

precisely because the man whose name he mentioned was
such a great one it was hardly to be expected another
one like him would be born so soon, and that he had
been an exception which the present Hohenzollerns did
not appear to be likely to transform into a rule.

"Bismarck dreams of an united Germany entirely
given up to Prussian influence. This I could understand
if I put myself at his point of view; but what appears to
me to be quite impossible is that Austria will submit to
this elimination of its influence and importance in Central
Europe. I will go so far as to admit that in case of war
between Austria and Prussia, Austria will suffer a defeat.
What will this defeat change in the general situation?
Very little, I should say, because, if only on account of
their geographical position, the two principal countries
in Central Europe, Prussia and Austria, can hardly be
enemies, or, at any rate, remain so in perpetuity. One
of the two countries must take the lead, and it is difficult
to assume that Austria will allow her rival to do so; the
contrary seems to be more likely. Austria in continual
enmity with Prussia might not perhaps do any harm to
the latter, but it will certainly interfere with her plans
unless by some circumstance, unforeseen at present, she
will persuade the leaders of Austrian foreign affairs that
it is in their interest to work on the same lines as
Prussia. But this could be done only if they had a
common enemy against whom it would be necessary to
ally their respective strengths.

"Now this enemy can only be Russia, because France
will never put herself into direct opposition to the
Habsburgs except upon the Italian question, which does
not interest Prussia at all; and Prussian public opinion
would not allow its Government to entangle it at present

in the complications of a foreign war, unless it were one against Russia.

"It is difficult to foresee what will be the policy of the present Prince Regent after he ascends the throne; but should he ever take von Bismarck as his Minister he will, from what I have seen of him, most certainly try to make Prussia assert herself in the European concert very much more than has been the case in recent years. He has a fully defined programme in his mind, though, of course, he did not disclose it to me. What struck me in all our conversations was the animosity, real or assumed, which he displayed, not only against Buol, but also in regard to certain people in Berlin to whom he attributes, rightly or wrongly, feelings of dislike for his personality. I say real or assumed, because it seemed to me at times that what he wished was to accredit the idea that he could be a bad enemy, and thus to induce others to second his designs, for fear of being severely punished should they not do so.

"I do not think Bismarck will remain long in Petersburg, and certainly he is burning to return to Berlin and to measure himself there with those whom he accuses quite openly of mismanaging Prussian politics. Whether this applies also to the Regent, or only to the latter's Ministers, he did not allow me to guess, but if I were asked to proffer a judgment on this man about whom so many conflicting opinions are heard, I should say that he was at heart a Revolutionary in spite of all his protestations of Conservatism, but Revolutionary in the sense that he is so sure of being able to build up anew the old edifice he desires to pull down that this allows him to speak of his Monarchical convictions, inasmuch as he aims not at overthrowing his King, but only the

political system to which that King clings and which
this strange man does not consider to be favourable to
the interests of his Fatherland, which he has made his
own in quite a remarkable degree. What he will become
in future is difficult to say. Either a great Minister or
a country gentleman. There is no *via media* for him.
Perhaps I am wrong in writing the word ' great ' Minister ; I should rather have said ' powerful ' Minister,
because I am convinced he would not care for the greatness unless it were associated with the power. In a
certain sense he is as unselfish as he is interested—' *il est
aussi peu égoiste qu'il est intéréssé!* ' "

Reading this judgment of a man who had certainly
great experience of humanity, one cannot but be struck
with that persistency in opinion which he notices, and
which remained one of the principal features in the
character of Bismarck throughout his career. He never
tried to hide it from the public, who most of the time
believed that he was deceiving them when, in reality,
he was absolutely sincere.

Bismarck is reported to have told someone once that
the " best way to mislead people is to tell them the
truth." And he spoke the truth far more often than
any other man placed in the position which he occupied
would have cared or dared to do. It was this habit—
which must not be confounded with honesty—that gave
him his great power. He would say disdainfully that any
of his plans might have been interfered with, and even
defeated, had one only taken the trouble to listen to
him, and to believe that they existed, and that he meant
to carry them out regardless of opposition and consequences. He used to complain—he even said so one
day to my father—that in Prussia Ministers persisted in

PRINCE VON BISMARCK

following a sentimental line of policy, which was the most fatal mistake a Government could commit. He had fully made up his mind to banish sentimentality from his programme, to care not whether he hurt or wounded the people with whom he had got to deal. There was in him something of the nature of that Brennus, the Barbarian chief, who, in throwing his sword into the balance in which the vanquished Romans were weighing the gold which they were offering to him as their ransom, had exclaimed the famous words, " *Væ victis!* " He had no mercy, and would have laughed at the person who dared mention such a word in his presence. For him politics was a game in which the greatest mistake consisted in not using and abusing the advantages which the clumsiness of one's adversary had put within one's reach. For him implacability was a virtue, the one virtue needed for the government of a nation.

Some people have said that Bismarck had been offered the post of Minister for Foreign Affairs during his stay in Petersburg, but that he had refused the offer and begged to be sent to Paris instead. This, however, is not exact, because if he had been left to follow his inclination he would have preferred to remain in Russia a few months longer, so as to bring before the eyes of Russian statesmen more prominently than he had been able to do the advantages of an alliance between their country and Prussia.

At that time Bismarck was a resolute partisan of an alliance with the Tsar, whose prestige he fully appreciated in spite of the Crimean War. That conflict, by the way, Bismarck did not consider was the great success for the Anglo-French entente which England and France believed it had been. He knew very well that

Sebastopol was not Russia, and that Russia would only consider herself defeated were she struck in a vital spot, such as Moscow or Kiev or Petersburg. He saw clearly that an alliance with Russia not only would considerably strengthen the position of Prussia in Germany, but would also bring advantage to the Empire of the Tsar, inasmuch as it would counteract the designs of Austria and oblige the latter to give some attention to what was going on across her Galician frontier, where, so far, she had refused to see a menace for the future. The game of Bismarck was to play one Power against the other, and this he succeeded in doing to perfection during the whole period he remained at the head of affairs.

Vast plans were maturing in Bismarck's mind which he did not want marred. During the Regency definite decisions were difficult, because there was always the feeling that the finality of authority invested in kingship was absent. Bismarck did not want to risk a reversal of any part of his policy. So, until the Regency lapsed, he was diffident of taking office.

He did not, however, abstain from pressing his convictions upon responsible Ministers. During a meeting which had taken place under the presidency of the Regent, at the latter's palace in Berlin, Bismarck had strongly advocated the necessity of a decided line of policy and of conduct in regard to Austria. He found a strong opponent to these views in the then Minister for Foreign Affairs, Baron von Schleinitz. The Baron staunchly advocated the need of maintaining good relations with Vienna, no matter at what cost. This he considered necessary in view of the possible danger of a Franco-Russian Alliance directed against the States of Central Europe, as had been mentioned in the Press recently. It is a curious thing to observe that this point, which in the years to come was to cause so much uneasiness and annoyance to Bismarck, was then simply ignored by him as quite an improbable contingency. On the other hand, Schleinitz, who, together with the Princess of Prussia, of whom he was the intimate friend, had been the first one to recognise its possibility, refused later on to admit the peril for the German Empire which might lie in such an alliance. The two men hated each other already at that time, and this enmity was to last until the death of Schleinitz, when Bismarck carried it so far that he forbade the members of the staff of the Foreign Office to be present at the funeral of their former chief.

In the meanwhile King Frederick William IV. died and his brother succeeded him. Even to a superficial observer it became evident that a great change was impending in the conduct of affairs, and that the new Sovereign would try to inaugurate a new system, about which the general public was in uncertainty, at least concerning its broader lines. At the head of the Cabinet stood Prince William of Hohenzollern, a very well-intentioned man, but neither a politician nor a statesman, who, besides, stood completely in awe of the War Minister, General von Roon. The General was the only man among his colleagues in the Cabinet who approached von Bismarck in intelligence, with whom he was upon terms of close friendship.

Almost the first day after the accession of the new King a conflict arose in the Ministry concerning the question of the oath of allegiance traditionally taken by the estates of the Realm on the occasion of the coronation of the Sovereign. Some of the Cabinet thought with William I. that the oath was compatible with his

well-known desire for a new constitutional law, whilst
others assured him that under the circumstances the oath
had better be avoided. Roon consulted Bismarck in a
long letter, in which, among other things, he asked
whether, in view of the seriousness of the crisis, he would
not agree to enter the Cabinet, seeing that the resignation of Baron von Schleinitz seemed to be certain. In
his reply Bismarck told von Roon, among other things,
that, in his opinion, " the principal mistake of Prussian
policy had been to consider too little the rights of its
own King and too much those of foreign Sovereigns.
It is," he added, "the natural consequence of the
dualism between the constitutional policy of the Ministers and the legitimistic direction given to our foreign
policy by the personal wish of his Majesty. It would be
very difficult for me to take upon myself the succession
of Schleinitz, and one of the reasons is that I do not feel
at present strong enough in health for the work which
such a thing implies; but if I accepted I should consider
it a necessity, even for reasons of home politics, to give
quite a different direction to our foreign policy. It is
only by changing entirely our attitude abroad that we
shall be able, in my opinion, to deliver the Crown from
internal movements which it would not be able otherwise
to resist, even though, I believe, if it would, it has at
its disposal the power effectually to crush any untoward
development. No one abroad would understand the fall
of the Cabinet on this question of the oath of allegiance;
it would be said that a long course of bad administration
of public affairs had exasperated the nation against the
Government to such an extent that the least breath of
wind was sufficient to kindle a destroying flame. . . .
For fourteen years now," he went on, " we have tried

to develop in the Prussian nation a taste for politics without allowing it to satisfy its appetite; is it to be wondered that to-day it seeks its food in the gutter?

"We are almost as vain as the French, and if only we believe that the foreigner esteems us we allow him to do what he likes in our own country. . . . Among the Royal houses of Europe, to begin with that of Naples and to end with that of Hanover, there is not one among them who feels thankful to us for the proofs of affection which we have given, and we practise in regard to them all a truly evangelical love for our enemies, to the detriment of the security of our own throne. I am as faithful to my own Prince as the Vendeans were in regard to their King, but I feel so indifferent to other Monarchs that I would never raise a finger in their defence. I fear that my point of view in this question is too different from that of our most gracious lord and master for him ever to think it wise to offer me a place among his advisers, and if he should decide to employ me at all I suppose it will not be otherwise than in home matters. However, I am quite indifferent, because, taken as a whole, I do not think that the Government can arrive at any brilliant results unless our attitude in regard to foreign affairs becomes clearer and less under the influence of dynastic sympathies. Hitherto we have had such want of confidence in our own strength that we have ever sought their help—aid which nearly always they could not give us, and which we did not in the least require."

This letter was still written from Petersburg, on the point of leaving for a short stay in Germany. When Bismarck reached Lubeck on July 9th he read in the papers that the crisis had come to an end, and that the King and his Ministers had left Berlin. On July 3rd the

Sovereign had published a message to the nation, in which he said that though he was determined to uphold the old tradition of the oath of allegiance, he had decided, out of respect for his brother's memory, to content himself with the ceremony of the coronation, which was linked with the principle of the direct succession to the Royal dignity.

A letter from von Roon, written on July 24th from Brunnen, in Switzerland, to Bismarck gave some details concerning the crisis and the circumstances that had accompanied it, and criticised severely the part which the Queen Augusta had played. "One of the reasons," said von Roon, "why it had been decided that a coronation had to take place was that, at the instigation of the King's Consort, the Royal robes to be used at it had already been ordered in the month of February preceding," and that the King was entirely under her influence and that of her friends, foremost among whom was Baron von Schleinitz. The latter at this time telegraphed to Bismarck asking him to come to Baden-Baden where the King was staying, and seemed to think that the former would use the opportunity to speak to the Sovereign in regard to home political questions. But Bismarck was far too clever to commit such an error, the more so that he immediately noticed that his arrival at Baden had been anything but agreeable to the King. He therefore merely told William I. that, in view of the coronation, he had come to beg the favour of a longer leave, as he wished to be present if allowed. William I. seemed quite relieved, and granted the request most graciously. Bismarck arrived in Königsberg on October 13th, where the coronation took place on the 18th. Before that day Baron von Schleinitz had tendered his resignation, which the King had accepted, and Bismarck noticed that the antagonistic feelings of the Queen in regard to himself had undergone a change. She even took the initiative in a conversation with him on the subject of a German national policy. Count Bernstorff had then assumed the direction of foreign affairs, and as he was not sympathetic to Augusta she showed herself more amiable toward Bismarck than she had been for a long time, going so far on one occasion as to stop and talk to him in the middle of some Court ceremony, much to the impatience of the King who unsuccessfully tried to draw her away. Bismarck, always attentive to everything that was going on around him, thought that he observed that relations between the Royal couple were slightly strained. William I. avoided him, probably because his consort showed herself gracious to him. Such incidents were of frequent occurrence in the *ménage,* and did not tend to make easier the position of those who were obliged to remain in close proximity to William and Augusta.

Bismarck did not return to Russia except to present his letters of recall; he journeyed back to Berlin in May, 1862, took rooms in a hotel, and remained there some weeks, feeling himself entirely out of place in the capital. He would not hear of entering the Cabinet, principally because he did not believe he would get from the King the support which he would have needed to carry through his plans. This lack of definitude on the part of William I. arose from domestic influences which he was unable to resist, and which were constantly at work around him. At last, disgusted—as he put it himself—at the uncertainty of his position, Bismarck applied to Count Bernstorff, asking him either to give him an appointment of some kind or else to allow him to retire altogether from the diplomatic

service. The reply to this request was his appointment
as Prussian Minister in Paris on May 22nd, 1862. Bismarck did not lose any time in starting for the French
capital, because on June 1st following he had already
presented his credentials to Napoleon III. at the
Tuileries.

The Emperor showed himself exceedingly gracious
in regard to the new Envoy; he had been nursing for
some time the idea of a Franco-Prussian alliance which
might help him to keep Austria in check, and he allowed
Bismarck to realise that such was the case in the course
of a conversation which he had with him at Fontainebleau, whither the Prussian Minister had been invited.
Napoleon suggested a walk, and during its progress
suddenly asked Bismarck whether he thought that the
King of Prussia might be induced to consider such an
eventuality. Bismarck answered that his Sovereign
entertained the best feelings in the world for the Emperor, and that the prejudices against France which
existed in Prussia at the beginning of the century had
almost entirely disappeared. But, he added, as a rule,
alliances were the result of circumstances, and that
circumstances alone decided their utility or their need,
because every alliance presupposed some determined aim
or motive. Napoleon objected, saying that some Powers,
without any ulterior reason for being so, were upon
decidedly friendly terms with one another, whilst others
could never be so. Napoleon continued that his idea of
an alliance was not inspired by the desire of launching
France into any kind of adventure, but because he sincerely believed that between Prussia and France there
existed well-defined common interests, and consequently
were present all the elements of an intimate and lasting

friendship and understanding. It would be a sad mistake, he agreed, to try to create certain events, because it was impossible to foresee either their direction or force. One could, however, make the necessary dispositions not to be surprised by them, and it was just as well to be prepared for everything, so as to be able to profit by one's chances when the moment to do so arrived.

The Emperor went on to develop this thought of a diplomatic alliance, whereby would grow up a mutual confidence and the conviction on both sides that each could rely on the other in moments of difficulty.

He went on to explain that a few days earlier Austria had caused certain overtures to be made to him in view of a *rapprochement*. So far as he could see this was owing to Bismarck's appointment to Paris, the news of which had provoked something like a panic in Vienna. Prince Metternich—the Ambassador—had told him that he had received instructions of such magnitude that on reading them he had been quite frightened. He had been given the most unlimited powers to come to an arrangement between the Imperial Government and France, no matter what the latter might require in exchange.

Bismarck was far too clever to engage in any undertaking either for himself or for Prussia; he merely thanked the Emperor for his confidence, adding that he must report to his Government the subject matter of the conversation they had just had. His personal opinion, which without scruple he explains in extenso in his Reminiscences, led him to believe that there was some truth in what Napoleon had told him, though he considered that the latter had been very imprudent in thus laying his cards before a comparative stranger. His own experience at Frankfurt had convinced him that Austria was ready to make any sacrifice, including even that of Venice, in order to assure its predominance over Prussia, and if it had not yet concluded an alliance with France this was not because it had hesitated to pay the price, but because the Emperor Napoleon mistrusted Austrian politicians and had an innate prejudice against a dynasty with which friendship had proved so fatal to his great uncle. On his return to Paris from Fontainebleau Bismarck wrote a long report to King William I., but instead of recommending the alliance which Napoleon had indirectly proffered he explained that the conclusion he drew from his conversation with the French Monarch was that it would be useless for Prussia to reckon on the help of Austria against France.

At the same time, by the back-stairs methods, he caused to be conveyed to the Foreign Office in Vienna the nature of the offers which he had received from Napoleon, thus poisoning with suspicion the relations between Austria and the French Court. Long after, when Bismarck was disgraced, Prince Richard Metternich recalled this incident, and owned that it had influenced him considerably in regard to his intercourse with Napoleon III., whom he had never been able to forgive the duplicity which had brought Austria such serious difficulties. Napoleon's indiscretion had justified the Prussian Government in advance in any betrayal of Austrian confidence it might make.

"And I was wrong to attach such an importance to it," added Prince Metternich, "because we should have fared better if we had not allowed France to be crushed in 1870. To be sure there was the remembrance of Sadowa, but, considering we had forgiven Prussia, there was no earthly reason why we should have gone on for such a long time resenting the action of France on that occasion, seeing that it was purely a passive one."

This was very well reasoned, only it was a remorse which came too late, and which he would have done better, perhaps, not to have mentioned, because by it he stood self-accused of want of foresight, which, in a man of his mental calibre, was inexcusable.

After the Fontainebleau incident Bismarck thought it wiser not to remain in Paris, but under the pretext of a summer holiday went to Biarritz. A strong current was setting in his favour, and his great friend General von Roon was continually pressing him to join the Ministry; so far he had objected, saying that he considered he had not been well treated by the King, who had markedly avoided talking with him the last time he had been in his presence. What he wanted was some certainty as to his future. When he had been sent to Paris this had been done under the implied understanding that his stay would be short, and that he would either be transferred to London or else called upon to occupy some important post in Berlin. But after his departure these fine promises had been forgotten, and Count Bernstorff had either not replied at all to Bismarck's inquiries or else done so in ambiguous terms. Roon was constantly assuring him that all that was needed to ensure his being called upon to take the direction of the Prussian Foreign Office was his presence in Berlin, but this was precisely what Bismarck did not care for, thinking it would be far more to his advantage if he were called by the King than if the latter found him at his elbow when he required him. Nevertheless, he was alive to every chance, and had assured himself of

allies in the capital. On September 16th he received a
telegram from Roon · "*Periculum in mora*, hurry up.
The uncle of Maurice Henning." This signature had
been agreed upon beforehand for use in case of necessity;
it told Bismarck that the time had come to return to
Berlin if he wished to be in " at the death." He arrived
in Berlin on the morning of September 20th. The
Crown Prince had been apprised beforehand of his
coming, probably by Roon, and at once summoned him
to his side. This incident very nearly cost Bismarck the
post which he coveted, because when the King heard
that he had seen his son first he remarked bitterly to
someone who ventured to praise Bismarck : " There is
nothing to be done with this one either; he has already
seen my son."

On September 22nd Bismarck was at last summoned
to meet the King at Babelsberg, near Potsdam, the
summer residence of the latter. William I. immediately
plunged into conversation, saying that he did not want
to govern if he was not allowed to do it according to his
conscience, and in a manner for which he could answer
before God, as well as before his subjects. This, he
went on, was impossible if he had to conform to the wishes
of the present majority in the Landtag. On the other
hand, though he had looked for them, he had been unable to find Ministers willing to take the responsibility of
the Government without considering Parliament. He
had, therefore, made up his mind to divest himself of
supreme power, and had already prepared his act of
abdication, as it was impossible for him to govern in
accordance with his personal views and opinions.

Bismarck replied to the Sovereign that he was quite
ready to enter the Cabinet, and that he was quite certain

that Roon would remain in it too, once he did so, and he added that he felt also convinced they would be able to discover others willing to co-operate if any of the present Ministers resigned. The King then asked him whether he would be ready to help him in a complete reorganisation of the army even against the majority of the Landtag. Bismarck, having given him his promise to that effect, William I. then declared that that being so, he thought it his duty to go on with the struggle and that he would not abdicate.

This is Bismarck's version of the incident. The King told a somewhat different tale to one of his personal friends a great many years later. His story was that, in spite of Bismarck's entreaties not to allow himself to be discouraged, he had felt rather nervous at the thought of embarking upon a struggle of such magnitude as opposing the wishes of the nation, and especially with the help of a man whom he knew well had not the sympathy of his colleagues, and whose personality was, moreover, particularly obnoxious to the Queen. But Bismarck had almost violently declared to him that he would not be doing his duty if he gave up the fight, and this appeal —always a powerful one with the old King—had decided him to tear up the abdication act he had already written and signed.

That same afternoon a long and earnest conversation took place between the Sovereign and Bismarck. This intimate talk gave Bismarck a much better understanding of the character of the King and inspired in him feelings of affection for the personality of William I., to which he remained faithful through many vicissitudes and trials. At the same time, that interview convinced him that he would always find one impediment he would never be able to get rid of, and that was the influence of the Queen.

Augusta was a very clever woman in her way, cleverer, perhaps, than her husband, and certainly more brilliant, but her unfortunate propensity for intrigue, and her conviction of her own importance and of her own intelligence, was bound to produce a permanent antagonism between her and the man who had undertaken to pilot the Prussian ship of State until he was dropped by a new captain. So long as the King had been the heir to his brother's throne he had shared his wife's opinions upon political matters, but when he became Sovereign, and was faced with all the responsibilities of his high position, he kept his own counsel— much to the Queen's chagrin. The Queen was given to excessive criticism, and was, moreover, very much disposed to take prejudices at the suggestion of the friends among whom she generally sought her inspirations. They represented things to her in a false light, always tinted with self-interest. She was obstinate, had no opinions of her own, but a very high conception of her duties as a woman and a Queen. She fully believed that she had the right to mix herself up in matters of government and of being informed in regard to all important questions of State. This the King did not like and was determined not to allow, but at the same time he lacked the courage to say so, and so much friction was caused all round.

At the same time the small, mean intrigues of the Queen never had the importance which Bismarck attributed to them, and it is surprising how such a powerful mind as his could not conceive their inanity and harmlessness. He would have fared far better had he ignored the Queen. This would have convinced the Court of her insignificance and considerably diminished her importance; it would have nullified any influence she might have had, and compelled her to give up a useless struggle. But the very fact that he continually opposed her and tried to thwart her transformed her, in the eyes of the enemies of Bismarck, into a formidable opponent; this she could never have been, and would never even have known how to be. Unfortunately for both, from the very first moment of Bismarck's assumption of power, his enmity with Queen Augusta assumed a scale quite out of proportion to her importance, and was to become the source of much unpleasantness and considerable strife in years to come.

CHAPTER V

Genius at the Helm

SEPTEMBER 23rd, 1862, was a fateful date, inaugurating a new era for Prussia and weaving into the web of circumstance for the world a new pattern in cruder colours and of sinister design. On this day the Royal Cabinet Order which appointed Bismarck to the functions of Minister of State and President *ad interim* of the Council of Ministers was published in the Official German Gazette. The maker of modern Germany, the moulder of the policy of its Emperors, came into power provided with a programme and armed with an indomitable will which was to carry his Fatherland to heights of which no one had ever dreamed. From the very first day that he took in hand the direction of public affairs he gave proofs of that moral courage, energy and brutality which were to remain the prominent features in his character until his death. He was absolutely sure of himself, as great geniuses have a way of being sure, and he was not to be persuaded to deviate one iota from any line of conduct he had thought out. His views as to the future were as simple as they were far-reaching and domineering. The Prussian army was to be reorganised according to the plans elaborated by the King and General von Roon; Austria was to be banished from the German Confederation, and Prussia was to become the leading Power in Germany. In a word, the Frankfurt programme was to become a reality after all, but under

Hohenzollern instead of Habsburg control—a very different matter.

To govern in defiance of a Constitution, Bismarck remarked to one of his friends, rather "tickled his fancy" —he deliberately used the English words because he felt they expressed the true state of his feelings on the subject better than anything he might have said in German or in French. He lost no time before he put into operation his ideas on the government of Prussia, and especially on the conduct of foreign affairs which, he declared with vehement impoliteness, had been atrociously managed for over half a century. He withdrew the Budget which his predecessors had laid before the Chambers a few days before his accession to office, and he caused the official Press to use words which left no doubt as to his intentions to administer the funds of the State independently of Parliamentary control and without an approved Budget. This revolutionary procedure was adopted almost as soon as Bismarck assumed office; he was nominated on the 23rd and the withdrawal of the Budget took place on the 29th!

The next day the Chamber protested against so arrogant an act, and on the motion of Max von Forckenbeck, a member of the Budget Commission, requested information as to the national Exchequer. Upon this Bismarck made one of the most sensational declarations that ever fell from the mouth of a responsible Minister of a Constitutional country. He began with the remark that the Budget, according to the Prussian Constitution, could only be accepted if the Government and the Chambers were in complete accord with the King as to its details, then went on to make the historical announcement—which Europe has never forgotten—that

" Prussia must gather together her strength and become prepared to grasp the first favourable opportunity instead of letting it slip by, as she has so often done in the past. The Prussian frontiers, as they have been fixed by the Treaty of Vienna, are not favourable to the healthy development of her existence as an independent State. It is not with speeches or with parliamentary resolutions that the great questions of the day are decided, as was mistakenly done in 1848 and 1849, but with blood and with iron."

One may imagine the impression which this fiery speech produced in Prussia and all over the Continent. Especially was this so in Austria, where it was interpreted as a direct threat against the dynasty of the Habsburgs. In France, too, the few people interested in the events which were taking place in Berlin began to wonder whither the new Minister of King William I. was intending to go and what was his ultimate object. Among these people was M. Thiers, who, however, was one of the few who did not hesitate to see in the declaration a foreshadowing of war with Austria.

Writing to my father on the subject, M. Thiers said :

" I am sorry that our Government here does not seem to realise that what is going on in Berlin is of a world-wide importance, and not at all the ' *querelle de clocher*' which some believe it to be. It is so strange to me that people who profess to have made a study of history fail to notice this important incident among all other important things, the development of a nation from the historical point of view. We are used to think of Prussia as a small and insignificant nation who has not yet recovered, nor ever will recover, from the blow which was dealt to her by the battle of Jena, and we have given no attention whatever to the methods of military expansion she has followed ever since with such unostentatious perseverance. Prussian diplomacy has always been of the intriguing kind; we have seen it at Frankfurt when, in defiance of the undoubted rights of the Emperor of Austria, the Imperial diadem was offered to Frederick William IV. That he refused it was a mistake which, unless I am very much mistaken, will only inspire in his successor or successors the desire to repair it.

"Prussia and Austria cannot exist side by side in Germany any longer. One of them must make way for the other, and the prize will remain in possession of the most clever and the most determined of the two rivals. I cannot imagine Austrian statesmen capable of being either clever or determined; I am speaking, of course, of those of to-day. Had Schwarzenberg been alive things might have turned out differently. They might, or they might not; because it is another thing to prove oneself clever when one has to do with fools than when one is confronted by persons as clever as oneself, if not more so. With all his intelligence, Schwarzenberg, so far as I can judge, only looked at the immediate consequences of a fact. Now it seems to me that von Bismarck thinks far more of its future effects; and quite right too. He takes office with the firm intention of wresting from Fate the place to which he thinks Prussia is entitled—foremost of all the other German States.

"This Bismarck will succeed because he is quite right in his appreciation of facts. It is impossible, in the long run, for Germany to remain the agglomeration of small States she is to-day. Unity is not only a necessity, but her unavoidable destiny. And every attempt toward unity must have someone to lead it. Do you admit Austria will ever become a leader? I think that there cannot exist any doubt as to the reply to this question. And if she is not a leader, then her position in Germany becomes an impossible one, unless she holds out the neck of her own accord to the noose which Prussia means to put around it. The struggle between the two countries is inevitable; do what you will you will not be able to prevent its being fought. Von Bismarck is but too well aware of this, and he disposes his batteries accordingly; he abandons nothing to chance.

" I can see, therefore, that Prussian administration will remain for the present more military than political in aim and effect. Politics and diplomacy will come later on, when the King begins to reap the fruits of the battles that others will have won for him. But the danger is not there. The danger resides in this taste for further expansion, which a victorious war is sure to raise in the minds and hearts of the Prussian nation. Once transformed into a military camp, she will necessarily want to show to the world what she is capable of, and then will come the dangerous moment for which I fear no one in France is prepared. If we were, consequent with our historical traditions, we should most certainly renew the system introduced by Richelieu, and go for Austria— *nous devrions courir sus contre l'Autriche.* As we shall not do so, we shall have to swallow the consequences of the inane diplomacy upon which the third Empire prides itself, and when the danger will become patent to the eyes of every blind man in the street we shall most probably try to stop the torrent that will sweep us away in its waters before we shall have had time to cry out.

No, my dear Count, do not call me '*un radoteur.*' I know that I am not mistaken, and that the Prussian danger, about which so many people keep laughing, is a very real and serious one."

As we have seen, Thiers was wrong in assuming that the Imperial Government had forgotten the principles to which Richelieu had remained faithful all through his Ministry. Napoleon III. had indeed made some move to ally himself with Prussia in an endeavour to put a stop to the inordinate appetites of Austria. It had not been his fault that the man to whom he had made the necessary overtures had not accepted them. He could not foresee that in the game which Bismarck began at Fontainebleau the French Empire was destined to become one of the stakes, and by no means the least important one either.

In Petersburg, too, the new Minister of King William I. was the object of suspicion, at least in circles where his wide intelligence had been appreciated, though not with sympathy. Those who, on his arrival in Russia, had treated him as a negligible quantity, had discovered before his departure that there was much more in him than had been imagined. There were persons, indeed, who had seen through his play and suspected that he wanted to buy the support of Russia against Austria. Among them was the Princess Orloff, *née* Gerebzow, my father's stepdaughter, a woman of alert intelligence who lived in close intimacy with the Imperial family. She knew more about the secrets of politics than perhaps any other woman in Russia, and shared the Francophobe feelings of her husband, Prince Alexis Orloff, one of the Russian delegates at the Congress of Paris, who had never forgiven the Government of Napoleon III. for the

humiliation which it had inflicted upon Russia as a consequence of the Crimean War.

The Princess had at the time, though I believed she
changed later, very decided German sympathies, based,
perhaps, on her personal relations with the Royal House
of Prussia, and she had very quickly discovered Bismarck's
game in Petersburg. When she heard about his later
appointment as Prime Minister she recognised how
pregnant it was with immense consequences in the future.
Having occasion to write to my father soon after, she
expressed herself in the following terms in regard to it :

"Your friend Bismarck is now a great personage,
and tries to become a greater one if we are to believe
all that we hear. It would be a curious thing if, after
all, the treachery of Austria at the time of the Crimean
War were punished, and if, after having helped to oust
us from Constantinople, she finds herself ejected from
Germany by this very Prussia who had to lick her feet
such a short time ago. The man's speeches in the
Chamber leave no doubt as to his intentions. It will be
a battle for life and for death, because Prussia will not
give way so long as he is there to push her along. What
I would like to know would be whether he really secured
something from our Emperor during his stay here. It
seems to me hardly likely that he would have adopted
such a resolute anti-Austrian policy if he had not had
something or somebody behind him to back him up. I
know that he had some conversations with our gracious
Sovereign about which the latter has not spoken to
anyone, and I have no doubt that he knew how to appeal
to all the remembrances of the past, and to speak of the
deceased Empress-Mother, and of all the Prussian relations we have always been so fond of. Whether he has

succeeded is another thing. I hope he has; for one thing, I always like people who know their own mind, and secondly, I believe that it would be to our advantage to see a strong Prussia in opposition to a weak Austria and a weakened France."

The great lady who had penned these lines evidently shared the mistake of that experienced politician, M. Thiers. They both believed that Bismarck required some foreign help to push through his extensive plans. In reality he did nothing of the kind, and his supreme ability consisted in persuading everybody but Austria— with whom he disdained to use any metaphors—that he wanted their aid, whereas he was already absolutely convinced that he would contrive, unaided, to emerge victorious out of one of the most entangled situations in which a statesman had ever found himself.

After the impudent declaration made in the Landtag on September 30th Bismarck was prepared to meet with violent reproaches, not only on the part of his enemies, but also from his colleagues, and he was not without some apprehension as to the impression that his speech might have made upon the mind of the King himself. Even General von Roon, who up to that day had always stood at his side, expressed to him after the sitting his displeasure, and told him in so many words that he did not consider such "witty digressions" likely to further the cause they had both at heart. But Bismarck remained unmoved and only protested against the words "witty digressions," saying that, on the contrary, he had never been more serious in his life than when he had made this memorable speech. He fully acknowledged, however, that the account which probably would be given of it to his Sovereign might dispose the latter against him; and

to counteract the effect of his words he had decided to
meet William I. on his way back from Baden-Baden,
whither he had gone for the celebration of the Queen's
birthday, so as to be able to have a quiet hour's conversation with him in the train before the Monarch's return
to Berlin.

The Chancellor has given us an account of this interview, so dramatic in its consequences. He waited for
some time at a small junction called Jüterbog for the
train in which the King was travelling, and had some
difficulty to discover William, who was in a reserved first-
class carriage. He was quite alone and seemed excessively
displeased at something. When Bismarck began explaining to him what had taken place and why he had been
led to make such strong declaration concerning Prussia's
future intentions, William I. interrupted him by saying :
"I can quite well foresee how all this will end. They
will cut off your head in the square before my window,
and a little later it will be my own turn."

To this impatient phrase Bismarck replied in words,
the grandeur of which was at the moment entirely lost
on his interlocutor :

"And what after, your Majesty?"

"How do you mean," answered the King, "afterwards? But afterwards we shall be dead."

"Yes!" said Bismarck "Afterwards we shall be
dead; but we must both die one day; and could we do
it better or in a more dignified way? I should perish in
fighting for my King, and your Majesty in sealing with
your blood the rights which God has conferred upon you.
Nothing would be able to change a fact so glorious and
so honourable for both of us—that we fell for the defence
of the rights which the Almighty has granted to your

crown. Your Majesty must not think of Louis XVI.; he lived and died as a weak man, and he is not a great historical figure. But Charles I. will always remain a splendid figure; remember how, after having drawn his sword and lost the battle, he nevertheless remained inflexible and sealed with his blood the Royal privileges to which he clung. Your Majesty is compelled to fight. You cannot capitulate; you ought to oppose yourself to the violence which is intended against you, even if by doing so you endanger the security of your own person.''

Bismarck had always been a profound student of the human heart, and he never showed it more than upon this occasion, when he was fighting for the triumph of ideas which none knew better than he might easily encompass the ruin of his Sovereign within the destruction of the hopes which they both had nursed and conceived. He was perfectly well aware that the one passion of William I., and the one principle which had always ruled him in life, was an over-developed sense of duty; once he thought his duty commanded to him to do this or that, he became inflexibly resolute, determined, firm, and even cruel if need arose. He was, as his Chancellor described, a true type of the Prussian officer, always ready to obey, but fearful of criticism when left alone to act on his personal responsibility.

As Bismarck explained the intricacies of the position, the King recovered assurance. The storms raised by the attitude of his Prime Minister made William wonder whether he had not gone too far in calling him to his side, and this feeling was accentuated by the hostility of the Queen and the latter's advisers. But, as soon as Bismarck had spoken with him—and this was the supreme ability of the future Chancellor—he looked upon

the situation from the point of view of a Prussian officer
entrusted with the defence of a place until death or
victory resulted.   Once he had been brought to look at
the position in that light there was no longer any fear
that the King would give way to weakness of any kind.
He no longer dreaded the criticisms of his wife or was
shaken by adverse public opinion; he did not even fear
the judgment of history.   When they reached Berlin,
after this conversation, William I. was perfectly calm;
he had recovered the good temper which was one of his
characteristics, and his Minister parted with him at the
railway station much relieved, convinced at last that he
would find in his Sovereign the support which he needed.

The struggle which had just begun under these circumstances even people well-intentioned in regard to Bismarck
declared to be dangerous enough to bring about his downfall and his material ruin.   A few months later, indeed,
the Landtag, by a majority of 274 against 45 votes,
declared the Ministers responsible in their persons and
in their fortunes for all the expenses to which they had
lent themselves without Constitutional sanction.   Some
people advised Bismarck to sell his landed estates to his
brother in order to save them from eventual confiscation.
He disdained to avail himself of this advice, and proudly
went on with the policy which he and Roon had elaborated
and the King approved.

A haughty page occurs in the Reminiscences where
the Chancellor outlines the future of his Fatherland
and the part Prussia was to play.

"I had never doubted," he says, "that the key to
German politics was in the hands of the reigning Sovereigns and dynasties, and not at all, as some people
thought, in possession of the press, the publicists, the

Parliament, or the barricades. Weak dynasties tried to find a support against the idea of union in nationalism, whilst the Royal Houses who thought themselves capable of resistance to the general movement were suspicious of it, because any development of the idea of German unity would, as a matter of course, diminish their independence to the profit of a central Power. The Prussian dynasty, however, could foresee that the hegemony of the future German Empire would inevitably belong to it. Since the time when during the Federal Diet of Frankfurt, the conception of a united Prussia-Austria had been replaced in my mind by the conviction that Austrian friendship, upon which I had relied formerly, did not exist any longer for Prussia. It seemed to me, therefore, that with Austrian treachery almost certain, it would not even be possible to regain, on the basis of the authority of the Federal Diet, the position which Prussia held in the German Confederation previous to the Revolution of 1848, and still more impossible to reform the Federal Constitution so as to raise the German people to the position of a great European nation.

" In spite of the humiliations of Olmütz, I arrived at Frankfurt with very good feelings in regard to Austria; but after I had seen certain documents which exposed the political aim of Schwarzenberg, which could be expressed in three words, ' degrade, then destroy,' I lost my illusions and realised that it was quite impossible to in a pacific manner the Gordian knot of the general German situation. It could only be cut with a sword. The King of Prussia must be won over to the national cause, and with him the Prussian army in order to , from the Prussian point of view, the unity of Germany as an Empire. So much became quite clear to me, hence my allusion in my speech before the Budget Commission to 'blood and iron.

"German patriotism, unless helped by its feelings of affection for a dynasty and the excitement of its rage or its enthusiasm, runs the risk of dying a natural death. Even in Prussia, where the national character is more formed than in any other German State, it is uncertain whether the integrity of the Prussian State could subsist were the Hohenzollern dynasty to disappear. As a result of this attachment of the individual German nations for the individual dynasties which rule them, this curious fact emerges that each German is ready at a given moment, if the chief of the dynasty gives the order, to do battle to the last extremity with his German neighbour. And though this often interfered with my plans, it yet helped them more than once in the case of our differences with Austria."

What a programme! and how strong and sure of oneself one must feel to flaunt it thus before the eyes of the world! Every one of the speeches of Bismarck can be considered as political acts more than anything else. At all events he never left his adversaries in the dark as to any of his intentions. When he was reminded of the Constitution he scornfully smiled and set it at naught. For instance, he did not allow the Landtag to make any use of Article 99 in the Constitution, whereby it had power to reduce the expenses of the State. He never waited for the Budget to be voted, but went on administering the kingdom on his sole responsibility. Finding himself at variance with the majority in the Chamber concerning the reorganisation of the army, he just went his way, knowing he now had William I. behind him. He never considered himself a Constitutional Minister in presence of a Parliament, only as the Minister of the King of Prussia. Once he disdainfully proposed a compromise, saying that the Crown, having consented to make some concessions, the Chamber had better follow its example. He expressed this opinion with such haughtiness that Count Schwerin interrupted, bringing upon himself the famous retort, "Might is better than right."

Bismarck afterwards declared that he had never said such a thing, but, nevertheless, it was the sense of his speech and the only way in which one could interpret it. When Count Schwerin accused him of having abused the power which he wielded, Bismarck maintained that he had only done so when the safety of the country required it, adding that, "as it is impossible for the existence of a State to come to a standstill, the man who is himself in possession of authority is under the necessity of making use of it in order to further the general interests of the nation."

The crux of the situation was that the whole existence of Prussia reposed on a military basis. The kingdom had always been ruled by a sword, and William I. did not mean to break this tradition. It appeared, indeed, to the King a monstrous thing that anyone should dare to question his right to advance the welfare of his army. Prussia was an absolute Monarchy so far as its soldiers were concerned. The King intended to keep within his personal control every matter connected with the military situation in his country. He carried this feeling so far that one evening, during a party which was given at the Royal Castle of Berlin, he accosted a Deputy who had voted against the military budget. Having received an invitation, the Deputy had thought it his duty to accept it; but William I. wrathfully told him that he could not understand how he had dared to appear in the presence of his Sovereign after his conduct of the day before, adding that he considered him as a rebel against the Royal authority. Bismarck found such outbursts not only a considerable help in his vast designs, but also an outward justification of his conduct all through his administration of the affairs of Prussia, and, later, of the German Empire.

All this while Bismarck never lost sight of his cherished plan to get into closer touch with Russia. The Polish mutiny of the year 1863 gave him the opportunity he had been seeking to establish upon a better basis a friendly understanding between the Romanoffs and the Hohenzollerns. He offered the Tsar the aid of Prussia in the repression of an insurrection which was threatening both countries. On February 8th, 1863, a Convention was signed in Petersburg which allowed Russian and Prussian troops to help each other for the purpose of re-establishing order in Poland and crushing the rebellion. This Convention, which received the name of Alvenslebem Convention, after the General who had signed it in the name of King William I., had been viewed with very favourable eyes by Alexander II., who had been irritated by the attitude of France, England and Austria, which showed that public opinion favoured the Polish cause. He found in Prussia a useful support to the line of policy he had adopted in regard to the Poles. England was not at all satisfied with this Convention, and its representative in Berlin, Sir Andrew Buchanan, told Bismarck that Europe would never accept it.

" Who is Europe? " sarcastically inquired the Prussian statesman.

"All the great Powers," replied Sir Andrew.

"Are they in agreement with one another?" further asked Bismarck.

And as it was impossible for the English Ambassador to give an affirmative reply, his interlocutor smiled significantly and the matter dropped. As things turned out, France was the only one who protested against the Convention, whilst Great Britain and Austria merely blamed it in a more or less timid and discreet manner. Bismarck had obtained his first great diplomatic success, the precursor of others which were to bring about the foundation of the new German Empire.

CHAPTER VI

Frederick III. and his Father

A GREAT deal has been said and written concerning the antagonism which at one time prevailed between Frederick III. and Bismarck; much of it is pure invention, and a goodly proportion of the balance mere hearsay. The Crown Prince Frederick undoubtedly dissented strongly—particularly on ethical grounds—from his Minister, but when all is said and done, and notwithstanding many things which must have painfully impressed the Crown Prince, he was grateful by nature, and fully recognised the services which Bismarck had rendered to his country as well as to his dynasty.

In a certain sense Frederick recognised them even better than did his father, because he was a convinced Imperialist. He had at heart a profound disdain for the independence of the smaller German States, which he looked upon as an anachronism; if he had been listened to, all the outward privileges which the Sovereigns in miniature—who believed themselves to be important factors in the German Empire—and which Bismarck had condescended to leave to them in about the same way that one throws a bone to a dog whom it is necessary to pacify, would have been abolished in 1871. One day when we were discussing the question Frederick expressed the opinion to me that the great mistake had been not to tell these crowned nonentities, initially, that they were only the Peers of the Empire, " *les Pairs de l'Empire.*"

To allow them to believe themselves indispensable factors in a situation which their pretensions only complicated to the detriment of its safety and welfare was to him an error which should have been extinguished as soon as it was born. Bismarck, however, did not share this opinion, having very well realised that the States of Southern Germany required some sort of pretty fiction to keep them in their proper place in the body of the new Empire, which, without them, could hardly have been expected to make progress. The great Minister and the heir to the Prussian throne were both Imperialists in the sense that they felt the necessity of an Empire. On the means whereby their desire was to be attained they were, however, at variance. This gave no reason, though, to conclude that the two were mostly at cross purposes. Each, indeed, had cause to be grateful to the other on more than one occasion. The Crown Prince not seldom championed Bismarck's policy, as, for instance, at Nikolsburg on the eve of the conclusion of peace with Austria, and it happened, too, several times that Bismarck came to the help of his future master and stood buffer —or peacemaker, if you will—between him and King William I., when the latter would have liked to show himself severely autocratic in regard to his heir's independence of opinions, in which Frederick displeased him more often than would have been either politic or opportune for the world to guess.

There is a circumstance which is very little known abroad, where the legend of the enmity of Bismarck with the Emperor Frederick III. has become an established fact, and this is that, among the people who insisted on Bismarck being asked to form a Cabinet, the Crown Prince had been one of the most pressing. Frederick had been predisposed toward Bismarck by his friend Max Duncker, whom the King had placed in close attendance on the Crown Prince, to initiate him into the management of State affairs. From the first moment the Crown had entered into conflict with the Chamber Duncker declared that Bismarck was the only man capable of pulling the Government out of the mire in which it had become entangled. Then again, Ernest von Stockmar, the private secretary of the Crown Princess, and the son of old Baron von Stockmar, the friend and adviser of Victoria of England and the Prince Consort, had also spoken in favour of the energetic statesman who had so well defended Prussian interests at Frankfurt. It naturally followed, therefore, that when the King had consulted his heir as to whether he should really entrust the presidency of the Cabinet to the clever diplomat who had been able to hold his own so well in the presence of Austrian arrogance at the Federal Diet, that Prince Frederick had expressed his agreement with the idea, and as soon as he heard that Bismarck had arrived from Paris he requested him to call upon him. The Crown Prince was a staunch Liberal at heart, and his sympathies were entirely in favour of the English system of government. He never for a moment imagined that the new President of the Council of Ministers would dare to rule in the despotic manner he immediately proceeded to put into force. On the contrary, he had hoped that he would use his best efforts to induce the Chamber to accept some kind of compromise with the Crown, and thus to put the governmental machine upon a sound basis, founded on a mutual understanding between the Sovereign and the elected Parliament.

This, however, was not to be, and soon rumours began

to be whispered that, among the persons who could not reconcile themselves to the new policy the King had sanctioned, the Crown Prince of Prussia was the most prominent figure. It was not remarkable that the very real unrest and indignation which arose out of Bismarck's high-handed methods of Empire-building gave birth to an opposition party who seized upon this foundationless gossip about Frederick and used it to "put spokes in the wheels" of the new Prime Minister.

Out of this agitation arose the conviction on the part of Bismarck that Frederick had become an enemy, which, however foundationless, the Minister resented deeply. Thus the rift began, and the wide differences of temperament between the two men did not tend to heal it. Things, however, might have gone on indefinitely in the sluggish condition into which they had lapsed if the incident which took place at Dantzig in 1863 had not brought everything to a crisis.

In the spring of 1863 rumours began to circulate that the Government had determined on a kind of *coup d'état* in order to put an end to the many expressions of discontent that had found their way among the public and in the Press. The Crown Prince had heard these grumblings, as others had done, and being on the point of starting for a journey of military inspection in Eastern Prussia he had written to his father before his departure, begging him to avoid, for the time at least, any too authoritative demonstration. This was on May 31st, 1863. On June 1st, however, was published a Royal decree limiting the liberty of the Press. The Crown Prince was incensed at it, and on the 4th addressed a long letter to the King, in which he expressed his disapproval of the measure, and complained that he had not

been invited to take part in the deliberations which had
led to it, and which concerned him as the future Sovereign
of the Prussian Realm.   On June 5th there was a reception in the Town Hall of Dantzig, where both the Crown
Prince and his Consort, who had joined him two days
before, were welcomed by the municipal authorities, and
where the Mayor of the town, de Winter, expressed in
his address his regret that the political situation of the
country did not allow the city to display the joy that
they really felt at the presence of its guests.   The Prince
was visibly moved, and replied :

"I also regret that my presence amongst you has
coincided with a most serious disaccord between the
Government and the nation, the news of which has surprised me considerably.   Personally I have not known
anything concerning the reasons that have brought it
about.   I have taken no part in the deliberations which
have led to such a sad result.   But all of you, and I too,
who, perhaps, am better aware than others of the noble
and paternal intentions and of the loftiness of feeling of
his Majesty the King, we all have the full conviction
that under the sceptre of his Majesty Prussia will go
forward with firm steps toward the glorious destinies
which Providence has in store for it."

The Prince, to give further weight to his words, sent
from Graudenz, where he was staying with the Princess,
an energetic protest to Bismarck against the decree concerning the liberty of the Press, requesting him to communicate it to the other members of the Cabinet.   This
course the King forbade ; instead, he wrote a most severe
letter to his son.   The latter instantly replied by asking
the Sovereign to forgive him for a step he felt he could
not avoid taking in the interest of his children and of his

own future, and begging him at the same time to allow
him to resign all his military commands and offices and
to retire into private life. William I. answered him on
June 11th, granted him the pardon he had asked for, but,
whilst saying nothing concerning his proposed resignation,
ordered him to remain silent for the future no matter
what could happen.

In a certain sense the irritation of the King against
his heir was legitimate, and at all events easy to understand; but Bismarck was too far-seeing not to perceive
that it would have been most impolitic to give vent to it
at a time when the Sovereign was already unpopular.
William I. wanted to have the Crown Prince confined
in a fortress as a punishment for his act of insubordina-
tion, and it was only with a great deal of trouble that his
Prime Minister succeeded in quieting his wrath. On
this occasion Bismarck decidedly proved himself a good
friend to the Crown Prince. The latter, therefore, might
have been expected to show himself, if not grateful, at
least better disposed toward his father's Minister. On
the contrary, Frederick thought it his duty to write to
Bismarck from Stettin on June 30th a rather violent
letter in which he expressed himself in terms of strong
indignation against the policy which the Minister of State
had persuaded the King to adopt and which, in his eyes,
was equivalent to a violation of the Constitution.

The strictures of the Crown Prince would have been
more than sufficient to incense an irritable man like
Bismarck, but his wrath was further excited by an unfortunate article that appeared in the London *Times* in that
same month of June, in which, among other things, that
organ declared that : "The Crown Prince of Prussia has
allowed himself, during a journey of military inspection,

to enter into open contradiction with the policy of the Sovereign and to express his doubts concerning certain measures adopted by the latter. The least that might have been expected from him after this grave offence would have been a public retraction of his words. The King wrote to him to that effect, threatening him with the alternative of deprivation of all his public functions. The Prince, having consulted with her Royal Highness the Princess, replied in a most dignified way to this demand. He firmly refused to retract anything of what he had said, and offered to resign all his dignities and commands, and to retire with his wife and children, somewhere, where no one would be able to suspect him in the future of the desire to mix himself up with any business of State. It seems that his letter was a most remarkable one, and one can only congratulate the Prince upon having a wife who not only shares his political opinions but who is also capable of being such a great help to him in such an important and critical moment in his life. It would be difficult to imagine a more painful situation than that of this princely couple in the presence of an obstinate Sovereign, a mischievous Ministry and an over-excited nation."

This article added fuel to flames that had not had time to burn themselves out. The King was absolutely furious and suspected his daughter-in-law with having inspired it. Bismarck had once more to intervene. He did not at all share his master's suspicions on the subject. His profound knowledge of human nature told him that the Crown Princess was far too intelligent and proud to have abased herself to the point of asking a newspaper to take up her cause and her defence. At the same time he felt suspicious of certain persons who surrounded her, such as her private secretary, Ernest von Stockmar, who had in consequence to resign his functions, an event which proved most unhappy for his Royal mistress, as his influence had been all the time in the direction of a policy of conciliation and abstention from party strife on the part of the Crown Prince. This Dantzig incident was but the prelude of several others which led to a state of chronically bad relations between the Crown Prince and Bismarck. When the Chamber of Deputies was dissolved, in September, 1863, the former wrote to the Prime Minister a curt letter :

"I have communicated to-day to his Majesty the ideas which I have already put to you in my letter from Stettin, which I had asked you, however, not to reveal to the King before I had done so myself. A very serious decision has been taken yesterday during the Cabinet Council. In the presence of the Ministers I did not wish to say anything to his Majesty. To-day, however, I have done so; I have explained my scruples, I have told my grave fears in regard to the future. The King is now aware that I am a resolute adversary of the Ministry.

"FREDERICK WILLIAM.

"*Berlin, September 3rd, 1863.*"

When one considers the natural violence of character which belonged to Bismarck one must come to the conclusion that he must have had singularly at heart the success of the vast plans which were maturing in his mind to have shown himself so patient in regard to this opposition. It would have been relatively easy for him to get rid of it by allowing the King to reduce Frederick to silence. But in this circumstance the genius of the statesman got the upper hand of the anger of the man. He was well aware that it was most essential for the security of the country as well as of the dynasty that the public should gain no real insight into the Royal quarrels. In his desire to be allowed a free hand in the measures which he saw and hoped would bring Prussia to glory and to fame, as well as to power, he went so far as to seek the Crown Prince, whom he asked direct why he refused to be present at the meetings of the Council of State, and why he systematically kept himself aloof from the Government. "It will be your Government in a few years," he added, "and if you hold different opinions from it you ought to try to smooth over the road to a change rather than to persist in tacit opposition." The Prince protested so angrily that Bismarck could not help becoming irritated in his turn. But, controlling his feelings, he merely replied that he had only spoken out of his attachment for the dynasty and in the hope of bringing about a reconciliation. He added that he had done what he could in the preceding June to prevent the King from taking violent measures against his son because he had wished for the welfare and the dignity of the Fatherland, and on account of the struggle in which the Government was engaged against Liberalism, to maintain harmony among the members of the dynasty. Bismarck concluded his remarks by declaring that he hoped that when the Prince ascended the throne he would find a servant as faithful as he was to the reigning King; but, whatever might happen, that servant would never be himself.

The conversation, however, ended more amicably than this might lead one to expect. The Crown Prince, nevertheless, persisted in his refusal to take part in the deliberations of the Council of State, and on that subject addressed a long memorandum to his father in which he sought to give reasons for his opposition. This only embittered relations that already had ceased to be cordial. William I. forwarded to Bismarck the document in which his son had unfolded his views, requesting him to make any notes thereon he considered to be necessary. Bismarck did so at much length, and with the evident desire to reassure his Sovereign as to the possible consequences of an opposition directed by the Crown Prince against his administration. The Minister rather feared the effect of any antagonistic step on the part of Frederick, perhaps because some people had persuaded him that this opposition was headed by the Queen, whom, in 1848, a certain party had wished to become Regent of the Realm in the name of her son when the abdication of Frederick William IV. had been expected.

The relations of William I. with his Consort were extremely curious in more than one respect. Their marriage had been entirely one of convenience, and they had never really agreed. Yet Augusta had contrived to acquire considerable influence over her husband, due principally to the fact that she worried him so much whenever something became a fixed idea with her that he gave way simply for the sake of peace. The Queen had a very high notion of her duties as a Sovereign, and William I., though he may not have loved her as much as she would have had the right to expect, yet respected her good qualities, and also the fact that she was the Queen, whose conduct it was his duty not to allow to be criticised. But the persistence with which she had always headed any opposition that manifested itself against his Government had made him suspicious of her and of their son, whom he would have liked to put beyond reach of his mother's influence.

Bismarck was very well aware of this state of things, and played his cards in consequence. His remarks concerning the memorandum of the Crown Prince were, therefore, so framed as to produce on the mind of the King the impression that it had to be treated as something without any consequence whatever, not worth contradiction. In a lengthy document he sought to persuade William I. that he was the only personage that counted in the State, that his opinions alone were to be taken into account, and that the position of the Crown Prince was an absolutely unimportant one which he had been foolish enough to take *au sérieux*, but to which no one attached any weight.

With such sophistries as the following the Minister succeeded in lulling the troubled mind of his Sovereign :

" The words ' tied hands,' used by his Royal Highness, have absolutely no sense. The country could never by any means identify his Royal Highness with any decision of the Cabinet because the country knows very well that the Crown Prince is not in a position which allows him to participate officially to the decisions of the Council of State. Unfortunately the position which his Royal Highness has chosen to take *against* the Crown is very well known in the country, and every head of a family, no matter to what party he may belong, will disapprove of it because it constitutes a refusal to submit himself to paternal authority. This wounds the feelings and the traditions of loyalty of the country. Nothing, therefore, could more harm his Royal Highness in public opinion than publication of his memorandum as he requests. The position of his Royal Highness Frederick is, no doubt, a completely false one, because it is not part of the mission of the heir to the throne to raise the flag of opposition against his King and his father. On the contrary, it is his duty to cease this opposition; he ought to make up his mind to play the part of an heir presumptive, as it should be, with submission and deference for his father and Sovereign.''

Among the many other clauses in this long and insidious reply the thirteenth is typical of the manner in which Bismarck uses the art of suggestion to get sufficient "sting" into his argument to cause his ulterior aim to be achieved without history being able to point a direct finger at him as the cause:

"There is no doubt that the work of the Ministers would be made easier if his Royal Highness did not take part in the meetings of the Council of State. But it seems to me that it is impossible that his Majesty should wish to avoid the duty his Majesty has to watch over the Crown Prince as far as is humanly possible and to insist on his becoming acquainted with the affairs as well as with the laws of the country. It would be a far too dangerous experience to allow the future King to remain a stranger to these policies and to these laws, because the welfare of millions of people depend on his becoming familiarised with them. His Royal Highness has given in the memorandum which his Majesty has seen fit to communicate to me the proof of his ignorance of the fact that the part taken by the Crown Prince in the deliberations of the Council of State is never a responsible participation in them, but only an educative one, and that on no occasion whatever can a vote be required from his Royal Highness. This is the point which the Prince has completely misunderstood, because if he were more

familiar with the affairs of State it would never enter
into his mind to threaten the King with the publication
of details of the deliberations of the Council which, in
itself, would mean a violation of the law and an offence
against the criminal code.''

Such incidents as these conspired to embitter the life
of Frederick and to make his path a thorny one.

CHAPTER VII

Playing with Austria

THE incidents which I have described regarding Bismarck's relations with the Crown Prince were, later on, to have a considerable bearing on the whole course of German politics, and the remarks of the future Chancellor upon the memorandum of the Crown Prince were to play a serious part in the relations of Frederick with his eldest son, the present Emperor William II. At the time that these comments were made to William I. Frederick remained in ignorance as to their import, and they only came to his knowledge through an indiscretion of the Queen Augusta.

One day when the old Emperor was unwell he had asked Queen Augusta to look out from his pigeon-holes some document which he required. In doing so she came across Frederick's letter to his father with the critical memoranda of Bismarck still attached to it. She quietly put both in her pocket and communicated them to her son. This occurred about the year '78 or '79, when the war which had always been raging between the Empress and Bismarck had reached a particularly active phase. She was the more delighted, therefore, to get into possession of a paper which she hoped would yet further irritate the Crown Prince against the Chancellor. Her hope, however, was not realised because the Prince at that time had, to an extent, reconciled himself with his father's Minister, and, at all events, had made up his

H   97

mind that it would not be to the advantage of the dynasty to lose Bismarck after the services which he had rendered to it.

In after years, when differences of opinion occurred between the heir to the throne and Prince William, he was glad to be able, on the strength of the remarks which Bismarck had made concerning himself, to require from the Chancellor his support in the exercise of his parental authority over a young man who seemed determined to set it at naught.

Of this, however, I shall speak later on in its proper chronological order. At present I must go on with my story, not without some shade of doubt whether I relate it quite correctly. In view of its importance I must ask my readers to forgive me if any inaccuracy has slipped into it. The incidents about which I am speaking did not take place under my eyes, and, unfortunately, at the time we discussed them were still too recent to be judged with the impartiality which they deserved. After 1873 I had opportunity personally to observe the development of the influence of the Chancellor and to watch the unequal fight which took place between him and the people who had foolishly imagined that they could drive him out of office in the lifetime of the Emperor William I. Of all that occurred in the years when I lived in Berlin I can speak with far more assurance than the events which preceded the war of 1870.

Now, to my story and the progress which, in spite of the opposition which his policy met in the country, Bismarck succeeded in making in the confidence of his Sovereign and among the extreme Imperialists in Germany who, tired of Austria, were but too willing and ready to enlist under the protection and leadership of

Prussia. Bismarck owed much to the help of this party, and William I. would have had longer to wait for his Imperial sceptre had not they been at the back of things. It was thanks to the Imperialists, too, that the Crown Prince gradually adopted a more peaceful attitude. Frederick was perhaps the most convinced Imperialist in the whole of Germany, and once he had become aware that Bismarck was working toward the restoration of the old German Empire for the profit of the Hohenzollern dynasty, he forgave him freely for the years of unpleasantness which he had caused him and even for the humiliating position into which he had thrust him—a Crown Prince without power.

A curiously anomalous position arose out of this change of feeling. Although King William I. had supported his Minister in all his enterprises, he was not always in accord with him concerning the means and the aims of Bismarck's policy, yet had not the courage to forbid him taking any particular course. The Crown Prince Frederick, who, on the other hand, had never been able to reconcile himself to the methods employed by Bismarck, yet supported him most cordially in many of his views from the moment that he had realised what they meant for the future of Prussia and of its dynasty. Between these two currents, equally favourable to him, the Chancellor was able to push through most of his conceptions and to maintain himself at the head of affairs for more than a quarter of a century.

Prussian statecraft during the first years of Bismarck's administration of foreign affairs was at once simple and complicated. Diplomacy was active in those years to keep Prussia absolutely free in all her movements, unentangled by any alliances with foreign Powers, no matter how

useful they might seem at first sight. It was on this
account that Bismarck turned a deaf ear to the propositions of Napoleon III., and that whilst willing to draw
Russia into the inner sphere of Prussia's politics, he had
not advised the King to conclude a treaty with France
directed against Austria. His plan was to use Austria
in such a way that she would co-operate in the work of
her own destruction. He ardently desired to see the
destruction of Austria as a German Power, but he fully
meant to make her realise her importance as among the
Slav nationalities. It had been on this account that he
had hesitated to enter into the views of the Tsar in regard
to the destruction of the Habsburgs whilst otherwise
lending himself outwardly at least to the Russian plans
concerning the settlement of the many perplexing questions of the day. By so standing aloof he would be free
to bend Austria to the task of weakening Russia in order,
ostensibly, to secure to herself the position as leader
of the Slav races. In reality Bismarck's far-sighted
machination did not arise from any sympathy with
Austria, but he saw in Russia the strongest and most
serious opponent of German unity.

The Cabinet in Vienna, however, understood that
Prussia was aiming at securing its dominance in Germany
by driving Austria out of the circle of its inner politics.
An interview which the Emperor Francis Joseph had with
King William at Gastein very nearly destroyed that plan,
because it elevated the relations of the two Sovereigns
with each other to a more personal and, consequently,
a more satisfying plane. This was a palpable check for
Bismarck's ambitions, and, as if to justify the proverb
which says that misfortune never comes alone, the
elections to the Prussian Chamber which took place

immediately after resulted in a considerable increase of the majority against him.

Bismarck found himself thus isolated in his own country, with nothing abroad to support him except the equivocal friendship of Russia; despised in Prussia for the struggle in which he had engaged with its parliamentary and constitutional traditions; and in direct conflict with the Royal Family, of whom not one would say a word in his favour. He began to wonder, indeed, whether he would be able to maintain himself in power when, suddenly, one of these events occurred which change the whole face of the world by their unexpectedness. King Frederick VII. of Denmark passed away at a moment when nobody had ever given a thought to his demise.

His natural successor in regard to the Duchies of Schleswig and of Holstein was his kinsman, Duke Christian of Sonderburg Augustenburg, who, however, had, so far back as 1852, resigned his hereditary claim to them for a sum of two and a half million thalers. This might have been a most excellent operation for him if it had received the assent of the German Confederation, and if his two sons had not strongly objected; the eldest, to the extent of making a formal declaration of his rights to succession, and declaring that nothing in the world would ever make him accept a renunciation which his father had had absolutely no right to make.

This was the beginning of the crisis. Lord Palmerston once remarked that there had been but three men in Europe who had really understood the Schleswig-Holstein question—one was dead, the second in a madhouse, and the third, who was himself, had forgotten it. Without, therefore, entering into the tiresome details which made war so acute a probability it is sufficient to say that what set fire to the barrel of gunpowder was the incorporation, in defiance of several Treaties, of the Duchy of Schleswig into Denmark by King Christian IX. immediately after his accession to the throne. This act of authority was immediately followed by a solemn protest from the Diet of Frankfurt in the name of Holstein and of Lauenburg against this violation of the autonomy of the Duchies and flaunting of the Conference held in London in 1852.

This protest gave Bismarck an opportunity to offer what French people call vulgarly "*Eau bénite de cour*" to Austria, whom he induced to declare jointly with Prussia its determination to uphold the rights of the German Confederation in Holstein as well as in Schleswig. Both the Berlin and the Vienna Cabinets declared that the Confederation was in honour bound to occupy Schleswig. Two members of the Prussian Chamber, Virchow and Stavenberg, thereupon proposed that the Confederation should also recognise the rights of the hereditary Prince of Augustenburg to the sovereignty of Schleswig as well as of Holstein, thereby ignoring and annulling the renunciation of Duke Christian, father of the Prince, in 1852. Bismarck immediately retorted that Prussia would consider the Treaty of 1852 as binding provided the King of Denmark expressed his willingness to conform to it. If he refused, the Prussian Government reserved for itself full liberty to act for the best according to its personal interests, and he added that upon this point it was in complete agreement with Austria. The Prussian Landtag was not satisfied with this reply, and declined to help him occupy the territory of Schleswig and also refused " contingency " credits for which he had asked.

There were some people who wondered what could

have produced this sudden change in the anti-Austrian feelings for which Bismarck was so well known. The public began at once to say that he was a man on whom it was impossible to rely, an accusation which, after all, was not so very wrong. Among these people was Baron von Goltz, then Prussian Ambassador in Paris, who took it upon himself to express to Bismarck his apprehensions concerning this renewal of friendship for Austria which had struck everybody as being so entirely strange. Bismarck's reply revealed much that was in his thoughts:

"You tell me," he said, "that you have no confidence in Austria. Neither have I; but I find that it is better for our present interests, and more opportune, to have Austria with us. Whether we shall drift apart, and by whose fault, time alone will show. I am not in the least afraid of war, and perhaps you will soon have cause to convince yourself that war is upon my programme. It is European Treaties that create European right, as a rule; if we wanted to interpret them in terms of morality and of justice we should speedily want to annul most of them."

What he did not add was that the crucial point of the whole Danish question lay in the acquisition of the Duchies by Prussia, for which every Prussian longed, with the difference that whilst the Chamber openly avowed it Bismarck wished to do it and to say nothing about it. He thought it his duty, however, to remind the King, on the day following the demise of Frederick VII. of Denmark, that all the ancestors of William I. had added something to Prussian territory, and that he ought to do the same. This took place during a meeting of the Council of State. The Ministers listened to him in silence, whilst the Crown Prince raised his arms to heaven in a mute protest.   The King only replied that "he had got no right whatever to take Holstein."

This reason was not the only one which made William I. hesitate.   It was far more the influence of the Queen Augusta which held him back, and the dread that she might be right after all when she had threatened him with the possibility of France seizing the opportunity which would present itself to occupy Rhineland as a compensation for the conquest of the Duchies. When this fear was communicated to Bismarck he simply laughed at it.   He carried the day, and an Austrian and Prussian army entered the territory of the Duchies, a step which was finally to give to William I. the military harbour of Kiel and the right to build the famous canal which was only to be completed by his grandson.   He had followed the example of his ancestors and added a priceless jewel to Prussian territory.

But what was Austria doing in the meanwhile? Austria had fallen into the snare which had been held out with an ingenuity which can only be compared with the orders that were given to her from Berlin in 1914, by which the whole of the world was thrown into the biggest war of history.   Her statesmen did not at all see the future.   They thought that they had matter for congratulation in the Treaty which they finally concluded with the Prussian Government ·at Gastein on August 20th, 1865, by which Austria remained in possession of the administration of Holstein, whilst Prussia took that of Schleswig, and Kiel became, potentially, the harbour of a German Imperial fleet still to be called into existence.   Both Duchies were to accede to the Zollverein, and the whole Constitution of the German Confederation was to be reorganised.   It is related that after the signature of this compact Bismarck exclaimed, "Now I have the pretext which will drag Austria into a war that will definitely exclude her from the position which she aspires to occupy in Germany."

The King of Prussia and Francis Joseph of Austria had a talk together after the Gastein agreement. Bismarck was present and, as a matter of fact, did most of the talking. He told Francis Joseph that whilst Austria had a great interest at stake in remaining upon good terms with Prussia it could not hope for any immediate advantages from the annexation of the Danish Duchies. The Emperor Francis Joseph refused to see things from the same point of view. Public opinion in his country, he asserted with emphasis, would not admit that a war which had cost so much in blood and in money would be unproductive of territorial expansion for the Monarchy. He bluntly inquired of Bismarck whether he meant to transform both Duchies into Prussian provinces, or whether he would content himself with exercising certain rights within their limits. William I. was asked for his opinion on the subject. The Sovereign felt embarrassed, but at last declared that " he had no right to take the Duchies, and that, therefore, he could not express an opinion as to what ought to be done with them." This put an end to any attempt on the part of the future Chancellor to persuade Austria to be a pawn in his game. History shows that he forthwith proceeded to obtain his end by other means.

This Schleswig-Holstein affair was, perhaps, the one in which the genius of Bismarck revealed itself most brilliantly, because his success laid the foundations of many other of his achievements. Public opinion in Prussia had been incensed against him because he had allied himself with Austria against Denmark. In reality, it had been the cleverest stroke of diplomatic skill he could have achieved. If the Prussian Government had acted independently of Austria it would undoubtedly have had Austria, together with England and France, and perhaps even Russia, against it. What was left for him to do then, except precisely what he did : obtain the complicity of Austria, dupe her later in such a way that she would accuse her ally of preparing in secret to annex Schleswig-Holstein to her own territory, thus provoking the *casus belli* for which he had been seeking ever since Olmütz. The plan was a magnificent one, if only by its unscrupulousness. Later on Bismarck declared that he had never had occasion to be more satisfied with himself than during the negotiations that had followed upon the war with Denmark. For one thing, the war in itself had strengthened his position by making Prussia proud of its military successes. At last Prussia understood the reasons which had caused the King to insist on the reorganisation of the army, no matter what the cost might be. This was already a gain for which one could hardly have dared to hope a few months before. What Prussia had required was to be launched with a firm hand on the road of her future victories, and to acquire the conviction that she was about to see fulfilled the glorious designs of the Great Elector and of Frederick II. Bismarck revived the self-confidence which Jena had shaken, and he well knew that the new appetites which he had awakened would never be satisfied.

The Gastein Convention had hardly been signed when Bismarck was already laying his plans how best to bring Austria to make some demonstration of hostility toward

Prussia. The question which appeared to his mind to
be most urgent for the moment was the weakening of
the Austrian Empire. He had said once that in " foreign
politics one meets with moments which never come back
if one has not been clever enough to profit by the advantages which they offer." This profound maxim which
all politicians ought to take to heart, and which Dr. von
Bethmann-Hollweg has so often forgotten, this maxim
was to inspire all his actions during those momentous
times when he had to contend not only with the difficulties which his powerful mind had foreseen, but also
with the unexpected hesitation of King William I., whose
feelings of loyalty feared the opprobrium that history
might attach to his name if he lent himself to such a
conspiracy against honour and truth. In order to find
some justification for the attack which his Minister was
meditating, William I. insisted on the latter making an
attempt to assure himself of the co-operation, or at least
of the disinterestedness, of Austria in regard to the future.
Bismarck accordingly proposed to Francis Joseph that
he and Prussia should divide the small German States,
whose independence was to be put an end to, and
together march against France, so as to conquer Alsace
and thus give to the new Central Empire that was to
be created out of the ruins of the German Confederation
the frontier line which was indispensable to its safety in
the future. As expected, the magnitude of the design
was beyond the intelligence of the man to whom Bis-
revealed it, and Francis Joseph recoiled with dread
and with suspicion from the temptation which was put
in his way.

The decision of the Emperor cleared the road before
the great Minister, whose genius was then able to give

itself free rein without being longer cramped by the scruples of William I. who followed him whilst not understanding him, and who was to become the instrument through which he succeeded in working out his boldest political conceptions. King William I. had become a partner in the perpetration of terrible injustices and iniquities which were disguised as absolutely righteous adventures, started out of the necessity of self-defence against aggressions no one had ever seen or heard of, but in which William I. came to believe in the most absolute manner.

The people who had the opportunity to approach Bismarck during that spring of 1866, which was to herald the humiliation of Austria before the Prussian eagles, and subsequently to lead to German unity, all agreed in saying that he had never appeared quieter and more impassive than during these anxious months.

He knew himself to be unpopular as no Minister had ever been before him in any country in the world. He had the Court against him, the Conservative and the Liberal parties, his own colleagues, with the exception of Roon, the Queen, the Crown Prince and Princess, the Royal family and public feeling in Prussia and throughout Germany. He treated them all with unconcern, because he felt sure that his King would stand by him, no matter what happened. That and his profound faith in himself was his great strength. Armed with these weapons he began, without hesitation and without remorse, the struggle which was to end in a war that would change the map of Europe. His whole conduct at this time can be compared to the discharge of a big gun that must take place once it has been fired, and which not even the will of those who have set the match can stop. Bismarck, too, had a trump card of no small importance in his game—that was the co-operation of Italy against interests with which Napoleon III. would never have consented to interfere. France had failed to play the pawn; she, therefore, must be checkmated. In March, 1866, King Victor Emmanuel, to whom William I. had sent the order of the Black Eagle a few weeks before, had been persuaded to dispatch a military mission to Berlin, composed of General Count Menabrea and General Govone, with powers to conclude an alliance with Prussia, which was signed for a duration of three months on April 8th, 1866, and June 7th following the troops of William I. entered Holstein. Austria immediately called upon the German States of Confederation to proceed to mobilisation against Prussia, whom it accused of having violated the treaties which it had signed, a thing, by the way, with which she was to become familiar in the future.

On June 18th the war began. It was to be one of the shortest that has ever been fought. On June 23rd the Prussian troops invaded Bohemia, and on July 3rd the battle of Sadowa saw the utter defeat of the Austrian army, not, however, without the Prussians having been for a short moment in extreme danger. Indeed, had it not been for the timely arrival on the field of action of the Crown Prince with his corps it is likely that the result would have been different. At midnight Crown Prince Frederick received from Colonel Count Finck von Finckenstein the order to march with all haste towards Königgrätz, and by a wonder of energy he contrived to arrive on the spot just as the Prussian troops already engaged in the battle were visibly weakening and being slowly driven back from the heights which they had occupied in the early hours of the morning. After a short but terrible struggle General Benedek had to retire in disorder, and Moltke, who, with a beating heart despite his impassive countenance, had watched the development of this tremendous fight, was able to say to his Sovereign in words that have passed into history: " Your Majesty has not only won this battle, but also the whole campaign."

The next day Austria appealed to Napoleon III. to intervene in her favour. She offered to cede to the French Monarch Venice and the territory appertaining to it in recognition. The latter, of course, handed it on to Italy, and indeed he could hardly have done anything else once he had made up his mind not to come to the rescue of the unfortunate Francis Joseph. In this Napoleon missed his opportunity, which would never again come within his reach, to become the arbiter of Europe; had he come to the aid of Austria, Prussia would never have been able to resist any attack seriously coming from the French frontier. Peace negotiations were therefore started; Bismarck was the first to recommend great moderation. This led to disagreements between him and the King, who wanted not only to annex Saxony, but also Anspach and Bayreuth, the two latter places because of family reasons and traditions— he considered them to have been the cradles of his race. The headquarters were then at Nikolsburg, a castle belonging to Prince Dietrichstein in Moravia, and it was there that the negotiations were carried through. Sharp quarrels took place between Bismarck, William I. and the Prussian Head of the Staff, General von Moltke. The King wanted to push forward and, if possible, to occupy Presburg in Hungary. Bismarck asked Moltke what he thought, adding, "If we could be absolutely certain that we should win the day a victory would certainly place us in a stronger position in regard to the peace negotiations. But if victory is doubtful it will be better to give up the whole enterprise rather than compromise our chances by a defeat."

Moltke replied that he thought the operation a dangerous one, and that he could not answer for its success. This determined Bismarck to recommend to the King the conclusion of an armistice from midday on July 22nd. This allowed him to send to General Fransecky, whose troops were engaged in an encounter with an Austrian corps, the orders to cease fighting, which arrived at a moment when it was hardly likely he could have come out with success from an engagement which the enemy had compelled him to accept. Diplomacy for once got the better of military science.

CHAPTER VIII

Austria Becomes a Pawn

HAD it been his immediate aim Bismarck might easily have realised his dream of an Empire at the Convention of Nikolsburg; but it would have meant the humiliation and subjugation of the whole of Germany under the heel of Prussia. An Empire so gained would have been compromised almost before it had been completed. The new Empire was not to arise out of the defeat of its future components; it had to be desired by them as the only thing which could give them, in their own eyes and in those of the world, an appearance of solidity. The vanity of the small States had to call it into existence, not their humiliation or defeat.

And what was to be done with Austria? Nothing at all, said the military party. Nothing at all, declared the King. She had been beaten; let her take the consequences of the reverses under which she had succumbed. But this was not what Bismarck thought; this was not, either, what he wished. With Austria as a perpetual enemy the very existence of Prussia as well as the unity of Germany would be endangered and compromised. Austria had to be transformed into an instrument of Prussian politics, into the useful pawn without which the game becomes impossible. She had to be treated with mercy, even with gentleness; and as vanity and self-indulgence were her besetting sins, these had to be appealed to so as to blind her to her future fate. A victorious entry of the Prussian troops in Vienna would naturally have been a source of immense satisfaction to the King and the military party, but was not a "political necessity," therefore it was avoided.

Many years later Bismarck confided to the one man, perhaps, from whom he had no secrets—Baron von Holstein, who was to become the *deus ex machina* of the German Foreign Office—that he had wished to give to the world, and to France especially, the idea that Prussia was a generous nation, and if she had shown herself merciless at Nikolsburg she would have awakened the anxieties of Europe, and perhaps have influenced Napoleon III. to the extent of interfering in favour of Austria. It was necessary for the success of Prussian policy for the whole world to be persuaded that Bismarck did not seek territorial aggrandisement; nothing more than the establishment of Prussian supremacy in Germany. So Bismarck had to keep his secret locked in his own breast, and meanwhile try as well as he could to moderate the appetites of his Sovereign, to assuage the impatience of the Prussian nation.

The conditions of peace which the King of Prussia mentioned in his telegram to Napoleon III., in reply to the information which the French Sovereign had given him of the cession of Venice to France by Francis Joseph, together with the latter's request for mediation, were so severe that one wonders how Bismarck could have allowed his Royal master to formulate them. Prussia required the reform of the German Confederation; that it should be placed under its authority; the cession of Schleswig-Holstein, of the Austrian part of Silesia which Frederick the Great had not contrived to wrest from Maria Theresa; the establishment of a frontier zone in Bohemia; **and** the deposition of the Sovereigns of Hanover, Hesse, Meiningen and Nassau, who were to be replaced by their presumptive heirs. Later on other demands were formulated which came partly from the King himself and partly from the military party. In these William I. asked for the annexation of Saxony, Hesse, and Hanover, and especially of Anspach and Bayreuth.

These terms, however, had to be modified. Austria declared that she placed, as a *sine qua non* condition of peace, the preservation of the independence of Saxony, whose Sovereign was a personal friend of Francis Joseph, and one of the Austrian plenipotentiaries who had arrived at Nikolsburg, Count Karolyi, categorically refused to consent to the slightest cession of Austrian territory. In spite of the opposition of King William, Bismarck gave way, because he wanted the preliminaries of peace to be signed as quickly as possible so as to avoid any intervention on the part of France, the one thing which he feared.

In the meantime Count Benedetti had arrived at the Prussian headquarters as the Ambassador and special envoy of Napoleon III. He explained the lines upon which his Government was prepared to recommend Austria to conclude peace. Prussia was to obtain territories with a population of about four millions, with the Mein as a frontier line. Austria was to retire from the German Confederation; King William I. was to have perfect freedom in Northern Germany, preserving, however, the integrity of the Saxon kingdom. Napoleon's great hope lying at the bottom of this proposition was that it might lead to the formation of a Confederation of the Southern German States, over which French influence would predominate. Nevertheless the proposal secured for Prussia latitude to move about freely in Germany, and that was

MARSHAL VON MOLTKE

Bismarck's aim. The King, however, was not of his opinion, and he decidedly opposed the plan. On July 23rd a Council took place at Nikolsburg under the presidency of William I., in which was to be decided the question whether one should accept the proposed peace or not. Bismarck was ill, and in consequence of this it assembled in his room. He gave the reasons why he considered it essential to accept the conditions offered by Austria, but he was absolutely the only one of his opinion. The officers of the Staff, not excepting Moltke, were all in favour of continuing the war until the fall of Vienna had put Austria at their mercy. The King agreed with this advice. Bismarck was so agitated that he became the prey of a nervous attack that brought about a crisis of tears such as no one would have expected a man of his kind to have been capable. The next day he had recovered sufficiently to go to the King. Whilst waiting to be received he met two colonels who had brought with them reports concerning the ravages of cholera among the troops in the field and the terrible figures which these reports revealed. This confirmed him yet more firmly in his resolution, and when he came into the presence of William I. he quietly went over all the political and military reasons which rendered the continuation of the war impossible, and for the first time revealed to William I. something of the gigantic conceptions which were agitating his brain. Later on he informed von Holstein that he told William I. : " Austria must be considered as a pawn in the chess of Europe ; if she is pressed too hard she will make alliance with France or Russia, and we shall lose the game. Moreover, we can do nothing with the German provinces of Austria, and should we annex them *in toto*, or partially, by doing so we should not add anything to our own strength. A fusion of them with Prussia is impossible; they would always remain a thorn in the flesh.''

This account is somewhat different from the one which the Prince gives in his Reminiscences, but the sense is the same. Personally, I am inclined to believe the one which I have reproduced as being the more correct of the two, as it was not destined for publicity. The King declared that he considered the conditions proposed as insufficient as well as unsatisfactory. He added a curious remark which proves how entirely he had allowed himself to be persuaded of the justice of the war which he was fighting : '' It is quite impossible to allow the guilty party in this war to get off scot free. Austria ought to be punished, not the German States it has persuaded to follow its lead.''

Bismarck very cleverly replied that it was not Prussia's mission to avenge the wrongs of others; what she had to do was simply to bring about the unity of the whole of Germany under the leadership of the King of Prussia.

What William I., who had a goodly share of the Hohenzollern spirit of vanity, disliked in the whole proposition was the fading away of his dream of a triumphal march into Vienna at the head of his armies; and being brutal, as all Prussians are, he could not see the subtlety of the reasonings of a spirit who always thought more of the possibilities of the morrow than the successes of the actual day.

At last the irritated King said that he had made up his mind and that the war would go on, and dismissed his Minister so coolly that the latter thought all was lost. Bismarck went back to his room and remained standing at the window, with the feeling that perhaps the best thing to do was to throw himself out of it to the courtyard beneath. The whole edifice he had been building had crumbled down like a house of cards, and, as he expressed himself in the picturesque language he used to people before whom he did not restrain himself, he would have liked "to wring the necks of all the idiots who did not understand him." Suddenly he heard the door open; someone came in and laid a hand upon his arm. It was the Crown Prince.

"You know that I have always been against war," he told him. "You considered it necessary, and the responsibility of it remains on your shoulders. If you are convinced that peace ought to be concluded, I am quite ready to help you and to discuss your opinion before my father."

The Prince then went to seek the King, and, after half an hour, returned to Bismarck, who had been waiting for him with an anxiety he could hardly control. "It has been hard," said Frederick, "but my father at last consented." And he handed the Minister a paper on which William I. had hastily written in pencil a few remarks which summed up the whole situation:

"As I find that the President of my Council of Ministers sees fit to abandon me in presence of the enemy, and as it is impossible for me here to replace him, I have discussed the question with my son. He has allied himself to the opinion of the President of the Council, and I find myself compelled, to my intense sorrow, after all the brilliant victories won by my army, to swallow this bitter pill and to accept a shameful peace."

With this message was concluded the first part of the task. The one which remained to Bismarck, though difficult, was neither so complicated nor so painful to perform.

It is of interest to compare the impression which the Battle of Sadowa and the peace negotiations that had followed upon it produced in the Southern States of Germany, whose future fate depended so entirely on their course. Prince Clovis von Hohenlohe, who was a keen judge of politics, and at that time had not entirely fallen under the influence of Bismarck, records in his diary on June 7th, 1866 : "I begin to fear that peace is not quite so near as people think. If it is true that Napoleon wants to impose too hard conditions on Prussia—as, for instance, the reinstatement of the German Princes, the evacuation of Bohemia, and so forth—then it is certain that the King of Prussia will refuse to accept them, and the natural consequence will be that Napoleon will invade the Rhine provinces. A good many things speak in favour of this, and very likely it would suit the plans of the Emperor if Prussia, by refusing the peace conditions, gave him the pretext which he requires to occupy Rhineland. This might bring a war between Prussia and France, and the general entanglement in which affairs would fall in the whole of Germany would reach its culminating point. I hope that I am mistaken, but it is quite possible that affairs may take such a turn."

A few days later he returns to the subject : "I think that though everyone longs for peace, Prussia is dragging out the negotiations as long as she can in order to gain time and ground. Should an armistice not be concluded, then we (the Bavarians) would find ourselves in the very difficult position of having to fight with France against Prussia, a position which, from the political point of view, I should consider dishonourable. The time would very soon come when the German conscience would react against such an unnatural alliance. On the other hand,

how can we fight against the French and the Austrians
at the same time?''

This extract from the diary of a man who, though a
stanch partisan of Prussia, was yet in close touch with
the popular feeling of his country at the time—that feeling changed considerably later on—proves how thoroughly
Bismarck had appreciated all the details of the situation
the victory of Sadowa had created, not only in Prussia,
but in the whole of Germany.

An amusing incident, if anything can be called
amusing in events of such a world-wide importance, is
the fear which Bismarck owned quite frankly he had of
a war with France. He had a very high opinion of the
strength of the French army. Napoleon III., on the
other hand, felt sincerely afraid of meeting the Prussian
troops. What is still more curious is that both of these
men changed their opinion in the four years which were
to follow; in 1870 Bismarck was absolutely certain that
the French would be beaten, whilst Napoleon thought he
could keep his ground against the soldiers of King
William I. In his favourite game of bluff the Prussian
had once more scored a triumph; the French Staff had
gathered a totally false impression as to the degree of
preparation the Prussians had attained: with very few
exceptions they believed that war would be a simple walk-
over from Paris to Berlin.

The one thing, however, which preoccupied the public
opinion of Europe at the time I am writing about was
precisely this attitude of France to which Prince von
Hohenlohe had referred in the passage which I have
reproduced from his diary. No one could understand
Napoleon III., not even his own advisers or Ministers.
The fact was that the Emperor had been led into a snare,

had realised that he had been entrapped into compromising his position, and thought that the best thing to do was to allow events to take their course.

How this trap was laid and baited is as follows. When, after his appointment as President of the Council and Foreign Minister, Bismarck had returned to Paris to present his letters of recall, he had not done so without intention. The fact was that he desired to sound Napoleon as to the possibility of his consenting to the annexation of Luxemburg by France, and eventually of Belgium. Napoleon had replied that it was impossible to discuss such a question at a moment when absolutely no complications with England threatened the peace of Europe. But he had asked the Prussian Minister to give him in writing his views on the subject. Bismarck had been far too clever to refuse : he replied that he would have to consult William I., whose views he had not yet had the time to ascertain. When, in 1865, he returned to France and visited Biarritz, Bismarck renewed his conversation with the Emperor and told him that, considering the gravity of the subject, it were perhaps just as well if he could have the French views compactly expressed in a *précis* so as not to make any mistake when talking about it with the King of Prussia. Napoleon, therefore, added a few words to a private letter which he gave to Bismarck. This letter was carefully put aside. During the negotiations that took place at Nikolsburg the question came up once more, whereupon Bismarck gave Benedetti to understand that Prussia would very willingly subscribe to any views which France might have in regard to Belgium. This was done in such a clever manner that the French Ambassador appeared to have been the one to formulate the demand which, in reality, had proceeded from Prussia itself, the terms of which were published in the famous paragraph that went the rounds of the European Press in 1870 as the expression of the desires of the Emperor Napoleon, and the price which he had required for his abstention from going to the rescue of Austria in 1866 : "We must have an ostensible Treaty granting to us the acquisition of Luxemburg, and a secret one stipulating an offensive alliance between France and Prussia, which would recognise the right of the former to seize Belgium when the Government of the Emperor should consider it as opportune and necessary to its interests."

The initiative in this iniquity seemed therefore to have belonged to France. That was all that Bismarck required, and we have seen the use which he made of it later on, when, for the advantage of his policy, he referred to this disgraceful negotiation. It has previously been made public that Napoleon wanted to protest against this half revelation and to disclose all the circumstances which had attended his conversations with Bismarck at Paris as well as at Biarritz, and the Empress, too, wished it. But—and here comes the supreme iniquity—the German Chancellor caused a message to be conveyed to the Sovereign to the effect that he still possessed the minute of his offer, written in the hand of Napoleon III., and that he should not hesitate to make use of it if necessary. With the alternative, therefore, of being made to appear either as fool or knave, the Emperor could only resign himself to his fate.

Feeling sure that he had muzzled France, and irretrievably compromised the Imperial Government, Bismarck proceeded to sign the peace Treaty as outlined at Nikolsburg. That was the second step toward his great plan of Empire. He could now proceed with calm and energy toward its development—the Prussian Chamber had at last recognised the wisdom of his conduct. In the new battle which he was prepared to fight in the Chamber he could claim liberty to lead his King toward an Imperial throne and his country toward the domination of a submissive Europe. For this was his aim, a submissive Europe; one in which the only god would be militarism, the only right that of the gun and of the sword, the only Monarch the King of Prussia, and the only law that of Prussia.

Part II

The Process of Union

CHAPTER IX

First Steps to Empire

I HAVE always wondered why it has become the custom to speak of the so-called will of Peter the Great, a document which has never existed, yet no mention has ever been made by historians of certain instructions left by the Great Elector to his successors, in which were formulated these principles of conquest and of compulsory annexation that have actuated his descendants. These instructions exist nevertheless, and though, of course, I have never actually read them, I often heard of them, not only through the late Frederick III. himself, but also one evening from the Emperor William I., when, in reviewing the different phases of the Austrian and French campaigns, he let fall some remarks concerning the fidelity with which his dynasty has conformed itself to the desires of its illustrious ancestor. The sense of this document, which, I believe, is always given to every Prussian Monarch to read immediately after his accession, is to the effect that Prussia ought never to rest until she had reached a preponderant position in Germany. Of course, the existence of this paper was known to Bismarck, and most probably he made use of it to touch the sentimentality of William I. so far as to bring that Monarch to believe in the plans of his chief Minister. Nevertheless, Bismarck knew that the unhoped-for result of the Prusso-Austrian war was but the

first step to the colossal work with which the Great
Elector charged his descendants.

An aspect of the new situation which Bismarck anticipated with no little anxiety was the way in which the
foreign Powers would view the sudden aggrandisement
of Prussia, and with what eyes they would look upon its
new importance as a factor in the European situation.
He was very well aware that a good many people considered that the internal position could only be temporary, if for no other reason, because of the discontent
which the new order of things was sure to arouse in the
Southern provinces.

But when it came to the foreign relations of Prussia
with the other great European Powers, the question was
sure to become even more complicated. Bismarck considered as absolutely certain that a war with France would
quickly follow upon the one he had just brought to a
succcessful issue; he never lost sight of eventuality. He
knew that the Southern States would infinitely prefer
the renewal of the old Rhine Confederation created by
Napoleon I., under the supremacy and the influence of
France, to an alliance with Prussia, and he therefore set
himself to the task of thwarting this possibility by culti-
vating good relations with certain important political
personages in the Southern States, with whose concur-
rence he hoped to be able to carry through his schemes.

The first step was the organisation of the North
German Confederation; the second without meanwhile
provoking the hostility of France and of Russia, or
giving occasion to Austria to develop a thirst for
revenge. Nor were these all the points needing careful
negotiation! At the same time Bismarck had to beware
lest King William I, should put forward too openly his

Prussian dynastic ambitions. A war with France was indispensable to the achievement of Prussian schemes, but it were wiser to wait a few years until the Prussian army, through its new military laws, had been reinforced by strong contingents from the newly conquered provinces of Hanover, Hesse and Holstein. He also hoped before war became inevitable to bring in the Southern provinces of Germany. Until this had been done Bismarck's policy was to prevent by every means a war with France.

Herein lies the secret of the entirely conciliating attitude of 1867, when the question of the cession of Luxemburg to Napoleon III. in exchange for a sum of money arose; for this reason Prussian troops evacuated the fortress of Luxemburg without hesitation. Bismarck was perfectly well aware that in the game he meant to play he could not count on the help of anyone. Italy would never have engaged herself to march against France. Russia also, in spite of the family ties which bound the Tsar with the Prussian dynasty and of his personal affection for his uncle King William I., was disinclined to favour any further accession of power on the part of a State which, in an incredibly short time, had risen from a subordinate rank to one of considerable importance. Prince Gortschakov in particular had always been suspicious of the intentions of the Berlin Cabinet, and if we are to believe a communication M. Drouyn de Lhyys, French Minister for Foreign Affairs, made to the Saxon Envoy in Paris, Count Vitzthum of Eckstädt, Gortschakov, during that eventful month of July, 1866, which had seen the Austrian defeat at Sadowa, had invited the Emperor Napoleon III. to join the Russian Government in a protest against the suppression of the German

Confederation. The French Sovereign had refused to associate himself with the idea, saying that the matter was a purely German affair with which foreign Powers had no right to interfere. But the fact that such an eventuality had been contemplated was more than sufficient to excite the apprehensions of such a shrewd and far-seeing mind as that of Bismarck, who felt the more worried in that he knew very well that Prussia would find no sympathy in London either. Yet, notwithstanding these perplexing omens, it was essential for him to make sure of the neutrality of all the Great Powers before he could hope to execute his deeply laid schemes against France without becoming entangled in most unpleasant complications.

At home, too, the Prussian policy of dominance was beset with serious difficulties. Although Bismarck's triumphs had won him a considerable number of partisans, and even some passionate admirers, he had not silenced all his former enemies, some of whom had the ear of the King of Prussia. Doctor Maurice von Bethmann-Hollweg, the grandfather of the present German Chancellor, was one such. He even went so far as to write to William I. detailing all the dangers which, in his opinion, were bound to follow on a policy that was tending to tear Germany asunder by a fratricidal war. The doctor even went so far as to tell to his Royal master that he felt sure Austria would show herself ready to comply with the Prussian demands if only the Foreign Minister were superseded.

Another great personality, Mgr. Melchers, Archbishop of Cologne, whose opinion the King had asked for through the intermediary of my uncle, Prince Boguslas Radziwill, also spoke in the same strain. I

mention the incident in order to reproduce the reply of
William I. The Archbishop begged his Sovereign to
stop before plunging the whole of Germany into a war
which might mean the total annihilation of Prussia. But
when his letter reached William I. Bismarck had already
persuaded the King of the absolute justice of his cause.
He replied, therefore, to the Archbishop by a long
epistle, explaining that the perfidy of Austria had brought
about the lamentable crisis which none deplored more
than he did himself. He began by stating that ever
since the Seven Years' War Austria had sought to force
Prussia into the position of a second-rate Power, and
even the results, the " glorious results," as he called
them, of the campaign of 1864 against Denmark had
not made her renounce this determination, though she
ought to have seen that if she had allied herself with
Prussia truly and sincerely they could together have kept
the whole of Europe in check. " Austria," added William I., " has accumulated lies upon lies, calumnies upon
calumnies, paid the Press in the whole of the world to
excite it against us, and has not hesitated before any
treachery, to rouse public opinion against Prussia, to
represent her as greedy for conquest, and, by this campaign of libel, to excite the whole of Germany against
her. This is the villainy that has brought us to the point
where we stand at present! No State that respects
itself," he went on, " could remain indifferent in the
presence of such facts. Austria suddenly, and without
any warning, concentrated troops on her frontiers.
During the last session of the Diet at Frankfurt, by her
action in bringing before the Assembly the question of
the Duchies—which, according to this Convention, was
to have been settled by Prussia together with Austria

alone—she has destroyed the Convention she signed at Gastein. Lies and perfidies have attended all her actions. I therefore turn my eyes toward God and, certain to be approved by Him, and to act for the best interests and for the sake of the honour of my kingdom and my people, I have decided to draw the sword. . . ." He ended his letter by asking the Archbishop to pray for him and for the success of the Prussian arms.

This curious letter proves how constant Prussia has remained throughout her political existence, to the hypocrisy of which she has given such proofs since the beginning of the present war. The remark that it was a lie to represent her as eager for conquest, in the presence of what was to follow, was perhaps the most terrible piece of irony in history.

The first action of Bismarck after the signature of the Treaty of Nikolsburg had been to try to conciliate the Prussian Chamber. A bill of indemnity for the expenses which the country had incurred on account of the war was presented by him and accepted without any trouble, the more so that he had taken good care to have its appearance heralded by a Royal message which informed the Deputies that Prussia had annexed Hanover, Electoral Hesse, the town of Frankfurt and the Duchy of Nassau, to which later on were added those of Holstein and of Schleswig. Indemnities were also imposed on Bavaria, Würtemberg, the Grand Duchy of Baden—notwithstanding the family ties which bound it to the Royal House of Prussia—and Hesse Darmstadt. Surely this was sufficient to satisfy even the most ferocious Prussian appetite. But the clever statesman wanted something more, and contrived to persuade Saxony, as well as the States of Southern Germany, to conclude

Treaties with Prussia, giving her control of their armies; a formidable clause which, even now, it is hardly possible to believe that he actually deluded them to accept. Having accomplished these things, Bismarck then entirely reorganised the new North German Confederation under the presidency of Prussia, consolidating her position so effectually that Prussia had no need to mistrust her ability to break down the line of the Mein, which Napoleon had hoped to establish as a barrier between France and the King of Prussia's ambitions.

At this period the French Government could have interfered, but French politicians would not believe in the danger which was hovering over their heads, and this in spite of warnings which they received from every side, and Napoleon began his negotiation with Holland for the acquisition of Luxemburg, which was to become so fatal for his future prestige.

Of course, it had never been in the intentions of Prussia to allow France to secure Luxemburg into her possession, and whilst Bismarck was encouraging Napoleon III. in his dreams of annexation he conducted an underhand intrigue at the Hague to bring Napoleon's plans to naught. The existence of the Treaties which he had concluded with the Southern German States was revealed by Bismarck, the knowledge of which frightened Holland, as he expected it would. He did more than this, he caused the Prussian Envoy at the Hague to signify to the King of the Netherlands that Prussia would consider the cession of Luxemburg to France as a *casus belli*. The Monarch hastened to break off negotiations. In case, however, Napoleon might be influenced by public opinion to enter into an open conflict with Prussia, Bismarck instantly proceeded to call together

a Conference in London, which settled the question of
the neutrality of Luxemburg, and insisted that the
Prussian troops in occupation of the principal fortress
in the Duchy should evacuate it. This settlement
allayed the irritation felt in Paris, but was very badly
received in Berlin. The situation did not trouble Bismarck, who knew very well that he had not been the
dupe in the transaction, the result of which had been
to engage an honourable nation like the French to respect
the neutrality of that same Luxemburg, the frontiers of
which were to be forced by the Prussian troops on the
very first day of the present war. Verily the most
solemn treaties were nothing more in the eyes of Prussia
than mere scraps of paper.

King William I. visited Paris in 1867, at the invitation of Napoleon, to see the great Exhibition which had
just then been opened. He was given a magnificent
reception. The appearance of Bismarck, who was with
the King, produced a great impression upon the people
of the French capital. His colossal stature, in his white
cuirassier uniform, fitted their ideas of his massive personality. He was immensely admired. One of the
features of this exhibition—so cynical is destiny—was
the success of the new Krupp field guns, which were there
shown for the first time to the people they were to
destroy three years later.

The three years following upon the Prusso-Austrian
war was perhaps the most fertile period in the whole of
that long struggle of Prussia for power and position.
Her chief Minister set to work to consolidate his task
and to lay the foundation upon which the German
Empire, which was to absorb the new Confederation, was
to be built. During those years every means was brought

to bear upon the task of winning the sympathies and the help of people who could prove of use to Prussia. Especially was this propaganda active in the South of Germany, where Bismarck knew that few cared for Prussia, and all would have been only too glad to escape from the chains she had contrived to wind around the recalcitrant States. In Baden the thing was relatively easy, but in Bavaria it is doubtful whether anything would ever have been achieved had it not been for the activity of Prince Clovis von Hohenlohe, the future German Ambassador in Paris, and later on Chancellor of the German Empire.

Prince Clovis was a very shrewd man, a statesman of experience and of weight, who, though not a political genius, had yet a very clear outlook upon the difficulties of his time. He was a grand seigneur of the old type, one whose position was so great that he could afford to ignore snubs and criticisms, and who, thanks to his family connections and to his intimacy with the Prussian Royal family, was better able than any contemporary to make his voice heard in his native Bavaria, where he was a great landowner and a most important personage at Court. One of his brothers was the famous Cardinal Hohenlohe, whose political activities in Rome during the Kulturkampf, and especially in the years immediately preceding it, were so strongly criticised. It was said, by the way, that at one time Bismarck seriously thought of putting forward, and backing with his influence, the Cardinal as a candidate for the Papal throne. If this were so it would have been at the suggestion of the Duke of Ratibor, who was the enterprising and pushing man of the family. Another of the Hohenlohe brothers was High Chamberlain and Master of the Household of the Emperor of Austria, whilst the eldest, the Duke of Ratibor, was perhaps one of the most influential persons in Berlin and in Silesia, where he possessed vast domains.

In spite of his Bavarian origin, Prince Clovis at heart was a convinced Prussian and a stanch partisan of a close union between Bavaria and Prussia. For three years he held the office of Bavarian Minister President, and directed the affairs of this country entirely upon Prussian lines : he really believed in the necessity of the restoration of a German Empire under the protection of Prussia. Without him it is hardly likely that the adhesion of the German Southern States would have been secured so easily as, from his Memoirs, they proved to be. The Prince recalls the negotiations that passed between Berlin, Munich and Karlsruhe, and in which he was one of the principal instruments. He it was who signed the secret Convention with Prussia which gave full control of the Bavarian troops. At the same time it must be remembered to his credit that he stipulated for the preservation of the integrity, as well as of the Sovereign rights, of Bavaria. Bismarck did not dissent, because he knew that otherwise it would be impossible to persuade King Ludwig II. to give his assent to the new military arrangement; and, after all, that was the only thing which was wanted by the wire-puller at Berlin.

Prince Clovis made a curious report to the King of Bavaria on the matter. He argued that it was a necessity not only to support Prussian politics, but also to conclude a treaty of alliance with her; such an alliance, he emphasised, would be the best guarantee for the future peace of Europe and for the welfare of the Bavarian State. Whether he was really convinced of this or not it is difficult to say. Prince von Hohenlohe, though essentially an honest man and incapable of anything mean, yet was a decided opportunist, as all his career proved. Whether he acted out of what he believed to have been true patriotism, or in view of a high ambition, is, of course, unknown to us. My personal impression, and I have known him well, always was that, in a marvellous manner, he could conciliate his honesty and his convictions with political necessities such as they appeared, but not always such as they were. His remarks, for instance, concerning the tragic death of King Ludwig II. of Bavaria. This tragedy, which at the time occupied the attention of the whole world, is dismissed with half a page of trite, uninteresting reference in his Memoirs.

During the years Prince Clovis remained at the head of the Bavarian Ministry he contrived to inspire Bismarck with a high idea of his prudence and self-control, allied to a rare discretion; he always thought twice before starting and a dozen times before doing anything. Without his manipulation of public affairs in Bavaria Bismarck perceived quite well that his task would have been much more difficult than was actually the case. The Prussian Minister found in Prince von Hohenlohe the best ally he could have wished for, and it is interesting to watch the consummate art which the latter brought to bear upon the task of persuading his own Sovereign to decide for or against Prussia without giving Ludwig II. the least suspicion that such a pronouncement could only be academical, as, for instance, was the Luxemburg affair.

Of course, the real aim pursued by Bismarck was to decide the Bavarian Government to burn its ships and to compromise itself to such an extent that it could neither hesitate nor draw back. Once this was done he could sleep quietly and await, if not exactly with indifference, at least without apprehension, the development of events. The question of Luxemburg gave him the opportunity he required, and Prince von Hohenlohe, as we shall see, became the instrument whereby the opportunity was wielded to Prussia's benefit.

CHAPTER X

Welding the Southern States

AS soon as peace had been concluded with Austria, Prussia devoted her whole attention to the complicated question of winning over the German Southern States, among which Bavaria was, of course, the most important. Bismarck's natural genius for intrigue had at once told him that the first thing to be done was to put at the side of the King of Bavaria a man on whom he could absolutely rely, and who at the same time could not be suspected of being his tool. It was then that the Duke of Ratibor, with whom he had always stood upon excellent terms, mentioned to him his brother Clovis, whom Bismarck knew but slightly, but about whose character, opinions, and general ideas he was very well informed. The Hohenlohes were all ambitious, and the Schillingsfürst branch of that family was not over-burdened with worldly goods, except the eldest of the four Hohenlohe brothers, the Duke of Ratibor, who had inherited part of the fortune of his uncle, the Landgrave of Hesse-Rothenbourg, together with the castle of Rauden, in Silesia, and the title of Duke of Ratibor. The second brother, Prince Clovis, by a family arrangement, found himself in possession of the entailed estate and castle of Schillingsfürst, but found it so encumbered that he had great trouble to make both ends meet, notwithstanding the fact that he had married a relatively rich woman. This was one of the reasons which had made him choose an official career, knowing

very well that his name and title would easily ensure for
him lucrative appointments.   Very possibly the Duke
suggested to Bismarck that his brother Clovis would make
an excellent Prime Minister, able to guide in the desired
direction the young King of Bavaria, whose originalities
had already attracted the notice of the public.   The difficulty was to make Clovis acceptable to the Monarch, as his
liberal ideas were widely divergent from those entertained
by the Bavarian Royal Family, who were ultramontanists
and clericals.   At this juncture Count von Holnstein
comes on the scene.   He was then Master of the Horse
to Ludwig.   He it was who, many years later, played such
a sinister part in the tragedy which brought about the
terrible death of the King.   Holnstein was always in want
of money, and it became an easy thing for Prussia to make
a friend of him.   He quickly agreed to mention the name
of Prince von Hohenlohe to his Royal master.   Not long
afterwards Ludwig II. called Prince Clovis as his adviser,
and entrusted him with the task of forming a Cabinet.
Deluding himself that the idea had been exclusively his
own, Ludwig became most eager to carry it through, the
more so that it had reached his ears that Hohenlohe had
not shared the general opinion in Bavaria, that the exile
of Wagner, who was at that time in full favour with the
King, was a necessity.   Even if no other reason had
existed, this was sufficient to make Ludwig II. eager to
have among his Ministers a man whose great name, position, and general reputation would make him independent
of party influence.

The appointment of Prince Hohenlohe, which was
opposed not only by public opinion in Bavaria but also
by the Royal family, sealed the fate of his native country,
and definitely gave it up to Prussian influence.   It had

been very cleverly worked. Bismarck had contrived to imbue several people who were in constant communication with King Ludwig II. with the conviction that it was the best choice the latter could make, inasmuch as the personal character of the Prince put him entirely out of reach of any interested motives. Although financial matters had nothing to do with the eager consent of Prince Hohenlohe to assume the direction of Bavarian politics, he was not above the satisfaction of seeing his income, which was most moderate for his rank, increased in a comfortable manner. His was of an eminently practical nature in that respect, as he later on gave many proofs, especially when upon being asked by Bismarck to take upon himself the functions of Vice-Chancellor, he declared that he could not do so unless his salary as an Ambassador was maintained. This, however, occurred when he was already an old man, and suffering from a tendency to stinginess that increased as time went by.

In 1866 I think the principal aim of Prince Clovis was to establish Prussian influence in Munich upon a firm basis. He was a convinced Imperialist, and a decided adversary of Austria and of Austrian politics. The programme which he laid before the King of Bavaria when, on the last day of December, 1866, he assumed office as Minister of the Royal Household and President of the Council, was in itself a revelation, and it corresponded so well with Bismarck's own ideas on the subject that the latter caused the Duke of Ratibor to write congratulating his brother upon his efficient co-operation, and to convey a promise to remember always the good services which he had rendered to the Hohenzollern dynasty by his handling of Ludwig II.

In February, 1867, conferences between representatives of the Southern States took place in Stuttgart, under the presidency of the Wurtemberg Minister for Foreign Affairs, Herr von Varnbüler, and, owing to the influence of Prince von Hohenlohe, these conferences settled the broad lines upon which the future union with Prussia was to become an accomplished fact.   The items were formulated in a long report, which the Prince addressed to the Grand Duke of Baden, a personal friend of his, who for that reason had been selected by mutual consent between Prince Clovis and Bismarck.   The conference was to assume the appearance of an absolutely independent assembly, actuated by pure patriotic motives in its resolutions and decisions, and therefore Bismarck stood outwardly aloof from its deliberations.   The Grand Duke of Baden was the son-in-law of King William I., and a decided partisan of Bismarck.   Hence the choice of the Grand Duke as a mouthpiece before the Conferences. It was astonishing, indeed, how long Bismarck was able to speak undiscovered through other lips.

Among the resolutions voted by the Stuttgart Conference was one connected with secret Conventions between Prussia and the Southern States, which gave to the former full military control.   At first the existence of such an agreement was not disclosed or suspected.   Then the Luxemburg affair cropped up, and, in view of the impression this would produce in Holland, Bismarck deemed it advisable to publish its terms.   He advised the Duke of Ratibor to write in that sense to his brother, and the latter then mentioned it to the Grand Duke of Baden, asking him for his views in regard to this important affair.   In the meanwhile Bismarck had summoned Prince Reuss to Berlin, whence Henry of Reuss wrote in the following terms to Prince Hohenlohe :

"Berlin, February 20, 1867.

" I arrived here yesterday morning, and saw Count von Bismarck at once. I related a lot of things concerning you and affairs in Munich. I need not tell you that he wishes you all kinds of good luck and full success in your handling of your Ministry; he will do everything in his power to give you all the support you may need. I have discussed with him the wishes which you have expressed to me concerning the disclosure of the existence of the secret Treaty. Count Bismarck recognised that it would be pleasanter for you and for the Würtemberg Government, as well as advantageous for your position in regard to your country, to admit the secret Treaty. Personally, he has nothing against that course, but he would like to wait until after the debate in the French Chambers concerning the announced interpellation in regard to the foreign policy of the Imperial Government.[1] Then he thinks the matter had better leak out through apparent indiscretions in the newspapers. He would like to learn your opinion on this subject, and to know whether you would like publicity to be given to the affair in some other way. Count Bismarck has further commissioned me to tell you, that should you feel the necessity or the wish in this, or in any other kind of business, to address yourself directly to him, he would most willingly enter into private correspondence with you. He has absolute confidence in Werthern,[2] but believes it would be perhaps advisable, until you had learned to know W. better, to address yourself directly to him (Bismarck). He considers Montgelas[3] as a good business man, and an honest one too; but this

[1] This took place from the 14th to the 18th of March.

[2] Baron Werthern had just been appointed Prussian Minister in Munich, in place of Prince Reuss.

[3] Count Montgelas was the Bavarian Envoy in Berlin.

is all, and it is hardly possible to enter upon more intimate relations with him."

When one reads between the lines of this letter, the design which lurks behind such a letter is seen. Apparently a businesslike communication, it is couched in terms which could only flatter the personal vanity of the man to whom it was addressed, and open to him at the same time the road to further intimacy and acquaintance with political schemes of high statesmanship.

As a complement to this letter we have one of the Duke of Ratibor, who, in a certain sense, was the *deus ex machina* entrusted with the mission of urging his brother to lend himself to the vast designs of the man with whom the whole of Europe was learning to count.

" *Berlin.*

" I have been at a ball at the house of Putbus, where I had opportunity to talk with Bismarck. He began the conversation by offering me a glass of champagne and asking me to drink to your health and success. I then related to him what you had written to me, and he agrees that you ought to proceed with great caution. One does not require here anything more from Bavaria than what she is willing to give. The material interests of the South of Germany require a Treaty with the North German Confederation, because, without such a Treaty, the Customs Union and the whole welfare of the Southern States would be compromised. This is the point which one cannot sufficiently put before the eyes of people there. Bismarck, however, advises great caution and no undue haste. He takes the greatest interest in everything which goes on at Munich.

" The Queen also spoke with me yesterday in the same sense, and she asks me to give you her best regards. Field-Marshal Wrangel also wishes you much luck in all your enterprises, hopes all will go well in the future as it has done until the present day, and sends you his compliments. Herr von Wincke has also had a word concerning you, and is very glad to know you are doing so well. You can see from this that you are in favour here with all parties. Bismarck also considers as a matter of course the conduct which Bavaria has held in regard to the other South German States, and he has refused to accept all the propositions made by Würtemberg and Baden, when they were not presented in agreement and simultaneously with those formulated by Bavaria."

In the present case Bavaria meant Prince von Hohenlohe, and the reader will draw his own conclusions regarding the cleverness with which Bismarck contrived not only to win him over to his point of view, but also to transform him into the very best political instrument he had ever had at his disposal.

One may perhaps wonder why the future Chancellor took such trouble to reconcile to his policy individuals instead of States. He knew that it is easier to convince men than nations, and that certain men have dominating power. In the case of Prince von Hohenlohe there were psychological reasons which rendered him liable to be allured by the prospect of becoming one of the pillars of the new Empire. These reasons were connected with his position and standing in Germany. Few people abroad have got an idea of what it meant to be a mediatised Prince in Germany at the beginning of last century—the period of Prince Clovis. He had not yet had time to be relieved of the conviction that he was in nowise relegated to a different status to that of any Royal family with whom, indeed, he could still marry on a footing of equality. The Hohenlohes, Solms, Salms, Bentincks, Wittgensteins had each been Sovereigns once upon a time of a State. Small and insignificant, it is true, but Sovereigns all the same, and considered as such by the Habsburgs, Hohenzollerns and Wittelsbachs. Circumstances had deprived them of certain of their rights, but of none of their privileges, and certainly of none of their arrogance. At heart they had never reconciled themselves to the change which had overtaken their independence, and they had in consequence been more accessible than private individuals would have shown themselves to the idea that what had befallen them ought also to befall those other German Princes who had escaped becoming mediatised. They never for one single moment admitted in their hearts that they were but the subjects of the Kings of Prussia, Bavaria or Würtemberg, and they took great care to keep up certain advantages of rank and of station which had been left to them. For instance, they conserved the right of notifying to the other German Sovereigns every family event that took place among them, such as births, marriages and deaths, and of doing so in the ceremonious terms fixed at the Congress of Vienna, which carefully preserved their former Sovereign status and permitted them to address as equals those German Monarchs who had kept their independence. Prince von Hohenlohe had succumbed to this weakness, though his ambition had told him that it would be in his interest to conceal the fact. But conscious that, had things been different, he might have been a Sovereign, he was not sorry to see in the new developments that all the German Princes, whether Kings, Grand Dukes, Dukes, or merely Princes, would become no more than the Peers of the new Empire.

Among the various people who, during these eventful years which followed upon the war with Austria, took an active part in all the negotiations that were taking place in the South of Germany, the Grand Duke of Baden displayed the greatest activity. He had strong personal reasons for his hostility to Austria, where he had met with slights that he could not bring himself to forgive. Bismarck, with whom he was in complete accord until the accession of the present Kaiser, but whose bitter enemy he was to become later on, used the Grand Duke whenever it became necessary for him to convey either to the King of Prussia or to some other Sovereign an idea with which he did not think it wise or opportune to associate himself. It was principally on the initiative of the Grand Duke, indeed, that the military Conventions which in the long run, and in spite of the opposition which they encountered in Bavaria as well as in Würtemberg, were accepted by the Government of both these countries, though never viewed with contented eyes by their population.

The work of pulling through these secret Treaties was not such a light one as even Bismarck himself had imagined. In Munich the King, who was influenced by the members of his family, and who personally hated Prussia and everything Prussian, did not wish to hear anything concerning the handing over of his army to the control of a nation which he detested, and of which his father on his death-bed had advised him to beware. At no time had the Imperialist idea exercised any fascination

K

on the mind of Ludwig II., and he did not wish in the least to be considered as a German Prince, being quite content as a King of Bavaria. Later on, when he was induced under false pretences to write the famous letter which decided the proclamation of the Empire at Versailles, it was because he had been told that this Imperial dignity he was helping to revive would be alternately the property of the Hohenzollerns and of the Wittelsbachs, and that it was only the great age of the King of Prussia that had caused him to be the first to wear an Imperial crown. At that time Prince von Hohenlohe was no longer Bavarian Prime Minister, having been obliged to abandon office before the war of 1870 owing to the unpopularity of his Prussian policy. No responsibility, therefore, for this error of Ludwig can be attached to Prince Clovis, but whether during his years of power he had whispered something of the kind in the ear of the King is a point which I should not care to deny.

What is certain is that reports which Prince Clovis presented to his Royal master during the time that he remained his adviser were couched in terms emphasising that the only means by which Bavaria could escape the dangers with which she was beset was its union with Prussia. He characterised these perils as terrifying, but always evaded saying in what direction they lay. On March 20th, 1867, he penned a long document to his Sovereign on that theme, in which, among other things, he said · " The danger which awaits the kingdom, should it remain in its present condition, is twofold : First, every European complication, no matter to the advantage of whom it begins and ends, once it touches Germany, will put in the greatest danger the welfare as well as the independence of Bavaria. Then the longing of the German people

to fulfil its national destiny, in spite of the opposition
which it may meet on the part of those who rule it, can
only bring about a civil war that would imperil the
existence of the dynasty. Therefore the efforts of the
Bavarian Government ought to be directed toward the
following desirable achievements :

" (a) To contract alliances that would nullify the
danger of European complications, and

" (b) To bring about a national unity of the whole
of Germany which would satisfy the just requirements
of the nation without infringing the Sovereign rights of
your Majesty or touching upon the integrity and the
independence of Bavaria."

Prince Hohenlohe proceeded, in this lengthy document, to develop arguments which he believed to be the
more likely to convert the King to his point of view,
and then attempted to explain what, in his opinion, had
been the real purport of the peace between Austria and
Prussia as accepted at Nikolsburg and finally signed at
Prague on August 23rd, 1866.

" Article IV. of that Treaty," he wrote, " stipulates
that Germany is to be reconstituted without any interference, and with the exclusion, of Austria . . . that
the South-Western German States are left at liberty to
ally themselves with the North of Germany, but that . . .
the South-Western States are to retain an international
independent existence, notwithstanding their having
entered into the new Confederation."

The King allowed himself to be influenced by this
report as well as by the personal arguments of Prince
Hohenlohe during the several conversations which he had
with him on that same subject, and he agreed that negotiations should be opened with Prussia on the basis

indicated to him by his Minister.   His family, however, did not agree with him, and bitter controversies between them took place in consequence.   The Bavarian aristocracy also was entirely against Prussia, and considered Hohenlohe almost in the light of a deserter, the more so because of his unorthodox religious opinions.   Taking all these facts into account, one can but feel surprised that the Prince, who later on abandoned office on much slighter provocation, held firmly to it at a time when he found arrayed against him not only public opinion, but all the political parties in the kingdom; and the thought involuntarily occurs that he must have had very powerful reasons to ignore the attacks to which not only his political conduct but also his personality were subjected from every side.

Once Ludwig II. had given Prince Hohenlohe the authorisation to begin negotiations with Würtemberg and Baden upon a more definite basis than had been talked about during the Stuttgart Conference, Clovis lost no time in forcing matters along, and they progressed more or less satisfactorily, though the Delegate of Würtemberg, Herr von Varnbüler, admitted that it would not be an easy thing to get the country unanimously to acquiesce.   Perhaps Bismarck also saw that Bavaria would raise objections to the Prussian propositions, because it was just about that time that he let loose the Luxemburg complication which, as he expected, would give to the hesitating spirits, who had failed to grasp the extent of the so-called advantages which a closer union of the Southern States with Prussia might bring, the necessary impulse they required to accept the inevitable

The first knowledge that something was wrong reached Munich through a telegram dispatched by Bismarck to the Prussian Envoy in Munich, Baron von Werthern, on April 1st, 1867, in which he told him that :

" It would be desirable if your Excellency could ascertain and let me know what impression the proposed selling of Luxemburg to France produces on the Bavarian Cabinet, and what would be the feelings of that country in case we came to an understanding with France on this subject."

Werthern consulted with Hohenlohe, and then replied :

" Public opinion expects that Prussia will uphold the rights of Germany in regard to Luxemburg."

That this, however, was not so certain as the Prussian Minister tried to make out can be surmised from a remark of Hohenlohe that Werthern ought not to lay too great a stress on the last point, as public opinion might easily be turned. On April 2nd the Prince telegraphed to Count Montgelas, the Bavarian Envoy in Berlin, a dispatch which must have caused considerable pleasure to Bismarck, because it furnished him with the very weapons which he needed to bring pressure upon the Southern German States to accept, however unwillingly, the alliance and military readjustments about which they still felt some hesitation :

" Last night Baron von Werthern spoke with me concerning the desire of Count von Bismarck to ascertain the views of the Royal Government in regard to Luxemburg. I have hastened to confer on the subject with his Majesty the King, my gracious Sovereign, and I herewith communicate to you the desires which he has expressed, but, at the same time, Count von Bismarck ought to realise the difficulty which I encounter in giving him any definite opinion concerning a thing of which I have no official knowledge, and which I have only heard through newspaper rumours and the telegraphic account which we received last night of his declarations in the Reichstag.

" As far, therefore, as it is possible to judge under these circumstances, the Royal Government shares the point of view of Count Bismarck, and only desires to add that, considering the Treaties of April 19th, 1839, and July 27th, 1839, every alienation of the Grand Duchy of Luxemburg, without the free consent of the Walram line of the House of Nassau, its eventual heirs, would be considered by it as impossible to accept. The Bavarian Government hopes that, at all events and in all cases, Count von Bismarck will not fail, and has not failed, to assert the legal rights of Germany in regard to this question, but that this will be done in a manner not likely to endanger the peace of Europe.

" Should, however, which God preserve, things assume a serious turn, the Royal Government expects that Count Bismarck will, without delay, give it all necessary information on the subject.

" Your Excellency will please communicate to Count Bismarck the contents of this dispatch."

On this day also a telegram passed from Bismarck to Werthern, asking him to try to ascertain, through the Bavarian Government, what attitude Austria would be likely to adopt in case of a war between Prussia and France in consequence of the Luxemburg question. Hohenlohe telegraphed immediately to Vienna, but before even he could get a reply Bismarck gave Werthern the following instruction on April 3rd :

" Will you please tell Prince Hohenlohe, quite confidentially, that rumour has it that the Treaty in regard to Luxemburg is already signed. The Emperor Napoleon has declared that it is impossible for him to withdraw at present, though I have told Benedetti that, in view of the public opinion in Germany, we cannot yield and will not do so. On the other hand, Count Perponcher telegraphs from the Hague that the Treaty is not yet signed, and that he hopes to prevent its being done. In regard to the state of things in Germany, we must, according to my opinion, risk a war, however little this question of Luxemburg is worth it. The manner in which the nation, whose feeling of honour has been wounded in the business, has taken the thing is most decisive, and leaves us no other alternative. At all events, we ought to use this particular incident to consolidate our national strength, so as not to be surprised from the material point of view by a war which may still easily and soon break out.''

Baron von Werthern at once sent this telegram to Prince von Hohenlohe, who was dining at the Palace, and for whom it did not probably constitute a very great surprise. The latter replied to it on the following day :

'' I have had this morning an audience of the King, to whom I have exposed all the details of the Luxemburg question, and from whom I have asked what reply I ought to give to Count Bismarck in regard to his telegram of yesterday's date. His Majesty has authorised me to declare that, in case of a war, Bavaria would side with Prussia in accordance with the secret Treaty which exists between them, but that it seems to the King that the interests of the South of Germany urgently require that Bismarck should wait for the reply of Vienna to our inquiries before taking any extreme decision.''

And on April 5th Prussia was informed through a

note which was sent to Baron von Werthern that, in case a conflict arose between Prussia and France on account of the Luxemburg affair, the Bavarian Government would side with Prussia, and considered that the other South German States were bound to do the same according to the terms of the Treaties.

This was all that Bismarck required. A few days later the Luxemburg affair, which in reality had never assumed the threatening aspect it had pleased him to give to it, was arranged by his proposal to refer the whole matter to a conference that met shortly afterwards in London; the question of neutrality of the Grand Duchy was settled at that Conference.

In the meantime Prussia had acquired the assurance that, in case of war, the South German States would remain faithful to their engagements. Once he was reassured as to this most important point, Bismarck could go forward with confidence upon his campaign of Imperialism. He was not, however, to bring it to realisation without many difficulties.

CHAPTER XI

The Process Continues

THE whole aim of Bismarck in this Luxemburg affair, as seen from the preceding chapter, had been to determine the position which the Southern German States would take when it became opportune for him to begin the war with France that occupied such an important place on his programme. He had also wanted to do away with the hesitation which existed in the Southern States concerning the publication of the secret Treaties they had entered into. Bismarck imagined that the secrecy arose out of a desire to be able to deny their existence later on if it suited the States to do so. The Luxemburg incident gave Bismarck a proof that Bavaria, at least, meant to stick to its obligations and would help him to exact the same thing from Würtemberg and Baden, which were, perhaps, even more hostile than any in Germany to alliance with Prussia. It procured also for Prussia the right to call on her unwilling allies when danger knocked at the door—an immense advantage to Bismarck in the delicate and dangerous game he was playing.

Bismarck had never for a moment contemplated the possibility of going to war for the sake of Luxemburg, and he had known very well that he had the means to prevent the Emperor Napoleon from doing so. The whole scare had been raised to procure for Prussia the advantage of ascertaining whom were her friends and

whom her enemies.   At the same time, it led public
opinion in Germany to believe that Prussia would always
uphold every German right, and had further consolidated
the influence of King William I. by presenting him in
the light of a resolute champion of every German
Sovereign whose rights or privileges were threatened
by foreign interference.   There seemed at that time
hardly any possibility of the Biebrich branch of the
Nassau family ever being called to the throne of Luxemburg, as the King of the Netherlands had two sons who
were young men and likely to marry; but the very fact
that there existed a remote chance that one day it might
succeed was enough to procure for the line a defender
and a champion in that very King of Prussia who, only
a year before, had confiscated the German Duchy of
Nassau!   The comedy was admirably played, and produced everywhere the impression which Bismarck had
expected it would do.

All these incidents, however, did not make him lose
sight of the principal aim he was pursuing, and, as
soon as the emotion consequent upon the Luxemburg
incident had subsided, he proceeded to call together at
Berlin a conference of the different State Ministers of
Southern Germany to discuss the lines upon which it
was intended to organise the new Union.   Bismarck
presided over this conference, and did it in a masterly
way, emphasising to his colleagues points which would
at once receive their assent, and skipping over with consummate ability those which might excite their opposition.   The Jesuitical nature of the arguments which
he used to persuade others that white was black can
best be appreciated by the perusal of the report which
Prince Hohenlohe drew of the work of the conference,

and which, upon his return to Munich, he submitted to his Ministry and, later on, to the King of Bavaria.

"I arrived in Berlin," he writes, "on June 3rd, 1867, at twelve o'clock in the forenoon. Count Montgelas received me at the railway station, and accompanied me to the Hôtel de Rome, where I found an invitation to attend a Ministerial conference which was taking place that same day at two o'clock. Before that time I received the visit of Baron Varnbüler, who explained to me the broad lines of the Prussian proposals. At two o'clock I drove with Councillor Weber to Count Bismarck. There we found the Ministers Varnbüler, Dalwigk and Freydorf, also the Private Councillors Delbrück and Philipsborn, and also the Councillor of Legation von Nordeck who had accompanied Freydorf to Berlin.

"Bismarck began the proceedings by a short report on the matters we should have to discuss, and then handed us the Protocol which explained the point of view of the Prussian Government. I immediately replied by remarking that I had arrived in Berlin to express the willingness of the Bavarian Government to take part in the negotiations concerning the reconstruction of the Zollverein (Customs Union) and done so, though I had absolutely no knowledge either of the programme or of the plan upon which these negotiations were to be conducted; but that I must observe, before proceeding any further, that the point of view of the Prussian Government, such as it was exposed in the Protocol, did not at all correspond to the one entertained by Bavaria.

"The entry of our Deputies into the North German Parliament was also an arrangement with which Bavaria could not agree. Upon this, Baron von Varnbüler asked

how and in what way the Prussian Government thought
of constituting the new legislative organisation it wished
to call into existence, to which question Bismarck replied
that the distribution of voices in the Bundeszollrat would
be the same as in the former Bundestag. The legislative
body was to be on the lines of the North German
Reichstag, elected directly by the population at the rate
of one Deputy for 100,000 inhabitants. The franchise
would be settled by the Treaties. He declared that if
we had doubts as to the wisdom of having a Zoll Parliament (Customs Parliament), Prussia would prefer that
we should constitute our own Customs Union, which
would work quite amicably with the North German
Zollverein. But Prussia would not give up its plan, and
the dissolution of the Zollverein would be the consequence if its proposition came to be negatived. In
regard to the system of the election of the Deputies,
Bismarck was in favour of direct elections, but left us
absolutely free in that respect to do what we liked best;
he only advised us not to grant any remuneration to
the Deputies for their services.

"I retorted that we had imagined the constitution of
a Customs Parliament as something absolutely different
from what we were now told. We had had in view an
Assembly to which the North German Parliament and
the South German Chambers would have to abandon
some of their rights, especially those concerning Customs
and commercial matters, but not an assimilation with
the North German Parliament. After Varnbüler and
Freydorf had declared themselves in favour of the Prussian propositions, and Dalwigk had remarked that in
such a case there was nothing left for him to do but to
follow their example, Bismarck once more proceeded to

explain to us the advantages which a Customs Parliament would have over the present state of things.

" I recognised that in regard to pure Customs matters I could not dispute the existence of such advantages, but that I must make reservations from the political point of view. The arrangements proposed would, little by little, draw us into the circle of the North German Union, and this was a thing which was repugnant to us and to our ideas. If we had wanted to enter into the union we should have done so of our own accord. I therefore repeated my proposal to call together an Assembly to which the North German Parliament would abandon some of its rights in regard to the Zollverein and the South German States some of their privileges as to other matters. Bismarck, however, declared that he would never agree to such a thing, because it would mean the dissolution of the North German Union. No matter how much he would like to organise a Customs Union, he would not sacrifice to it the North German Bund. Minister von der Heydt agreed with him on this point.

" Bismarck then said that when people wished to come to some common arrangement they had to make up their minds to abandon some of their personal independence. He recognised the sincerity and frankness with which I had spoken, and in return for it he would say here what he would never declare publicly—that Prussia would never cause any inconvenience to the South German States. The Prussian Government did not care at all for our joining the North German Bund, because it would only be put to great inconvenience by the entry of eighty new Deputies in the Reichstag. Varnbüler then said that the Assembly could be called the Customs

Deputies Assembly—in German *Zollabgeordnetenver-sammlung*—and Dalwigk reminded us of the English Constitution, saying that the Reichstag could, after the English fashion, resolve itself into a Committee. Though we did not arrive at any decision Bismarck read to us an extract of a Convention agreement, after which discussions were continued until nine o'clock in the evening and a Protocol drawn up, to which the Würtemberg and Baden plenipotentiaries agreed on the next day, whilst I contented myself by handing in an explanation of the motives which had actuated my opposition to the scheme. There is not the slightest doubt but that Prussia will rather give up the Zollverein than abandon the idea of a Parliament. It is difficult to guess what, under these circumstances, will be the decision which it shall please his Majesty to take. In favour of the Prussian scheme it can be urged that when once we have got the Zollverein we can avoid the discussions of a further constitution of the North German Union, and also the dangers attendant on a dissolution of the Zollverein. Should the King wish, with the help of another Minister, to try to bring about the dissolution of the Zollverein, then I am quite ready to hand in my resignation to his Majesty.''

Nothing cleverer than this report could have been penned, inasmuch as it threw on the King of Bavaria the entire responsibility for the decision which events required the Bavarian Government to take. At the same time it proved that the cause of the Southern States in general, and of Bavaria in particular, had found in Prince Hohenlohe a warm defender. The Prussian comedy engineered by Bismarck was being performed with wonderful skill, and in such a masterly manner that the specta-

tors of it could never discover the concealed artificiality
which pervaded its enactment. When the time came
for signing the preliminary Treaty of Union, Baden and
Würtemberg did so at once—that is, on June 4th—whilst
Hesse-Darmstadt only assented to it on the 7th, and
Prince Hohenlohe declared that he could only look at
it in the light of a Prussian proposition, in regard to
which he must reserve the opinion of his Government.
In Munich they considered that the seventh clause of
the Treaty was unacceptable, but at last, after long
debates, Bismarck, who had all the time quietly waited
for the opportune moment to come out with the offer,
declared himself ready to make some concessions to the
Bavarian susceptibilities, consented to its having six
instead of four voices in the Zollbundesrat, and also
agreed that, when negotiations began with Austria to
induce her to join the Customs Union, representatives
of her neighbouring States should take part in the
negotiations. He further consented to the Assembly
being called the "Zoll Parliament." Matters being
finally settled in that form, the Treaty of July 4th was
drawn up, and its signature by the representatives of all
the participating Powers took place in Berlin on July 8th.
This part of Bismarck's task was thus fulfilled to his
complete satisfaction.

Prince Hohenlohe, too, could look back upon the
work which he had performed with a certain pleasure.
He had fairly launched Bavaria on the road leading to a
complete union with Prussia, and he did so in a manner
which did not excite the susceptibilities of his own
Sovereign, who, on the contrary, felt grateful to him for
having stood up with such energy for the rights and
the independence of his country and of his Crown.

Ludwig II. had been at last persuaded that there was no escaping his fate, and that he had better submit to the inevitable, trying only to save what he could out of his former Sovereignty. He had never been a militarist, and this, perhaps, made him more indifferent to the abandonment of his army into the hands of Prussia. At the same time the proverbial dignity of the Wittelsbachs prevented him from bowing the head to the Prussian yoke without, at least, some tacit kind of protestation. He allowed a free hand to Prince Hohenlohe to Prussianise Bavaria, but when he was asked by the Grand Duke of Baden to meet the King of Prussia at the Castle of Mainau, where the Baden family used to spend the summer, he absolutely refused to do so.

When, at last, Prince Hohenlohe, in the Bavarian Landtag, announced that he had concluded, in the name of the Government, a military alliance with Prussia, the emotion to which this acknowledgment gave rise was even stronger than Hohenlohe had foreseen. The Deputies heaped reproach upon him, one of them going so far as to speak of the chains and of the slavery in which the Prince wanted to keep Bavaria in regard to Prussia.

Hohenlohe remained unmoved, and proceeded to bring into execution the two principal points of his programme—the reorganisation of the army and the struggle against the ultramontane elements in the country. He knew beforehand that he would be beaten on the second point, but he had never reckoned upon making a political career in Bavaria, considering his appointment of Prime Minister as only a stepping stone to higher things. He had quite made up his mind to enter the service of Prussia at the first opportunity, and in a manner befitting his great rank and position as a German mediatised Prince. This was what lay behind the efforts Prince Hohenlohe so consistently made to get into favour with Bismarck, whose genius he had guessed even when others had denied it, and whose long tenure of power he had foreseen.

Hohenlohe, though not of the wideness of views which distinguished Bismarck, was far-seeing enough to know that it was the determination of Prussia to go to war with France as soon as she thought she was ready for the struggle. And he was not the only one. Even the Crown Prince of Prussia, whose aversion to military aggression was well known, recognised the impossibility of avoiding a new fight if the advantages earned in the two preceding wars were to be retained. In April, 1868, on his road to Turin, whither he had been sent by the King to attend the wedding festivities of the Crown Prince Humbert of Piedmont with his cousin, the Princess Margherita of Savoy, Frederick passed through Munich, spending two days at the Royal Castle, where he received Prince Hohenlohe in a long audience. Prince Clovis describes the interview as follows :

" We discussed questions of general politics. I took an opportunity which Prince Frederick gave me to warn him that Prussia must not show itself too oppressive toward the Southern States, and advised him not to lose sight of the republican and ultramontane tendencies in Würtemberg, of the state of public opinion in Bavaria, and, above everything else, of all that was going on in France. He seemed to agree with me, and spoke at length of Würtemberg and the political leanings which had become predominant there. He did not mention Baden, and showed himself in general extremely reserved in all that he said. At one moment, when the conversation turned on the subject of the Prussian intrigues in Austria, it seemed to me that he disapproved of them entirely.

" In regard to a war with France, he remarked that the alliance of the Southern States with Prussia implied, of course, a common action between them and Prussia. Who, therefore, he inquired, would be the Commander-in-Chief of the Bavarian army? This led the conversation to the military efficiency of Prussia, which, he assured me, was at least as high as in France. On the whole, Prince Frederick showed himself of a very peaceful disposition. He declared that he hated war and the very idea of it, but that sometimes one could not avoid it, though he could never recommend it as a means to reach any aims one might have. He seems to consider inevitable the unity of Germany under the protectorate of Prussia, but it appeared to me that he would not care to see it brought about by violent means, only through moral persuasion."

The Crown Prince had illusions which Prince Hohenlohe did not attempt to dissipate. The words of Frederick prove that even a man so averse to violence as the heir to the Prussian throne did not see the possibility of escaping the conflict which Bismarck had contrived to persuade the whole of Prussia would be unavoidable. There were some, however, who saw through this policy of intrigue. A woman of great talent and intelligence, long dead—the Countess de Mercy d'Argenteau—who had occasion to see Bismarck at this turning point of his public career, when the edifice which he had built was yet to be completed, made some remarks about him which seem now almost uncanny in their exactitude.

" No one seems to care for Bismarck in Germany, at least outwardly ; you meet more people who prophesy that soon he will be compelled to retire than those who maintain that his influence is increasing not only with the King of Prussia but also with the country. My impression is decidedly the latter. Bismarck's star is not in the least on the wane. He is working energetically at the organisation of the army down to its smallest details, strange as it may seem to find a man who has never been a soldier remain absorbed to the extent that he does in military matters. His enemies say that he does so to win the good graces of the King, but he is not the kind of man who cares for the favours of Sovereigns. The secret is that he considers the army an indispensable corollary of his political plans, and this is sufficient for him. He is upon excellent terms with General von Moltke, he is the intimate of General von Roon, and the three men have got not only the King but also the whole of public opinion in Prussia on their side.

" As for Germany, Bismarck thinks less of its feelings than he says. He knows that the Southern States are condemned beforehand to fall under Prussian influence ; the only question is when. He would prefer this not to be delayed too long, because King William I. is already old, and that his son may not entirely follow his father's views. The Crown Prince is an Imperialist and cares only for the Empire, of which he firmly believes Prussia will become the head. The King does not care for the Empire, and would prefer its chief to remain the King of Prussia, without any additional title to add to a glory which seems to him to be inherent to the dynasty of Hohenzollern. The Crown Prince hates war; the King says he does, which is something different, but he would plunge into its horrors without any repugnance if he thought it his duty to do so. This is the difference in the character of the two men. One would sacrifice a great deal not to see blood flow, whilst the other would not even see this blood, should its spilling be in accordance with his principles and his appreciation of the divine right of which he believes himself to be the representative.

"Bismarck plays upon this difference of temperament and of conception of right and wrong between father and son, and does it in a masterful way. Between these three personages the condition of public opinion in Prussia—I do not speak of Germany, because it is Prussia alone that counts—is absolutely terrifying. We stand before events of an incalculable gravity, of an incommensurable importance. Unfortunately no one will see it, not even the Prussians, who have been reduced to the condition of a well-oiled machine that slowly grinds down the corn it has been given to thresh, but that does so unconsciously and unreasoningly, passively obedient to the hand that presses the lever and causes millions of men to respond to the mechanical appeal he makes to them from time to time. Some people tell me that Bismarck, the man who is behind all this, is inferior to Cavour, and that his methods of statesmanship are not beyond discussion. This may be, but does it count, and will it count in the presence of success? We live in an age when success is everything; no one looks at the means, the result is all that is observed. And Bismarck's policy has already brought about most tangible results. Look at the position of Prussia when he was called at the head of the Cabinet, and look at what it has become to-day. That man knows what *he* wants, and it is a pity that our own French politicians will not see it, and a still greater pity that they cannot make up their minds as to what *they* want. If Napoleon III. were wise he would either start without delay to crush this Prussian danger which so very few appreciate yet, or else he would risk everything in order to conclude an alliance with this Prussia of whom we have heard so much recently, and will hear so much more in the days to come. A Richelieu would do so. Some such bold stroke as this might perhaps protect France from the catastrophe that is hovering over the world, the consequences of which our children and grandchildren will feel even more acutely than we shall do. But there must be no delay, because the day is indeed drawing near, and we shall soon see it break in all its fury; and upon us, unless we take our precautions to divert it on other heads than our own."

Madame de Mercy was a keen judge of the human heart She had predicted the political situation of Europe better than many so-called politicians and statesmen had done at the time. Her cry of warning was unfortunately unheeded, as she expected it would be. But it is curious to reproduce it here, when history has proved its prophetic truth and shown that this woman of talent had been able to appreciate to his real value the man of genius whom events were so soon to transform into the real master of Europe.

CHAPTER XII

New Light on the Ems Dispatch

MANY persons have said, and not a few have thought, that the candidature of Prince Leopold of Hohenzollern to the Spanish throne had been put forward by Prussia with the intention of manufacturing an "incident." Personally, I do not believe it for one moment. The policy of Bismarck was far too wide, and far too clever, to resort to such means to provoke war. He knew very well that something was bound to occur to disturb the good relations between Prussia and France. Judging from what I have heard, the first news of this unfortunate candidature came upon Bismarck as a surprise. On the other hand, I would not at all feel inclined to affirm that the Prussian Foreign Office was entirely a stranger to it. I have heard a story which is curious enough to deserve mention, though I should be sorry to take the full responsibility for its veracity. There was at that time at the Wilhelmstrasse a young man who was later on to become the most important personage in that complicated machinery. At Versailles, where he was on the staff, his work was destined to attract the attention of Bismarck to an extent none of his colleagues had ever done. This young man was Baron von Holstein. Early in 1870 he had gone to Spain on a holiday. At Madrid he saw many political personalities, and became acquainted socially with a lady who was supposed to exercise a considerable influence over the

mind of Marshal Prim. She questioned Holstein about
the possibility of inducing Prince Leopold of Hohenzollern to accept the Spanish crown. The idea had been
first raised during the autumn of 1868, but had fallen
through because the King of Prussia did not care for
a member of his family to run the risk of becoming a
dethroned monarch. This was what the proposed honour
really amounted to, as no one with the slightest political
experience could be so lacking in wisdom as to imagine
that a foreign Prince would have the slightest chance of
remaining for more than a few months on the Spanish
throne. William I. had therefore discouraged his cousin
from acquiescing in the proposed plan.

It seems, however, that there were people in Spain
who still nursed the opinion that it would be for the
interest of that country if Prince Leopold could be induced to accept the throne, and the lady in question said
as much to Baron von Holstein. The latter retrenched
himself, of course, behind his total ignorance concerning
the ideas of Count Bismarck on the subject, but he
suggested that a certain Bernhardi, a secret agent
of Bismarck, might canvass the candidature in Berlin.
The lady understood, and it is very probable that Marshal
Prim understood too. A few days later Baron von
Holstein returned to the Foreign Office, but spoke to no
one at the Wilhelmstrasse, not even to his immediate
chief, of his conversations at Madrid; indeed, when asked
concerning them one day by Bismarck himself, who had
been told at Versailles, he merely replied that he had not
considered himself important enough to think that anything he might have heard or said could interest the
Minister, but that he had tried in Spain, as well as
everywhere else, to serve him and the intentions which

he supposed him to have. The story says that Bismarck merely remarked that he did not often find people willing to do so. But after this the career of Baron von Holstein prospered in an amazing manner, though he was never given a post abroad, except that of Councillor of the Embassy in Paris under Count Arnim and Prince von Hohenlohe, when we shall see him playing an important part in the war scare of 1875. Afterwards he returned to Berlin and never again left the Foreign Office, where he was almost as powerful as Bismarck himself.

Even if this incident took place, I feel inclined to think that the zeal of the Baron had been entirely due to his personal initiative. But it is certain that in the course of the month of June a former secretary of the Spanish Legation in Berlin, Senor Salazar y Mazarredo, arrived in the Prussian capital with the intention of conferring not only with Prince Leopold of Hohenzollern, but also with Count von Bismarck, and, thanks to the interference of Queen Augusta—this last fact, I believe, not being generally known—the King was induced to consent to his cousin Leopold embarking upon the adventure.

The Queen, whose everlasting quarrels with Bismarck strongly influenced the last years of William I., was a clever woman, very fond of intrigue. She knew very well that her husband had married her for convenience, whilst his heart was entirely given to someone else. For her part, whilst pretending a deep attachment to William I., she nevertheless had on more than one occasion intrigued against him. She had very decided ideas on certain matters, and was apt to get enthusiastic without any reason for doing so. The

thought of having a German Prince on the throne of
Spain had appealed to her, and she had encouraged the
movement from the very first. At any rate, she argued,
Prince Leopold's proposed adventure was not more
risky than the one in which his own brother, Prince
Charles, had engaged himself in Roumania. William I.
had been all the time averse to both of these enterprises,
but, as his wife had made him confess, what it pleased
his distant kinsmen to do did not, after all, concern him,
and it was not his business to try to save them from
themselves. He therefore signified his consent, and on
July 3rd the Havas Agency announced to the world that
Prince Leopold of Hohenzollern had accepted the
Spanish throne.

It seems that before the news became official someone
at the Prussian Foreign Office had suggested the advisability, in publishing it in the official organ of the
Government, to add that the Prince Leopold meant to
pay a visit to Paris, so as to consult Napoleon upon his
future course of action. This was on the point of being
done when another person telegraphed Count Bismarck
on the subject. The Count indignantly replied that such
a course should not be thought of for one single moment,
as the Hohenzollerns were in no way dependent on what
the Emperor of the French thought.

In his Reminiscences Bismarck does not mention
this incident at all. It is, however, perfectly true. He
says instead that he had always fancied that Prince
Leopold in Madrid would have been rather inclined to
side with France against Germany than with Prussia
against France. But we may be forgiven for thinking
that he was not quite sincere.

Bismarck's affirmation that France was seeking a

quarrel with Prussia is also absolutely unjustifiable, because it was Prussia, and especially Bismarck, who was
trying to trap the Emperor Napoleon into a quarrel. He
played admirably the part of an indifferent spectator. He
caused the Foreign Office to answer in an evasive manner
the first questions addressed to it by the French Government, and to have replied to them that it knew nothing
at all about the whole affair, which did not concern
Prussia or the North German Confederation, but simply
the head not of the Royal House of Prussia but of the
whole Hohenzollern family and the Princes of that name :
a subtle distinction which it is quite impossible for history
to accept unreservedly.

We touch here upon a point of history that has never
been properly ascertained, because there are to this day
some people in Spain who pretend that representations
were made at Madrid by the Cabinet of the Tuileries on
the subject of the possible advent of a German Prince
in Spain, and that there they met with a *non possumus*.

What is certain is that, whilst in Berlin Bismarck
was proceeding with great caution, Paris was accumulating
mistake upon mistake and allowing chauvinism to sub-
merge reason. Looking back upon that time, by the
light of all which followed upon it, the questions arise :
Had not this chauvinism, which brought France on the
verge of ruin, been fomented from across the frontier?
Had the Press been paid to give way to ultra-patriotic
feelings? And whether all those who shouted so fiercely,
" À Berlin, à Berlin ! " were all genuine Parisians.

The French Minister of Foreign Affairs at that
moment was the Duc de Gramont, and the fact was
counted to be a great misfortune for France by a certain
section who scarified the Duke as one of the most incap-

able, vain and unreasonable politicians the second Empire ever employed. The Duke had rallied himself to the cause of Napoleon, much to the indignation of the Legitimists who had not forgiven him for deserting the Comte de Chambord, after having accepted the splendid inheritance which the Duchess of Angoulême had left to him—something like seven hundred thousand francs a year. He it was who made in the French Chamber the famous declarations which inflamed the country and made it look upon the Hohenzollern candidature as an outrage directly addressed to the French spirit of independence as well as to its self-respect.

Nevertheless, in spite of these reproaches, which in some slight degree were justified, it is a matter of doubt if, even with another than the Duke in his place, it would have been possible to avoid the war which Bismarck had made up his mind to provoke. The only advantage which a cleverer politician than the Duc de Gramont might have obtained would have been to leave the odium of the declaration of war on the shoulders of Prussia.

The King of Prussia, however, who knew absolutely nothing of the machinations that had brought about these complications, was doing all that was in his power to prevent hostilities. The Queen, too, had been thoroughly frightened by the mischief which her ill-timed interference had brought about, and was beseeching William I. to insist upon the Prince of Hohenzollern withdrawing his candidature. She wrote herself to Leopold's father, Prince Anthony, begging him to restrain his son from throwing Europe into difficulties, of which she was at last beginning to appreciate the importance. On his side, Bismarck was in direct communication with the Prince, secretly encouraging him to

remain firm and not to yield to pressure, which he
described as being without purport or necessity. On
the other hand—and this is again a point which has been
overlooked by the many historians who have described the
story of these eventful days—the Queen, through a friend
of hers, a lady in whom she had perfect confidence, had
caused a message to be conveyed to Paris, in which she
had implored the Emperor Napoleon to send Count
Benedetti to Ems. King William liked and appreciated
the Count, and she thought that with him as intermediary
the two Kings might be able personally to disentangle
matters.

In consequence of this confidential message Benedetti journeyed to Ems. His first conversation with the
King was most courteous and encouraging. After
Louis XIV., William I. was perháps the Monarch who
possessed the most complete conception of a Sovereign's
dignity. He would never have yielded to foreign pressure, however insistent, upon any question which touched
the Royal prerogative, yet, though he told the French
Ambassador that the matter concerned the Spanish
Government more than his own, William I. wrote to
the Prince of Hohenzollern, advising him, in the interest
of the dynasty, to desist. He did not wish for war,
and certainly among all the people who worked in favour
of it he cannot be reckoned. Owing to the news which
he had received from Ems, Bismarck deemed it advisable to confer personally with his Sovereign. So, leaving
Varzin, he travelled by way of Berlin to the famous
watering-place. In Berlin telegrams advised him that
the King was negotiating with Benedetti instead of
referring him to the Prussian Ministers. This angered
Bismarck beyond words. He decided not to go imme-

diately to Ems, but that same evening instead asked Moltke and Roon to dinner. The meal had just begun when a telegram was brought from Paris with the news that the Prince of Hohenzollern had relinquished his candidature because France had threatened to declare war upon Prussia. A man whom I knew personally, and who was at that time employed in the Foreign Office, was present. He described the scene to me. When Bismarck had read this dispatch his face had changed so terribly that those near thought he was going to have a fit and rushed to open the window, to give more air to the stuffy apartment. The Chancellor, in his account of the incident, declares that his first thought was to send his resignation to William I., as he did not wish to stand before the whole of Germany as officially responsible for so great a humiliation. There we see already quite distinctly his determination to bring matters to a bloody crisis.

He started to explain the position as he saw it, rather than it was in reality; it had, he said, become an impossible one. The King, under the threat of war, had, four days in succession, received the French Ambassador without the presence of one of his Ministers: he had personally conducted political negotiations of a first importance instead of refusing to enter into discussions with a foreign diplomat and simply referring him, as was his duty, to his Minister for Foreign Affairs. This, continued Bismarck, infringed his obligations as a constitutional Sovereign. The Queen, he asserted, was at the bottom of the whole affair, and he was not altogether wrong. Both Roon and Moltke begged Bismarck to reconsider his position, asking him at least to wait until he had heard in detail all that had taken place at Ems.

What had taken place at Ems? This is the historical point which Bismarck himself has cleared for us to his everlasting shame, and which I shall briefly repeat here. When the news of the retirement of Prince Hohenzollern reached the King of Prussia he could not hide the extreme satisfaction which it gave him. It is a curious thing that at St. Cloud the fact produced the same impression on the mind of Napoleon III., and that in France, as well as in Prussia, it was the responsible advisers of the Crown, and not the Sovereigns themselves, who brought about the calamity which was to send the Bonapartes into exile and to deprive France of two fair provinces. The Duc de Gramont, instead of telegraphing to Benedetti thankfully to accept the happy solution of a painful incident, sent a peremptory order to ask from the King of Prussia guarantees that in the future no German Prince would ever put himself up as a pretender to the throne of Spain. Had the Duke not been the man that he was, one could almost suppose that this piece of stupidity had been dictated to him by Bismarck himself. Almost at the same time the Prussian Ambassador in Paris, Baron von Werthern, telegraphed to Ems the copy of a note which the Duc de Gramont had dictated in collaboration with M. Emile Ollivier, in which were framed the words in which the King of Prussia was to formulate the promises which the French Government expected him to give. This note caused a profound irritation to William I., and he expressed his regret that Werthern had not, upon its communication to him, decided to leave Paris on his own initiative without waiting further orders from Berlin.

On that eventful day, July 13th, 1870, my brother-in-law, Prince Anthony Radziwill, was the aide-de-camp on duty. The King sent him twice on that day to Count Benedetti. The first time it was to tell to the French Ambassador that he fully approved of the retirement of Prince Leopold of Hohenzollern. The second time—it was already five o'clock in the afternoon—it was in reply to the message of insistence of Benedetti, to which the King answered that he refused to engage himself in new discussions, and could only refer once more to the promises which he had already given, but he did not say that he refused to see the Ambassador any more. On the contrary, he added that he would be glad to say good-bye to him the next morning at the railway station before his departure for Coblenz.

At the same moment that my brother-in-law was delivering this message the King caused von Abeken, the official of the Foreign Office in attendance upon him at Ems, to telegraph to Count Bismarck an account of the whole incident. This telegram reached the latter when he was once more dining with Roon and Moltke, whom he had asked the day before to share again his meal of the next evening. It was this telegram that brought about the catastrophe which so many people had tried to avoid.

This is the telegram :

" Ems, July 13th. 3.40 evening.

" His Majesty the King writes to me :

" ' Benedetti has accosted me during my walk and asked me in a most pressing manner to authorise him to telegraph that I engaged myself once for all never to grant my consent to the Hohenzollerns putting forward again their candidature. I have refused in a rather firm tone before putting an end to the conversation, because one

must not, and one cannot, take such engagements for ever. I told him that, quite naturally, I had not yet received any news, and that he could easily ascertain, as he was informed before me of what was taking place in Paris and in Madrid, that my Government was quite out of touch in this matter.'

"His Majesty," Abeken went on, "has received at this moment a letter from the Prince. His Majesty, having told Benedetti that he was expecting news from the Prince, has decided, in reason of the proposition which Count Eulenburg and myself have made to his Majesty, and in consideration of the opinions expressed before, not to receive Benedetti any more, and to let him know only by the aide-de-camp on duty that his Majesty received the confirmation of the news which have been communicated from Paris to Benedetti, and that in consequence his Majesty had nothing more to say to the Ambassador.

"His Majesty leaves it to your Excellency to decide whether this new exigency of Benedetti, and the refusal with which it has been met, ought to be communicated to our Ministers abroad and to the Press."

Bismarck silently handed the telegram to Moltke and to Roon. Both read it and said nothing. After a few moments of hesitation Bismarck once more took up the fatal paper and perused it with great attention, then, in sharp, ringing tones that contrasted with his discouraged one of a few moments earlier, he addressed a few questions to Moltke as to the state of the Prussian armaments and the rapidity with which war could open on the Prussian side. The General replied that if Prussia had to go to war, he did not see any advantage in delaying the hostilities. Even if it proved impossible to protect the left side of the Rhine against a French invasion, the rapidity with which Prussia could begin the campaign would bring into action a force far superior to any that France could display in the same time. He considered, therefore, that it would be more advantageous to Prussian arms for hostilities to begin at once.

This was more than sufficient to decide the course of action of Bismarck. Abeken had told him that the King was leaving him entirely free to communicate or not to the Press the contents of the message. The German statesman at once determined this should be done, but in his own way, and consequently he thought it better not to give publicity to the *whole* of the telegram, but simply to make extracts from it, so as to produce both in Germany and in France the effect which he required to force a declaration of war. The result was :

" Telegram received in Berlin at 5.9 evening, arranged by Bismarck and communicated by him to the Press and to Prussia's representatives abroad :

" After the news of the relinquished claim of the Hereditary Prince of Hohenzollern had been communicated to the French Imperial Government by the Spanish Royal Government, the French Ambassador has again requested at Ems, from his Majesty the King, the authorisation to telegraph to Paris that his Majesty the King engaged himself for the whole of the future never to grant his consent to the Hohenzollerns in the case these should wish once more to put forward their candidature. Upon this his Majesty the King has refused to receive again the French Ambassador, and has ordered the aide-de-camp on duty to tell him that his Majesty had nothing further to communicate to him."

After using the long pencil he generally used to this

terrible effect, Bismarck read the revision to his two companions with the remark that, "If, in obedience to the orders of his Majesty, I communicate this telegram as I have worded it to the Press, and if I have it at once telegraphed to our different embassies, it will be known in Paris before midnight. It will madden them. Our success depends entirely on the first impressions that the origin of the war will provoke at home and abroad. It is most essential that we should appear as the attacked party. Now let us drink to the success of our arms."

And such is the true story of the Ems dispatch.

CHAPTER XIII

Sedan and Paris

IN reducing the Ems telegram Bismarck displayed his knowledge of human nature. And with what psychological accuracy he could grasp all the intricacies of a situation! One cannot sufficiently regret that Napoleon III., already worn out by the illness to which he was to succumb three years later, had not the energy to oppose the mistaken enthusiasm of his subjects, by explaining—as, indeed, Benedetti did years later—that " no one had been insulted at Ems, and no one had wished to insult anyone else." Certainly such an idea was far from the mind of William I. Napoleon III. also did not care to enter into a conflict with Prussia, which, if unsuccessful, he realised but too well would mean the fall of his dynasty. The Empress also, in spite of the accusations which have been launched against her, did not foster the war spirit; indeed, she no longer had any political influence. Emile Ollivier did not care for her, and the Duc de Gramont, however much he may have admired her as a woman, did not trust her as a Sovereign. I know from a personal source that he had begged the Emperor not to tell his Consort of the Ems negotiations until they were completed. The Duke had the naive idea that by his own direct influence at the Hofburg he would be able to draw Austria into an alliance with France against Prussia, a plan which he knew Prince Metternich would oppose, and he feared the latter could

hear something about it through the Empress who might
confide in Madame de Metternich. Eugénie knew that
in case of a war breaking out she would be called upon
to assume the functions of Regent, but it is a cruel
injustice to accuse her of having urged the Emperor to
declare war.

Everything conspired to favour the success of Bismarck's plans. On that same evening of July 13th the
official organ of the Prussian Government, the *Nord-
deutsche Allgemeine Zeitung*, published extra sheets con-
taining the altered telegram, and the population of Berlin
feverishly discussed with the utmost indignation the so-
called insult to which King William I. had been subjected
by the French Ambassador. About that same time the
Paris boulevards were filled with an angry crowd scream-
ing and yelling that the honour of France required that
they must wipe out with blood the insult offered to its
representative by the King of Prussia, who had ordered
him out of his presence. In both countries the excitement was no longer to be restrained.

The next day William I. returned to Berlin. To
his own surprise he was met by wild acclamations and
the enthusiasm of a delirious multitude, urging him to
defend the honour of the Fatherland. At the railway
station Moltke and Bismarck were awaiting their Sovereign, and the former presented to him the order for
the general mobilisation of the army, which the King
signed immediately. He was by that time fully persuaded that war was the national desire and that his
duty as a Monarch commanded him to go forward without flinching. All his hesitations of the day before had
disappeared amidst the shouts of the Berlin population,
who pressed around his carriage, kissed his hands, and

showered blessings upon his head. The enthusiasm which pervaded Prussia on that day had been kindled in an entirely artificial manner, but it had become a really genuine thing, and it was to continue until the end of the war which, among the many things it destroyed, put an end to the old Kingdom of Prussia which William I. loved so well, and raised in its stead a German Empire whose existence will probably be neither so long nor so successful a one as that of its predecessor.

On July 20th Bismarck had the audacity to declare to the Reichstag that in all the sad tragedy which was to cause such bloodshed he had only received one official document, and that was the French declaration of war.

In mentioning the telegram which he had sent on the evening of July 13th to the Prussian representatives abroad, Bismarck affirmed that it had only been a simple message of information and not at all a provocation as it was sought to make out in France. He accused the latter of having taken the initiative of the war by spreading a lie concerning the King of Prussia and thus wounding the national feelings of the whole of Germany and directly offending his Majesty. And after these words, which were neither an excuse nor even an explanation, but which could be one and all contradicted in every point and particular, the Chancellor closed the Reichstag.

The amazing thing in this whole terrible story, the consequences of which we see to-day in the struggle which is devastating Europe, and which might never have taken place but for it, was the utter indifference with which other nations surveyed it. Russia remained silent; Austria crossed its arms and said nothing ; Italy did

not move; and England, who, there is no doubt, would have liked to prevent the war, nevertheless remained neutral. The fact was that the poison instilled by Bismarck into the mind of the whole world was working. No one sympathised with France, because everybody believed her to have been a silly aggressor. The Empire was paying for its former mistakes; for having allowed Prussia to crush Denmark and Austria; for having looked with disdain upon the Prussian armaments; for having neglected to secure for itself useful and strong alliances; for having tolerated the disorders of its military administration.

On July 15th, 1870, France had scarcely 240,000 men under arms, whilst the Germans could dispose immediately of an army numbering over 450,000, which would in a few days have been reinforced by 400,000 soldiers more. What chance had France? Sedan has been too often described for me to linger over its incidents. The few points concerning it which I wish to point out here are connected with the personality of Bismarck. He gives at length the incidents of the capitulation. What Bismarck forgets to say is that he arranged matters in such a manner that he prevented, until the capitulation had been signed, an interview between his Sovereign and Napoleon. He feared that, in his feelings of compassion for a brother Monarch, William I. might show himself more lenient than his advisers. It is absolutely certain that if the two men had met the conditions under which the capitulation actually took place would not have been as hard as Moltke with his inflexibility and Bismarck with his unscrupulousness framed and imposed them. The Chancellor handled matters so skilfully that it was only after General Wimpfen had put his name to the awful document, which sealed the fate of the Imperial dynasty, that the King of Prussia was informed that the Emperor had been waiting for him since the early hours of the morning. The old man, who had a heart if his Minister had not, angrily resented having been kept in ignorance. His first impulse would have been to rush to his erstwhile enemy, and by the cordiality of his welcome help him to forget as far as possible his sad position.

When Napoleon reached the palace, where he was to remain a prisoner until the end of the campaign, he found the kind protection of a woman who had taken upon herself the task to soothe his great misfortune. From the first moment that she had heard of the destination of the Imperial captive Queen Augusta had occupied herself with all the details concerning his establishment in that castle where his uncle, the King of Westphalia, had once held his Court. Indeed, had she been permitted to do so, she would have repaired herself to Wilhelmshöe to receive him there with all the honours due to a Sovereign. But Bismarck was watching, and he proceeded to represent to the King, in the worst light possible, the delicacy displayed by the Queen, and to accuse her of political intrigues. His was a soul capable of tenderness in regard to his nearest and dearest, but not of generosity for a fallen enemy. The respect which he showed to Napoleon III. on the morning following' the battle of Sedan did not proceed from pity so much as from triumph.

Once the capitulation had been signed the position of Bismarck became in some respects more secure than it had been before. I say with intention "in some respects," because in others he found that his word did not bear so much weight in war as it had done in peace time. The General Staff did not like his way of making the military operations dependent upon the general political situation. The Chancellor understood very well what other gain for Prussia than annexation of territory or a large contribution in money was brought within reach —an imperial crown for his King. This was of greater import to Bismarck than even the occupation of Paris.

Headquarters had been transferred to Versailles after the battle of Sedan, and here Queen Augusta's influence became felt as much if not more than it had been at home. She determined to try and persuade the King that he ought to conduct the war in a gentlemanly, chivalrous way. It reached Bismarck's ears that, together with her daughter-in-law, the Crown Princess, she had tried to prevent the bombardment of Paris by representing it to William I. as a useless act of cruelty, and he could not bring himself to forgive her for this piece of womanly interference. When, too, the bombardment was mooted, some friends of the Queen represented to certain officers of the Staff that the results of a bombardment would never legitimatise its expense. General Roon, who did not share this opinion, one day spoke about the matter to Bismarck. He at once offered to furnish the necessary funds out of the Federal Exchequer. Roon accepted, and one morning the Prussian batteries attacked the forts of the French capital, much to the astonishment of the King, who asked how such a decision could have been taken without its being expressly referred to him for consent or disapproval. He was so angry that even Moltke felt embarrassed and had to call Bismarck to the rescue. The latter thereupon unblushingly told William I. that he had agreed to the suggestion, and a bombardment would accelerate the capitulation of the great city and thus bring peace. No plan had ever been submitted to the Sovereign, but he did not contradict the flagrant untruth.

Nor was it only the King whom Bismarck deceived. In the course of January Bismarck had occasion to speak with the Crown Prince, with whom his relations had become quite friendly in consequence of the proclamation of the Empire respecting the rumours from Berlin, that both the Queen and the Crown Princess were doing their best to prevent the bombardment of Paris. The Crown Prince protested that such was not the case, whereon the Chancellor retorted that many people believed it, and in consequence the Crown Prince's popularity in the army was bound to suffer, that therefore the best thing would be for the Prince to do his best to bring about an immediate bombardment. He failed. Frederick William was also against a measure which he considered useless and mischievous; he briefly replied that it was not his business to interfere with the decisions of the General Staff, and Bismarck had better let Moltke mention the matter to the King.

Bismarck bit his lips, but worked away at his plans. He tried to enter into negotiations with Napoleon III. The Emperor declined; the Empress Regent also refused to enter into any negotiations the result of which would have been the cession of a portion, however small, of French territory. These rebuffs did not disconcert Bismarck. He, indeed, had more than enough to occupy his undivided attention if the Empire, at the construction of which he had laboured for so long and with such perseverance, were to be proclaimed at last and put outside any possible danger for the future.

CHAPTER XIV

Inauguration of the Spy System

IT is an interesting fact that the strong hostility which existed between the General Staff and the Foreign Office in Prussia in 1870 is also manifest during the present war. In both campaigns each accuses the other of compromising success by meddling in matters which ought to be left entirely in the hands of the people directly responsible for them. In 1866 the Staff already hated Bismarck, whom it accused of having stultified the success of the Austrian campaign by his interference. It decided, before starting for the French front in 1870, that this time he would not be allowed a free hand; that they would keep him in the dark concerning the military dispositions. Bismarck himself relates that whilst he was travelling in the King's train to Cologne he heard in the next compartment a conversation between Generals von Roon and Podbielski, of which he formed the subject, and which was clear enough to make him understand that he would not be informed of any of the decisions taken by the Staff.

Despite this general feeling, however, when the capitulation of Sedan had to be discussed Moltke himself asked Bismarck to assist him, and after this he was called more than once to give his opinion on occasions when some important decision had to be taken. But the rivalry between the two departments responsible for the conduct of affairs during war continues fierce and unabated to the present time. The Staff to-day is just as loud in its denunciations and accuses the Foreign Office of all the mistakes which have taken place, and brought about the crisis that is shaking the whole of Europe, whilst the subordinates of Bethmann-Hollweg are loud in the denunciations of the hurry displayed by the Staff, who gave no time for negotiations in its impatience to go forward to crush enemies the real strength of whom it undervalues in quite a lamentable manner.

Bismarck, however, was a very different man from the present Chancellor of the German Empire. His powerful personality could not be set aside so easily, and though he was made the object of a kind of military boycott, he contrived to be at the King's side whenever he thought that the security of public affairs required it. He considered that the work of the army was to destroy the enemy, but that the aim of every war ought to be a peace that satisfied the policy of the State engaged in it. The political problem of every campaign, according to Bismarck, was by far the most important, and in the long run the question of peace and war always depended on the people in charge of the foreign affairs of the different belligerent countries. This was what the Prussian Staff refused to understand; this was what Bismarck intended to teach them. At Versailles, where so many grave interests absorbed his attention, he resigned himself with a better grace than could have been expected from him not to be informed of the details concerning the technical conduct of the campaign. But as he was the responsible adviser of the King he had to try to procure for himself the information which he needed. This, however, was not easy. With all his intelligence Bismarck did not see how to begin, when one of his lieutenants, that von Holstein who figured in the Hohenzollern candidature in Spain, stepped upon the scene. He proceeded to explain to the Chancellor a plan at which he had been working since the beginning of the war. This plan was nothing more nor less than the organisation of the formidable *bureau d'espionage*, which became such a powerful weapon in the hands of Bismarck and to the ability of which he owed more than he would have cared to own of his successes.

Von Holstein was a genius in some ways and one of the most extraordinary men that have ever lived. He had one great ambition : to know everything about everybody and to rule everybody through fear of the disclosures which he could make were he at any time tempted to do so. He was absolutely indifferent to high position, titles, decorations, or money. His tastes were of the simplest, his wants but few. He could appreciate a good dinner, but he could be content with a dry crust and never feel unhappy about it. During the years he worked at the side of the Chancellor he proved a most admirable helpmate, and his administration of the special department in the Foreign Office, of which he became the head, was perfect; but when Bismarck, at whose side he had remained for something like twenty-five years, was dismissed in the way we know, von Holstein did not show him the slightest sympathy, parted from him as coldly as he did everything else in his life, and continued his own special work in which he was engaged with the equanimity that had never deserted him at any time of his existence. Later on, however, he could not get on with Bismarck's successors, in whom he did not find the appreciation of his services to which he considered that he was entitled, and at last retired from active service, to

die a few years afterwards the possessor of far more
political secrets than any living man in his time could
boast of having learned.

Bismarck held Holstein in high esteem, and when he
came with his plan for the establishment of a vast
organisation of almost universal spying, Bismarck had
grasped immediately the advantages he could obtain from
it; but even he did not then realise how powerful such
an organisation could become. Holstein recruited his
spies in every class of society—men and women, rich and
poor, high and low. No matter the social condition or
the material resources of the people whom he took in
hand, he compelled them to execute his orders, which
for the most part consisted in the obligation to bring to
him certain knowledge which he required. His first care,
whenever any individual capable at a given minute of
playing a part, no matter how humble, in the great drama
attracted his attention, was to ferret out all that could
be learned concerning him or her. With but few exceptions he contrived to lay his finger on a hidden secret.
Once this preliminary step had been done to his satisfaction the rest was easy. The unfortunate victim was given
to understand that he would be shamed in public at any
time unless . . . unless . . . Well, this must be left
to the reader whose intelligence will readily enable him
to understand.

Thanks to this simple system of, let us call it, in-
timidation, the Secret Service which proved so useful
to Bismarck was instituted with much trouble but with
magnificent results. Not only Berlin and its society,
but in a certain sense the whole of Europe was subjected
to an inquisition that left them absolutely no loophole of
escape. Bismarck knew everything, heard everything.

made use of everything. After the war Holstein was for some years secretary to the Embassy at Paris, where he worked at the installation of the different branches of his service with such secrecy that neither Count Arnim nor Prince Hohenlohe ever suspected his occupation. Later on Holstein obtained entire control of the Secret Service, and became so jealous of his work that he never confided its details to anyone ; and when he retired the edifice which had been so very near to perfection when he stood at its head lost its importance, became, indeed, rather a source of bad information for Bethmann-Hollweg and his officials.

At the Foreign Office Holstein, when he was called from Paris, was officially the director of the political department. He was not only considered with great respect by his colleagues and subordinates, but also held in high esteem by all the German diplomats and am-bassadors abroad, who often came to him for advice and relied on him for giving them hints as to how they were to proceed in regard to Bismarck and what they were to say to him. Even men like Prince Münster and Prince Hohenlohe were very careful to ascertain through Hol-stein the disposition of their great chief before venturing into his presence, and often asked him to smooth the way. He was always polite, always ready to oblige, but only did so when he found it useful to his political interests. He used to spend his days in a small, narrow little room, which served to him as office and where two chairs and a huge desk composed the whole furniture. He never went out into society, and though he knew everybody very few people knew him even by sight. He was a demon for cleverness and unscrupulousness, and the fact that personal ambition was a thing utterly unknown to him rendered him all the more dangerous to his foes.

Holstein engineered the Hohenzollern candidature; he arranged the war scare of 1875 when Gortschakov was rendered ridiculous and poor Vicomte de Gontaut Biron made to play such a sorry part; he organised the vast conspiracy which resulted in unfortunate King Ludwig II. of Bavaria ending his days in the blue waters of the lake of Starnberg; he caused secretly the famous forged documents which were handed to Alexander III. to be fabricated, in order to provoke on the part of the Tsar a demonstration of sympathy in favour of Bismarck; he spent his life in intriguing, plotting, working in silence and in the dark.

The great fear of Bismarck during this period was that, if the siege of Paris dragged on too long, Europe might make some demonstration of sympathy in favour of France. The visits of M. Thiers to the principal Continental capitals also caused him some sleepless nights. Count Beust, too, whom he hated so cordially, was agitating to provoke the Russian and English Cabinet into making a collective intervention in favour of peace. It was this fear which caused Bismarck to shout with joy when Russia asked for a revision of the Treaty of Paris. Through Prince Peter of Oldenburg, a *persona grata* both at Petersburg and at the Berlin Court, who was a cousin of Alexander II. and a great favourite of his, it had been insinuated that such a request would meet with favour. Prince Peter was very glad to avail himself of the hint that he could prove of use in Russia's aspirations towards the East by suggesting that Petersburg could profit by the helplessness of France by seeking to abolish the clause of the Treaty of 1856 which prevented any Russian Fleet cruising in the waters of the Black Sea. Russia had always thought it humiliating to its dignity, and the Tsar would have been but too glad to see the clause abrogated; but, to the general surprise, Prince Gortschakov did not receive the idea with enthusiasm. It was finally the Russian military attaché at the Berlin Court, General Count Kutusoff, who took upon himself to speak to the Emperor Alexander concerning the suggestion made by the Berlin Cabinet, and who decided him to take the necessary steps to enforce it by inviting the Powers which had taken part in the Congress of Paris to meet in conference in London. The result was what Bismarck hoped for; no longer did Russia take up the cause of France against Prussia, except in a purely academical manner.

Count Kutusoff, who was one of the most convinced partisans of a complete understanding between Berlin and Petersburg, was one of the puppets of whom Bismarck made most use. An excellent and worthy man, but not at all intelligent, he took himself far more *au sérieux* than anyone else, and liked nothing better than to be entrusted with what he thought were diplomatic missions. He had got an excellent memory, and could be relied upon to repeat with exactitude all that he had been told. He did so with the full persuasion that he was merely giving expression to his own personal ideas. Very often this was precisely what was wanted. Without him, and without the Grand Duke of Saxe-Weimar, it is quite possible that Alexander II. would have allowed himself to be moved by the pleadings of M. Thiers or the letter which the Empress Eugénie wrote to him from Chislehurst, asking him to intervene in favour of France.

In this way did Bismarck blind Alexander II. to the direction in which his duty should lie.

I cannot conceive why nobody except Bismarck has drawn attention in the numerous accounts which have been written concerning the siege of Paris to the fact that, whilst it lasted, the Prussians suffered from a decided shortage of ammunition.

Now, who was responsible in 1870 for this want of organisation in the Prussian army? Was it due to the simple fact that ammunitions really were lacking, or to the want of haste in forwarding them? Bismarck attributes it to the last circumstance, and perhaps he is not very wrong in this appreciation. In 1870 the Prussians were not quite the barbarians they have become to-day, and among the higher officers of the Staff there were many who thought that the bombardment of Paris was a useless cruelty, and would result in the loss of art treasures and monuments of inestimable value that nothing could ever replace.

One wonders really what it was that Bismarck had hoped from this wanton ruthlessness. Holstein, who spoke about it one day, declared that the Chancellor had wanted the bombardment to distract public attention from the important negotiations in which he was engaged in regard to the proclamation of the Empire. This may be true and it may not. The real object of this unwarranted action has never been ascertained to this day.

On January 23rd Jules Favre repaired once more to Versailles. This time it was to settle the conditions of the fall of the brave city. Jules Favre consented to everything. His consternation was so great that he and the officers of the French Staff entirely forgot to include

N

in the armistice the Army of the East commanded by Chanzy, and neither Bismarck nor Moltke, of course, mentioned it. This fact, almost monstrous in its unscrupulousness, allowed the Prussians to continue its march against it and to crush it. Jules Favre afterwards declared that he had never thought of having this army mentioned in a special paragraph in the armistice convention because he had understood that the latter would include all the French armies in general, and William I., in his telegram to Queen Augusta, mentioned expressly " All the French armies." But of what value were the private opinions or thoughts of the Sovereign against the determination of Bismarck?

Such were the broad lines of the tragedy out of the pangs of which a new Empire was born and several great reputations marred. And if we are to believe von Holstein, Bismarck's first words after the proclamation of the German Empire at Versailles had been words of despondency. Throwing himself into an arm-chair and unbuttoning his uniform, he exclaimed. " It is very fine, but how long will it last?"

A King becomes Emperor

THE North German Confederation never had any chance of being considered as anything else than a provisional arrangement. Everybody had known in the latter 'sixties that, war or no war, the Empire which was in the air would, within a few years, become a reality. Germany, together with its various small States, would have to be moulded to it. The brilliant successes which had attended the French campaign brought matters to a climax, and the whole of Northern Germany had become eager for the elevation of the King of Prussia to the rank of an Emperor. In the Southern States, however, as we have already seen, this was by no means the same thing. Bavaria did not in the least care to become a Prussian province, and Wirtenberg felt averse to it. Bismarck therefore, had to arrange matters in such a way that the consent of both the Kings of Bavaria and of Wirtenberg should not only be obtained but appear in the eyes of the man in the street as the expression of their willingness that a new order of things should be established.

On the question of the Imperial title William I held that the value of the Prussian crown was above that of Emperor. The latter had been borne in succession by so many dynasties who had not contrived to keep it for any length of time. The Imperial title appeared to him as something in the light of a function in the armistice the Army of the East commanded by Chanzy, and neither Bismarck nor Moltke, of course, mentioned it. This fact, almost monstrous in its unscrupulousness, allowed the Prussians to continue its march against it and to crush it. Jules Favre afterwards declared that he had never thought of having this army mentioned in a special paragraph in the armistice convention because he had understood that the latter would include all the French armies in general, and William I., in his telegram to Queen Augusta, mentioned expressly " All the French armies." But of what value were the private opinions or thoughts of the Sovereign against the determination of Bismarck?

Such were the broad lines of the tragedy out of the pangs of which a new Empire was born and several great reputations marred. And if we are to believe von Holstein, Bismarck's first words after the proclamation of the German Empire at Versailles had been words of despondency. Throwing himself into an arm-chair and unbuttoning his uniform, he exclaimed, "It is very fine, but how long will it last?"

CHAPTER XV

A King becomes Emperor

THE North German Confederation never had any chance of being considered as anything else than a provisional arrangement. Everybody had known in the later 'sixties that, war or no war, the Empire which was in the air would, within a few years, become a reality. Germany, together with its various small States, would have to be modified to it. The brilliant successes which had attended the French campaign brought matters to a climax, and the whole of Northern Germany had become eager for the elevation of the King of Prussia to the rank of an Emperor. In the Southern States, however, as we have already seen, this was by no means the same thing. Bavaria did not in the least care to become a Prussian province, and Würtemberg felt averse to it. Bismarck, therefore, had to arrange matters in such a way that the consent of both the Kings of Bavaria and of Würtemberg should not only be obtained, but appear in the eyes of the man in the street as the expression of their willingness that a new order of things should be established.

On the question of the Imperial title, William I. held that the value of the Prussian crown was above that of Emperor. The latter had been borne in succession by so many dynasties who had not contrived to keep it for any length of time. The Imperial title appeared to him as something in the light of a function rather than of a dignity; Bismarck, on the other hand, differed from his Royal master. He considered that the adoption of the Imperial title by the King of Prussia had become a political necessity, because it represented to the mind of the German people the unity which was indispensable for the development of the Empire, and also as an important factor in deflecting attention from the Prussian superiority which was looked upon with such animosity by so many people. The first time that the subject was seriously mentioned to William I. his reply was characteristic : " What do you want me to do with this title? " he had exclaimed, to which Bismarck had replied, " Your Majesty cannot remain for ever a neutral substantive and be called ' *das Praesidium* '; it is an abstraction, whereas the title of Emperor will always exercise a fascination upon the masses," and he philosophically added, " the masses are what is called public opinion."

This, however, did not convert William I. He never cared for the title of Emperor, and he never could get used to it so long as he lived. Whenever I had occasion personally to hear him speak of the Empress Augusta, he always called her " the Queen," and he would not have in the least resented had other people done the same. And, indeed, among the persons who were admitted into the intimacy of the Imperial couple they were never mentioned otherwise than as the King and the Queen. Augusta, however, not because she cared for it, but because she thought it to be her duty, was always very particular to say " the Emperor."

With the Crown Prince it was different; he was essentially an Imperialist, though Bismarck is not quite correct when he pretends in his Reminiscences that

Frederick had not shown himself favourable to the creation of an Empire, and would have preferred his father to assume the title of King of the Germans. This might have been so in the sense that, like William I., he was very proud of the old kingly appellation which had been won with so much trouble by his ancestors; but he would have contented himself with it only on condition that the other German Sovereigns renounced it and declared themselves satisfied with being called Dukes, as he told Bismarck, or Peers of the Empire, as he told me personally one day when we discussed the story of this eventful time at Versailles. The Crown Princess was decidedly Imperialist in the widest conception of this word, and quite against any Federated Empire, which, to her mind, seemed to be only an anomaly. The very idea of the other Sovereigns reliuquishing their titles was, of course, absolutely Utopian. " Children must be left in possession of their playthings," Bismarck had said brutally one day when a friend of the Crown Prince had mentioned this view. Still, Bismarck had fully made up his mind beforehand that these titles should remain nothing more than playthings, empty of power or dignity.

The King of Bavaria was not to be persuaded. He had always hated Prussia. During that month of December, indeed, when he was pressed on all sides to play the uncongenial part which was expected from him, he showed himself so irritable that one day when his own mother, who was by birth a Prussian Princess, asked to speak to him he replied, " I do not feel inclined to see a Princess of Prussia."

Bismarck, however, was not the kind of man to allow himself to be discouraged. He therefore quietly pro-

ceeded with the underground work in which he had been
engaged ever since the beginning of the war. He had
the free disposition of the income of the so-called Guelph
fund—the confiscated fortune of the King of Hanover—
without indiscreet control from a third person. These
funds he used among certain personages at the Bavarian
Court. He also caused to represent Bavaria at Versailles
Count von Holstein—the only man in whom the King
of Bavaria had confidence—and the Chancellor set
himself the task of persuading the Count that the most
advantageous thing which could occur, both for him and
for the future welfare of Bavaria, would be that King
Ludwig should be induced to look with favourable eyes
on the revolution—because it was nothing else—it was
intended to bring about in the constitution of Germany.

At this particular moment the question of the restoration of the Empire had reached a very critical stage, and
might even have collapsed entirely. To this danger
contributed the haughty silence of the King of Bavaria,
and the extreme repugnance of the King of Prussia to
consent to what appeared to him to be a diminution of
his Royal prerogative and dignity in favour of one that
had not received the sanction of divine right. At this
juncture Baron Holstein—who already then had begun
to assume the function of those confidants of mighty
personages which we see introduced in the Greek
tragedies and later on in those of Racine or Corneille—
then took it upon himself to suggest to Count Holstein
to ask Bismarck to write a personal letter to Ludwig II.,
in which he would explain the reasons which made it
expedient to offer to a Hohenzollern the crown of Bar-
barossa and of Othon. The Count, of course, caught
at the idea, the more so that it flattered his vanity to,

be able to say later that it had been his advice which
had influenced Bismarck at such a grave and anxious
moment. He therefore presented himself at the Chancellor's residence at Versailles. Bismarck, who in questions of grave importance had absolutely no vanity,
seemed to become lost in thought for a few moments,
just to impress Holstein's vanity, then took up a pen
and wrote to the King of Bavaria a letter which he
had had elaborated in his mind for the last day or two,
and the terms of which had been settled long before the
Bavarian nobleman had craved an audience. The sense
of this missive was that he quite recognised it would be
impossible for the Bavarian Sovereign to grant to the
King of Prussia the presidential rights and privileges,
which had been already offered to him in an official way
by Bavaria, without wounding the national feelings of
the people of that country, Prussia being a neighbour of
Bavaria. A German Emperor, on the contrary, was not
a neighbour belonging to a different race, but a German
compatriot of the Bavarian people. According to his
(Bismarck's) opinion, King Ludwig could with far more
decency consent to concessions if he made them to a
German Emperor than to a King of Prussia. As we
shall see, the psychological instinct of Bismarck had once
more proved to be right.

Count Holstein left for Hohenschwangau, where
Ludwig II. was residing, on November 27th. Bismarck,
in his Reminiscences, says that the King, who had at
first refused to receive him, had him shown into his
presence when he heard that he was bringing to him a
letter from the Chancellor, and that, after having read
this communication, he wrote immediately and signed
the message which the latter had asked him for. This

is not, however, quite true. Count Holstein remained for three days in Hohenschwangau before he was admitted into his Sovereign's room. It was only after the Monarch's private secretary, Herr von Eisenhardt, who was completely won over to the Prussian cause, had warned Ludwig that if he refused he risked being dethroned in favour of his brother or his uncle, Prince Luitpold, that the harassed Monarch at last, after considerable hesitation and resistance, signed what he called his own " *déchéance.*" As it was indispensable that the consent which had been wrung from him by such unworthy means should have the appearance of having been entirely spontaneous, it was given out at Versailles—and the untruth was repeated by the Chancellor in his Reminiscences—that, owing to the bad state of the roads and the difficulty of communications, the journey of Count Holstein had taken seven days instead of three. It is thus that very often history comes to be written.

So far Bismarck had been successful. The more local trouble remained. The opposition of the King of Prussia, as time advanced, grew more violent every day. The old man at last declared that he thought the whole idea preposterous. If he became Emperor he would have to give up the simplicity of life which he loved and in which he had been born and bred. The title of Emperor would only embarrass him, but if he were compelled to accept it, he wished to be called Emperor of Germany and not German Emperor, which was neither the one thing nor the other. Upon seeing that the Crown Prince agreed with Bismarck, William I. became the more determined to oppose them both to such an extent that, in the deliberation which took

EMPEROR WILLIAM I IN 1871

From the Painting by Winterhalter

place on January 17th, 1871, on the very eve of the day chosen for the proclamation of the Empire, he declared that he absolutely refused the title of German Emperor, and that if he could not be Emperor of Germany he would not be Emperor at all.

Bismarck then had recourse to the argument that if the appellation of Emperor of Germany was used it might offend the German Princes, who would consider that it implied a certain right upon their territories. At last, after a long discussion, William I. allowed himself to be persuaded, but insisted on his protest to be recorded in the protocol of the proceedings.

Another discussion ensued on questions of precedence. The King would not admit that the place which the Congress of Vienna had awarded to the Russian Grand Dukes and the Austrian Archdukes before the Prussian Royal Princes could be interfered with. At last he got into a perfect passion, struck the table with his fist, and exclaimed that he would not give way, and commanded things should be left as they had been in the past concerning this matter. It was only a few days after January 18th, when the irritation which the ceremony that had taken place on that day had given rise to had more or less subsided, that the King was persuaded to grant to his son the title of Imperial Highness; but all the supplications and entreaties of the various members of his family did not make him change his mind on the subject of a change in their status. He declared that, in spite of their desire to be called also Imperial Highnesses, they were Princes of Prussia and would remain such, because the fact that he had become an Emperor had nothing to do with them, and could not influence their position. Later on a delibera-

had succeeded in saving it from the Prussian maw. The
German Emperor, having discovered after the preliminaries of peace had been already agreed upon that
the battlefields of St. Privat and Gravelotte were to
remain French territory, insisted on their being handed
over to him, as he did not wish the places where so
many of his brave soldiers had fallen to be in the hands
of those who had slain them. It was a sentimental
reason, but it was connected with the Sovereign's love
for his army, and, therefore, was not to be refused.
Thiers was clever enough to see the advantage that he
could obtain out of this circumstance, and he offered
both St. Privat and Gravelotte in exchange for Belfort,
a request which William I. granted spontaneously after
Thiers had written to him personally on the subject; and
this notwithstanding the protestations of General von
Moltke and of the whole Staff.

Bismarck was clever enough not to go against William in this little matter. Indeed, he would have liked
to show himself more generous in regard to a vanquished foe, and would have repeated the tactics that
had proved so profitable in 1866 at Nikolsburg. But
this time he had to do with a far stronger opposition
which, apart from the military leaders who insisted on
being heard, comprised most of the German Princes
who at Versailles surrounded the King of Prussia, being
all convinced that the war which had just terminated so
brilliantly had never been wished for by Prussia. They
all of them thought they must have guarantees against
the possibility of another attack on the part of France.
Bismarck, of course, could not disabuse them, and he
began then to reap the fruits of some of the untruths
he had forced down the throat of the German nation as

well as of Europe. His sin was beginning to find him out.

At last the Treaty of Peace was signed at Frankfurt on May 10th, 1871. The enormous contribution of five milliards, which the financial experts whom Bismarck had consulted thought would cripple France for years to come—at least ten years, because he never believed that after a defeat such as she had experienced, and after the horrors of the Commune that had followed upon it, France would be able to hold to her engagements. For once he was mistaken in his appreciation of not only the material riches and resources of the fair country which he thought he had crushed for a long time to come, but also of its patriotism, its courage, and its spirit of self-denial. The Treaty of Frankfurt, which was to be the destruction of France as a great nation, proved its regeneration. Without it she would never have risen to the heights of sacrifice she has attained to-day; the heroic defence of Verdun was due to the tears which have been shed over the loss of Strasburg and of Metz.

It is not generally known that a request to grant autonomy to the conquered provinces was made to Bismarck by the Crown Princess Victoria. He decidedly refused to entertain such an idea, declaring that in that case one could have reason to fear an attempt at reunion with the mother country. He was haunted from the very day of the signature of the Treaty of Frankfurt with the fear of another war with France. His genius told him that in such a case she would find strong support among other Continental Powers.

The first thing to which Bismarck applied himself after his return to Berlin was to make the Reichstag vote an augmentation of the military expenses for a

space of three years, together with the general budget of the army for seven years. This measure would allow such manipulations of the public funds that would not be advisable for the Reichstag to control. He thereafter directed the whole brunt of his Foreign Policy toward the one object of isolating France. The period of time which extends itself from 1871 to the day when he was disgraced by William II. was spent by Bismarck in preparing the German Empire for the new war which he knew was unavoidable. It was to prove, perhaps, the most interesting period of his whole life, if only on account of the fact that it was to be marked by as many reverses as successes. Bismarck was feared, respected and worshipped by the whole of Germany. No King ever wielded a greater authority than his. His fortune had never deserted him during the whole course of his extraordinary career : can one feel surprised that he never thought that for him there could come a day when his Emperor would send him away in disgrace?

Part III

Development of Militarism

CHAPTER XVI

Bismarck and the Empress

THE war of 1870 and its outcome constitutes the greatest of Bismarck's triumphs: the German Empire was the visible evidence of his constructive genius in statesmanship. He was far too clever, however, not to realise that there was no real stability in the edifice which had taken him such pains to raise, and that its strengthening would be the most difficult task he had ever faced. As time revealed the different flaws which marred his work, the irritability which always marked his disposition developed to a still greater degree. But his temperament was essentially of the fighting order, and he was not happy unless struggling against something or somebody. Then again, the full consciousness which he possessed of his own superiority, with its corresponding belief that all those who surrounded him, and with whom he had to work, were but pigmies compared with himself, combined to make him suspicious, mistrustful, and desirous of sweeping away all obstacles which beset his path. Out of this sprang an ever-increasing impatience with the "stupidities" of others, and violent outbursts of rage at any opposition which he encountered to any of the vast designs which his active brain was continually evolving. He was essentially revengeful, and the tenacity with which he pursued all those who had ventured to cross or oppose him led, in many instances, to a useless expenditure of his strength.

Chancellor. He served the Empress in the capacity of private secretary, and Bismarck attributed to him first the composition of Madame Adam's famous book. "La Société de Berlin," and, secondly, the crime of being the particular friend of the Vicomte de Gontaut, which also was not true—the latter would most certainly never have chosen a red-hot Republican such as M. Gérard as secretary to Empress Augusta.

The Chancellor had several "pet enemies." The Empress was one, and the former Minister of Foreign Affairs, who during the last twenty-five years or so of his life had filled the functions of Minister of the Royal Household Baron (later Count) Schleinitz, was another. He became the *bête noire* of the Chancellor, who accused him of all kinds of black intrigues of which, nine times out of ten he was perfectly innocent. Bismarck believed him to be the person who furnished the Empress with information. But in this again he was wrong, because the principal source of the gossip which reached the ears of the Empress was her maid, Mademoiselle von Neundorff, who had been with her for something like half a century. Mademoiselle von Neundorff hated Bismarck as only an old maid can hate, and whenever she could thwart him or do anything likely to displease or to anger him she never missed the opportunity. All the enemies of the Chancellor were her friends, and she it was who used to keep the Empress aware of all that was said in Berlin society, the greatest ladies of which visited her and did their best to win her favour and good graces. Bismarck with all his genius failed entirely to appreciate the importance of this feminine rival of

He never could bring himself to look objectively at things or at people, and this it was that made him at times such a particularly unpleasant individual. The least thing put him out of patience, and he never would make any allowance for others, or bring himself to treat with disdain the attacks of those weak foes of his to whom he attributed an importance which they never deserved. He used also to take absurd and unreasoning dislikes of certain people; for instance, in the cases of the first French Ambassador at the Berlin Court after the Treaty of Frankfurt, the Vicomte de Gontaut Biron, and the Empress Augusta. The latter he pursued with an inveterate hatred which, instead of frightening her by its intensity, only amused her, and gave her an exaggerated idea of her own importance. The Empress, though a clever woman, never could get rid of her love for intrigue, and allowed herself to be influenced by a small coterie of persons whom she liked simply because they pandered to her love of gossip and brought her all the tittle-tattle of the day, true or untrue. She detested Bismarck because he had never appreciated her at her own value and never consulted her, but, on the contrary, did all in his power to keep her outside affairs of State. She was instinctively " *un personnage d'opposition*," and even at the time when she had been simply Princess of Prussia, with but a distant prospect of becoming Queen, she had always set herself up as a criticising power in the State, and all the enemies of the Government of the day had found a friend in her. Her extreme affection for everything that was French had always jarred on the nerves of Prince Bismarck, who reproached her for having French servants around her, for preferring to talk French rather than German, and especially for always having Frenchmen about her; one at least, M. Gérard, became the object of the special hatred of the Chancellor. He served the Empress in the capacity of private secretary, and Bismarck attributed to him first the composition of Madame Adam's famous book, "La Société de Berlin," and, secondly, the crime of being the particular friend of the Vicomte de Gontaut, which also was not true—the latter would most certainly never have chosen a red-hot Republican such as M. Gérard as secretary to Empress Augusta.

The Chancellor had several "pet enemies." The Empress was one, and the former Minister of Foreign Affairs, who during the last twenty-five years or so of his life had filled the functions of Minister of the Royal Household, Baron (later Count) Schleinitz, was another. He became the *bête noire* of the Chancellor, who accused him of all kinds of black intrigues of which, nine times out of ten, he was perfectly innocent. Bismarck believed him to be the person who furnished the Empress with information. But in this again he was wrong, because the principal source of the gossip which reached the ears of the Empress was her maid, Mademoiselle von Neundorff, who had been with her for something like half a century. Mademoiselle von Neundorff hated Bismarck as only an old maid can hate, and whenever she could thwart him or do anything likely to displease or to anger him she never missed the opportunity. All the enemies of the Chancellor were her friends, and she it was who used to keep the Empress aware of all that was said in Berlin society, the greatest ladies of which visited her and did their best to win her favour and good graces. Bismarck with all his genius failed entirely to appreciate the importance of this feminine rival of his, and in his prejudices and blind hatred of Schleinitz attributed to the latter the sins of Mademoiselle von Neundorff.

The Empress had always sympathised with the Roman Catholic Church, though the rumour that she had joined it had no justification. But she had many Catholic friends, and she was by nature adverse to any kind of persecution, be it religious or political. The *Kulturkampf* had been for her a source of great sorrow. During the whole time that it lasted she never attempted to hide her disapproval of a policy in which she saw a considerable danger to the security of the German State, and she never missed an opportunity of showing the nature of her feelings on the subject.

Her expressions of irritation in regard to the *Kulturkampf* did not advance the cause of the Catholic party, and it is probable that if she had not been there Bismarck would have wearied of this struggle much sooner than was the case, which did not originate with him, but owed its birth to the discussions which had taken place in Bavaria during the administration of Prince Hohenlohe between the Liberal parties in that State and the Roman Catholic Church. He continued them in Prussia, not so much out of hatred for the Catholic religion or clergy, but out of dislike for certain people, in whom he feared to find not rivals, but adversaries of his political views, and out of hatred for the Poles and everything which concerned Polish aspirations. The *Kulturkampf*, indeed, would never have taken place but for Poland and for the Polish question. It was this Polish question which prevented the *Kulturkampf* from coming to an end quicker than was the case. It was not so much the Catholics whom Bismarck disliked to see about the King and Queen, as the Polish elements, in whose midst all his other enemies found a friendly welcome, and in whose houses they were received with open arms. When I first married I remember that the feelings of hostility between my husband's family, and everybody even remotely connected with the household of the Chancellor, were about as violent as they could be. The Radziwill Palace, which by a strange irony of fate was to become two years later the residence of Bismarck himself, was a centre of reunion for all the members of the Opposition in the Reichstag, and it would be useless to deny that it constituted a centre of animosity against the person of the Chancellor. He was not very far wrong when he attributed to the many intrigues which took place under its roof a certain influence on the deliberations of the Chambers in regard to the so-called "Falk Laws," the promulgation of which was to raise such a storm of indignation in Ultramontane circles.

Personally, however, I took no part in these intrigues, which, as I was told by my father, whose judgment was in many respects an unerring one, could lead to nothing, and only end in ridicule. My Russian nationality put me outside the sphere of Polish intrigues, with which I must say, however, I never sympathised, having seen too much of them in Russia. I therefore made an exception to the rest of my family, and actually visited Princess Bismarck, who always showed herself excessively kind to me, and who went so far as to invite me to her house, where I had the opportunity to talk with the mighty Chancellor, who at that time did not seem to consider me in the light of a possible adversary, probably because I was far too young to attain any importance in his eyes. Yet once or twice I had the opportunity to hear his remarks on some important event of the day; and these, when remembered later, helped me to form my own opinion concerning the causes of several happenings which occurred. After the Congress of Berlin I set up a salon of my own, where a violent opposition to the policy inaugurated by Bismarck was started, and as time went I found myself fighting him and his views on more than one occasion, and not altogether without success, as I shall endeavour to show.

To return, however, to the subject of the *Kulturkampf*. One of the persons who greatly encouraged Bismarck in his anti-Catholic policy was Prince Clovis Hohenlohe, together with his two brothers, the Duke of Ratibor and Cardinal von Hohenlohe, the latter of whom had at one time seriously hoped to be elected to the Pontifical throne with the help of Prussia. Those three personages, in addition to their family ties, were firmly united by their common hatred for the Jesuits, a hatred that was carried so far as to be almost ridiculous and childish in its expression of dread in regard to the influence of the famous Order, in which they saw poisoners like the Borgias and people capable of every crime. Prince Clovis, who in other respects was such a sound, and in a certain sense such a moderate, politician, completely lost his self-control whenever the name of Jesuit was mentioned, and he it was who first brought forward the Bill which abolished the Order in the whole of the German Empire. If he had confined his activity to the expulsion of the sons of Loyola the evil would not have been great, and he certainly might have earned the gratitude of all the moderate parties in Germany, who did not care for religious intrigues, but who at the same time objected to persecution in matters of faith becoming a political principle. Unfortunately, he believed himself to be admirably well informed as to all the political currents which surged about the Vatican, and this was not by any means the case. Indeed, no one in Germany, not excepting Bismarck himself, knew anything about them. How could they, in view of the utter incompetence of the people on whose information they relied? One wonders whether one is dreaming or awake when one reads the following remarks of Prince Hohenlohe when German Ambassador in Paris, and remembers that it is a statesman of importance and experience who allows his pen to run riot in such utter nonsense · " Michaud, a professor at the Catholic Faculty of Berne, has related to me to-day that most of the victims of the Commune who were shot by the insurgents during its last days were enemies of the Jesuits, among them the Archbishop of Paris—Darboy— whom the Jesuits detested on account of the attitude which he had adopted during the Vatican Council; Senator Bonjean, who was known to profess most Liberal Catholic opinions; de Guéry, a Liberal priest; Chaudet, the editor of the *Siècle;* then the Dominicans of Arcueil, who were the followers of the doctrines of Lacordaire, and all the Jesuits who belonged to the Liberal section of their Order, among others the Père Olivain. No one knows precisely how it came that they were taken as hostages by the Communists. The well-known Vicar-General of the Diocese of Paris, who had been sent to Versailles in order to negotiate the liberation of the victims in exchange for some prominent insurgents who had fallen into the hands of the Government, never returned to Paris, as he had promised to do, and when he did come back, after the city had been recaptured by the regular army, the indignation of the clergy against him was so great that he had to resign his position. Now Archbishop Guibert has again reinstated him. Guibert is entirely in the hands of the Jesuits, and protects all the religious orders in preference to the regular clergy."

A little later we find that Prince Hohenlohe writes again :

"During my conversation with the Cardinal [i.e. his brother] and other priests I have heard the following in regard to the Roman question :

"There are a large number of Italian statesmen who belong to the Jesuit Order by affiliation. Among others Ponza di San Martino, Ricasoli, the late Massimo d'Azeglio, and Silvio Pellico. The General of the Jesuits resides in Paris, and it is King Victor Emmanuel who pays his expenses there.

"The Jesuits have been allowed secretly to remove their books from the library of the Gèsu College. This was done by night during many successive weeks. The Italian clergy in general say that the Italian Government protects the Jesuits in quite a particular manner.

"The King of Naples says that he has proofs that the Jesuits have sworn the fall of the House of Bourbon, and that they are responsible for all the misfortunes which have overtaken it.

"Among the cardinals and prelates with whom one could negotiate, and who are enemies of the Jesuits, can be reckoned, according to the words of Gustave [i.e. Cardinal Hohenlohe] the following : The Cardinals Franchi, Guidi, de Luca, Mertel, Angelis in Fermo, and the Nuncio Jacobini in Vienna. The Princess

Caroline Wittgenstein is also an enemy of the Order, and might be induced to work usefully against it."

One cannot even smile at such inanities, and the idea of the Italian Government protecting the Jesuits to the extent of paying an annuity to their General is so ludicrous as to disarm anger. But the fact that Bismarck could believe such tales, and place confidence in the people who related them, sufficiently accounts for the collapse of the struggle between the Chancellor and the Church of Rome. He would have liked to see Cardinal Hohenlohe in the Chair of St. Peter, but what qualifications had he for such a position? How could one have trusted a man weak enough in intellect to tell anyone—as he did to me quite seriously—that when his trusted cook was ill he would not risk engaging another in his stead, but had lived only on eggs bought and cooked by himself, and this because he was afraid of being poisoned by the Jesuits! One may like or dislike the famous Order, and, personally, I certainly am not counted among its friends, but between this and believing that its members spend their time in concocting plots worthy of any Porte St. Martin melodrama, there is a wide difference.

Bismarck, with all his genius and his keen knowledge of human nature, was quite unable to gauge the importance which, by passive resistance, the Catholic clergy and Catholic faction in the Chambers would in time acquire. He treated the Roman Church as a negligible quantity, and fully believed that in the nineteenth century it had lost its influence over the masses, especially in Germany, where Protestantism had thoroughly permeated public opinion. He committed the great mistake of confounding Catholicism and Polish nationalism, and the result was that in the long run he had to resign himself to see one of these elements triumph and the other remain unbeaten. But, faithful to his principle of never acknowledging himself in the wrong, the Chancellor, in his Reminiscences, will not accept the responsibility for all the errors into which he was led by the development of the *Kulturkampf*. With great ability he throws this responsibility entirely upon Falk. After having praised him almost to exaggeration, he drops the remark that, having been obliged to allow him to retire from public service—as, owing to the feminine influences which had been intriguing against him at Court, Falk desired—he was enabled to start a revision of the work which he had done, but which, out of consideration for him, Bismarck had not wished to begin so long as Falk remained in office.

The remarks with which he accompanies this cynical utterance are also worthy to be recalled, as they prove, among other things, how intensely personal Bismarck could show himself, and with what persistence he recurred to a subject which had provoked his irritation.

"Falk," writes the Chancellor, "succumbed to the same intrigue that had been used, but without success, against myself. He succumbed to them because he was more sensitive than I had ever shown myself to the treatment at Court, and also because he was not protected by the personal sympathy of the Emperor to the same extent that I always was. The animosity of the Empress in regard to the Ministry had its source in an independence of character which prevented her from going hand in hand with a Government the direction of which was not left exclusively to her, and which during her whole life made her find a particular pleasure in following the road of a persistent opposition to the Government of the day, no matter what the latter happened to be. Whilst the *Kulturkampf* lasted this tendency of her Majesty's character was encouraged by her Catholic friends, who received from the Ultramontane camp their information and instructions. These personages displayed great ability and a deep knowledge of the peculiarities of the temper of the Empress, and understood admirably how to use the inclination which she had always possessed to exercise an influence on the decisions of the Government. Several times I persuaded Falk not to send in his resignation to the Emperor, but certain letters which the latter addressed to him, and the bad treatment meted out to his wife at Court, made him at last hold to his decision, much to my regret."

Whether this regret was sincere I shall not pretend to judge, but what I do know was that later on Bismarck complained that he had been led into error by Falk, whose sole aim whilst in office was to destroy the Catholic Church, which the Chancellor pretended had never been his intention. He had merely wanted to fight against the separatist tendencies of the Poles, and to him Poles and Catholics were one and the same; that his persecution of the Roman Church had been a political and not a religious struggle. That, at least, was how he tried to explain it, and in this manner hide the extent of the defeat which his plans had encountered.

As he was not a man to admit himself beaten, Bismarck forthwith proceeded, after the arrangement of the religious difficulties with Rome and the Vatican, to inaugurate the anti-Polish policy to which he clung with such pertinacity the whole time that he remained Chancellor of the German Empire. This, by a kind of aberration which can neither be explained nor justified, the Poles of the Province of Posen seem to have forgotten to-day in their enthusiasm for a so-called "restoration of Polish independence," which is certainly the dirtiest little "scrap of paper" to which Bismarck's successor, but by no means follower, Dr. Bethmann-Hollweg, has ever put his signature.

CHAPTER XVII

Juggling with War

I NOW come to an incident which at the time it took place caused some sensation, and which, by reason of the importance given at the Wilhelmstrasse to details which in other circumstances would never have demanded attention, was magnified to such an extent that it assumed the character of a grave international crisis. It affords an excellent example of the tortuous manner in which intrigues were engineered by Bismarck.

After the Treaty of Frankfurt the first Ambassador the French Republic sent to Berlin was the Vicomte de Gontaut Biron, a gentleman of high birth, unimpeachable connections, excellent education, a blameless character and moderate intellect. He was a Legitimist by conviction with a tinge of Clericalism, and he had been recommended to M. Thiers by a friend of the latter who held him in high esteem, and who had represented to the President that it would be advantageous to send to Berlin a man who was related to several influential personages at the Prussian Court and who for many reasons might soon become there a *persona grata*. Unfortunately he was no diplomat, and his patriotism was associated with political convictions which he thought it his duty to exhibit rather than to hide. He had been warmly recommended to the Empress Augusta by the latter's intimate and particular friend, the Princess Leonille Wittgenstein, a Russian by birth, who at the time was considered an old woman, though at the moment of writing is still alive and recently celebrated her hundredth birthday. The Princess was a clever woman, extremely fond of intrigue, a zealous convert to the Roman Catholic faith; she was a friend of all the Clerical party in France, where she counted relatives without number, and where her salon was the meeting-place of the leading members of the French clergy and of the influential Academicians. She asked the Empress as a particular favour to receive the Vicomte de Gontaut as warmly and cordially as possible, and Augusta had been but too glad to comply with this request. The Crown Prince and Princess also, who keenly appreciated the difficulties which were sure to beset the first steps of the new French Ambassador in Berlin, had done their best to smooth the way for him. His own relatives, too, such as the Duke and Duchess de Sagan, my sister-in-law the Princess Antoine Radziwill, and many of his former friends and acquaintances who had met him in Paris before the war, vied with each other in putting the Vicomte and his daughters at ease in the German capital. Had he availed himself in the right manner of all these advantages he might have done very well indeed; but, unfortunately for him and for all concerned, he wanted, from the first moment he arrived in Berlin, to make what he called "*de la haute politique*," and imagined this could be done irrespective of Bismarck. He went for his information to the very people Bismarck wanted to keep outside State affairs, such as Baron von Schleinitz, Count Redern—the Great Chamberlain, who was a personal friend of the old Emperor, and very Francophile in his sympathies—and—a crowning sin—the Empress Augusta. Vicomte de Gontaut had delighted the

Empress by asking her help to ameliorate the relations of France with Germany, and with whom she could make "*une politique personnelle*," as she liked to say. In justice to the Empress, however, it must be said that she was influenced by the highest of motives. She did not believe that Bismarck really wanted to re-establish good relations with the French Government; she imagined that by the personal intervention of the Emperor and herself this might be done in spite of the Chancellor. The Vicomte was fully persuaded that politics could still be made in the salons of influential personages and in the antechambers of kings and queens. This was very silly, but certainly it was not at all as dangerous as Bismarck represented. Had Bismarck, instead of making the recall of the Ambassador a diplomatic question, simply pointed out that his conduct was bringing ridicule not only on himself, but also on the French Government and the French nation, it is probable that he would have secured his removal without any fuss. But instead of this he represented him as a mischievous intriguer, and accused him of carrying on underhand manœuvres in Petersburg, whither de Gontaut used to retire almost every winter. It was not politics, however, which took him there, but his feelings of admiration for a most beautiful lady, the Princess Obolensky, at whose feet he had worshipped for very many years.

The Vicomte de Gontaut, on his part, was certainly wrongly influenced when he took too much *au sérieux* not only the gossip which was reported to him, but also some of the things which he heard in the Foreign Office in Berlin. Very often these were traps designed to induce him to make false reports to Paris which could be used to strengthen the demand for his recall. He was also wrong when, in his desire to make himself important, he asserted as a fact in 1875, that Bismarck was then planning a renewed attack on France. For once the Chancellor was telling the truth when he maintained that he had no thought of such a thing, though his pacific intentions existed merely because the reorganisation of the German army and its armaments, which had been proceeding *sub rosa*, and for which it had been using part of the French milliards, was not nearly completed. Had Vicomte de Gontaut been as well-informed as he pretended to be he would have known this essential fact; but neither he nor any member of his staff ever frequented military or parliamentary circles, relying entirely upon the Court circles for information on matters of which they knew nothing.

The strange part of the business was that the French Ambassador did not seem in the least to understand that his attitude was neither correct nor clever so far as the interests of his own country were concerned. He lived in a world of his own, full of preconceived opinions, not realising whither his blindness was leading him. He used to go to Ems and to Baden-Baden just at the time when the Emperor visited these watering-places for his annual cures, and, of course, whilst there had opportunities of meeting the Sovereign under less formal conditions than in Berlin. It is certain, however, that he did not discuss politics on these occasions, for William I. would have refused to do so under such circumstances; but he believed seriously that by putting himself within the reach of the King he was only doing his duty after the manner of the courtiers of Louis XIV. and Louis XV., who always went to Fontainebleau or Marly whenever the King visited these places.

Then, again, there was another matter which brought Vicomte de Gontaut into trouble without his ever realising why it had done so. Once, when he was at Baden-Baden, he allowed himself to be drawn into confidential conversations with the Russian Minister at the Court of Karlsruhe, M. Koloschine, a man possessed of inordinate vanity who always wanted to make himself important and who took it upon himself to propose to the French Representative common action on the part of France and Russia in the Near East, where complications were already arising which ultimately led to the war with Turkey. M. Koloschine's opinion was about the last to carry weight in Petersburg, but the poor Vicomte imagined that he saw in his communications a possibility for France to assert herself again as a great nation; his patriotism for once led him to a clear vision of future possibilities, and he urged his Government to try to help Russia in view of the renewed attack by Germany on France which was his nightmare, and against which Russia might prove such a useful ally. Unfortunately patriotism is not sufficient for diplomatic success, and the time for a Franco-Russian alliance had not arrived —it was, indeed, postponed for a considerable period owing to these very efforts from which Gontaut had hoped so much. He had, in his ignorance of statecraft, merely played to M. Koloschine's hand. The latter had imagined that, owing to the French Ambassador's encouragements, he would be able to report to Prince Gortschakov that France was willing to stand by Russia in the matter of the Eastern conflict, whilst de Gontaut fully believed that in mentioning to the Duc Decazes, then French Minister for Foreign Affairs, the overtures of M. Koloschine, he was laying at the feet of France the offer of an alliance with the Russian Government. If ever a *journée des dupes* took place it was upon this occasion.

When these incidents became known to Bismarck he declared that he would drive Vicomte de Gontaut out of Berlin, and he never rested until he had accomplished his purpose.

This was by no means so easy as it seemed at first sight. Even admitting that he asked the French Government—which, in fact, he did on more than one occasion —to recall its Ambassador, the request could not well be granted in view of the expressed desire of the Emperor, conveyed to Marshal MacMahon by some of the friends of the Queen, that the Vicomte de Gontaut should be left at his post. Prince Bismarck then tried to compromise the Ambassador by making him appear to be a man who sowed dissension where it did not exist, and of attempting to make himself important at the expense of the grave interests which had been committed to his charge. He had heard—probably through one of the servants of the French Embassy who had access to the writing-table of Gontaut—that the latter had sent to his chief in Paris a long report concerning a conversation which, according to him, had taken place between the Belgian Minister, Baron de Nothomb, and Marshal von Moltke, in which the latter had expressed his conviction that the recent addition of a fourth battalion to the strength of French regiments was an aggressive measure of France directed against Germany. The conversation had in reality had quite a different sense from the one which Gontaut had attributed to it, and anyone who knew Moltke well would have at once recognised its unlikelihood. The truth of the matter was that during a dinner at which both the Belgian Minister and the head of the German General Staff had been present, the former had made an allusion to the rumours of another war which were circulating among the public, and the old Marshal had made some playful remarks out of which Vicomte de Gontaut concocted a long report on what he did not hesitate to qualify as an exceedingly grave incident. This, however, was only the beginning of the story. Bismarck then suggested to one of his secretaries, M. von Radowitz (afterwards German Ambassador in Constantinople and Madrid), that he should at the first opportunity engage the Vicomte de Gontaut in a conversation which would lead the latter to raise an alarm as to the intentions of the German Government in regard to France.

M. von Radowitz found his opportunity at a dinner given by the English Ambassador, Lord Odo Russell, at which he and de Gontaut were present, and they soon engaged in a lively discussion on Franco-German relations. Radowitz began by expressing his satisfaction that these seemed at last to be re-establishing themselves upon an excellent footing, and referred to the gratification felt in the Wilhelmstrasse at the explanation given by the French Government concerning that unfortunate fourth battalion. Then he went on :

" You say that at present no one in France thinks about war. But can you give us a similar assurance as to the future? Can you affirm that France, after having regained its prosperity and reorganised its military strength, will not find then the alliances she needs to-day and the disposition to declare war against Germany? If we allow France to develop unhindered, shall we not, later on, have to repent for having done so? If France is always thinking of the day of revenge—and it can hardly be otherwise—why, on our part, wait to attack her until she has contracted alliances? You must acknowledge that politically, philosophically, and even from the Christian point of view, my deductions are right, and that it would be in the interests of Germany if she allowed herself to be influenced by them."

The amusing part of the story is that out of this specious series of arguments de Gontaut conceived, and conveyed to the Duc Decazes, the conviction that Germany was preparing to attack France, and this within the shortest possible time.

The French Government became at last thoroughly alarmed, and Gontaut then proposed that he should try to obtain the mediation of Russia, whose action he thought might stop the bellicose designs of Bismarck. The latter had not reckoned on this complication. He had wished to raise a war scarce, but had never meant it to extend beyond the French and German frontiers. He had especially never given a thought to the possibility of the Duc Decazes appealing directly to the Tsar. General Le Flo, the French Ambassador in Petersburg, who, on his side, had tried to trade on the well-known vanity of Prince Gortschakov, was only too delighted at the opportunity thus given him to be able to say that, through his intervention, he had muzzled the warlike intentions of Bismarck. The Russian Chancellor immediately proceeded to communicate the letter of the Duc Decazes to his Sovereign, and accompanied it with remarks calculated to arouse the susceptibilities of Alexander II. by representing that the peace of the whole of Europe was threatened by Germany. The Tsar, however, was even then meditating a war with Turkey, and he did not feel greatly interested in other international complications; but he

promised Prince Gortschakov to use all his influence in
Berlin, whither he was repairing on his way to Ems in
order to persuade his uncle William to give up any
aggressive intentions he might be entertaining in regard
to France.

Nevertheless the incident might have remained one of
these minor diplomatic disturbances that do not go
beyond Embassy walls had it not been for the determination of Bismarck to drown Gontaut in a sea of ridicule.
At that time Baron von Holstein was still in Paris.
Prince Bismarck summoned him to Berlin. Holstein
immediately proposed the advisability of suggesting to
the famous correspondent of the *Times*, Blowitz, a
rumour that Germany was about to attack France; if
war did not follow it could then be said that it was due
entirely to the spirit of moderation shown by the German
Government in face of the aggressive intentions of the
French Ambassador in Berlin, who had done all that he
possibly could to bring about a rupture between the two
countries. The Prince approved the scheme, and Holstein confided the story to the journalist under the seal
of secrecy. He concluded by telling the correspondent
of the *Times* that his paper would be doing a good work
by publishing all this in the hope of influencing some
Great Power, say England or Russia, to interfere in
favour of maintaining peace in Europe.

To those who knew Blowitz it will be easy to imagine
the joy with which he hailed these confidences of Holstein.
He was always on the look out for a journalistic *coup*,
and he recognised a great opportunity in Holstein's state-
ments. Nevertheless, he thought it well first to sound
both the French Minister of Foreign Affairs, the Duc
Decazes, and the German Ambassador in Paris, Prince

von Hohenlohe. Prince von Hohenlohe, under date of May 21st, 1875, refers to the matter :

" Blowitz went farther in his article than he had led me to expect he would do. His reasonings, which in the course of our conversation had seemed to be imbued with impartiality, became in his article what I had warned them they would be—an attack on Germany. The editor of the *Times* received his article on Wednesday, May 5th, and immediately telegraphed to its other Continental correspondents for information in regard to points raised by Blowitz, and it is also likely that he communicated on the subject with some leading political personages in London. It was only after the editor had become convinced, as he thought, of the accuracy of Blowitz's information that he allowed the article to appear. The supposition that it was inspired by Stock Exchange speculations is devoid of any foundation. It was simply a lapse from tact on the part of Blowitz which he committed in the interest of France, and by which he fully believed he was acting in the interest of the peace of Europe."

Bismarck was triumphant because he had contrived at last—especially after the visit of the Emperor Alexander II. to Berlin, some of whose remarks had been disagreeable to William I.—to persuade his master that de Gontaut was a mischief-maker whose stupidity had been used to their own ends by the Catholic and other Opposition parties in Prussia. The Emperor, though he continued to show himself most kind and gracious in regard to the French Ambassador, did not completely trust him any longer. Nevertheless, the Vicomte maintained himself at his post for something like two years longer, in spite of disagreements which any other person would have flown to the other end of the world to escape. Bismarck never again spoke to him, and carried his dislike of him too far. The common sense of Hohenlohe rightly gauged the situation. The Vicomte de Gontaut Biron thought himself a far more dangerous and clever personage than anyone else did. His vanity led him to consider every mark of politeness accorded to him as something quite out of the common, and he left Berlin with the conviction that he would be mourned there for ever by the Emperor, Empress, and the whole of the Royal family.

CHAPTER XVIII

Balkan Intrigues

IT sometimes happens that a man of moderate intellect has ideas worthy of a genius. Such was the case with the Vicomte de Gontaut, when in his mind there arose the faint and misty idea of a Franco-Russian alliance, or, at least—for his imagination did not go so far as that—of a Franco-Russian *rapprochement*. Unfortunately for him Bismarck became aware of the letter to Duc Decazes, and at once grasped the influence it might exercise over the political situation in Europe. How he heard of it is rather curious, and goes to show how very careful people occupying public positions ought to be in what they say or write. The Duc Decazes had mentioned the contents of the letter of the French Ambassador in Berlin to Marshal MacMahon, who in his turn had spoken about it to his *alter ego* and aide-de-camp the Marquis d'Abzac. The latter was married to a half-Russian, half-German woman, Mademoiselle de Lazareff, whose mother, the Princess Biron von Curland, was then alive and living on her estates in Silesia at a place called Dyrnfhurt. Her daughter, whose marriage with the fascinating French marquis had not been altogether a success, used to spend nearly all her time with her, going but rarely to Paris, the atmosphere of which did not altogether suit her tastes. The Marquis d'Abzac, one of the most charming and amiable of men it has ever been my fortune to meet, used to visit his wife once or twice a year in her Silesian home, and whilst there used to meet many members of the Prussian aristocracy allied to her family. He was popular everywhere, and in Berlin was a *persona grata* in Court circles, especially with the old Emperor, who was very fond of him, and appreciated the great loyalty of his chivalrous character. When with his relatives he sometimes allowed himself to talk politics with greater absence of self-restraint than was, perhaps, altogether wise.

Bismarck was aware of the fact, and he contrived to keep himself pretty well informed as to everything which was said and done in the Lazareff-d'Abzac household by the spying of a servant who, whilst pretending to know no other language than his native German, understood and spoke French to perfection. This move had been suggested to Bismarck by Baron von Holstein, who afterwards related this fact to the friend who repeated it to me with evident satisfaction. The idea of this possible Franco-Russian alliance haunted him to such an extent that he applied all his wonderful faculties to the achievement of another bond capable of counterbalancing its effects, and then bethought himself once more of the closer union with Austria.

He allowed himself to become so entirely absorbed by this dread of finding united against him the two European Powers which he believed to be the most dangerously inclined to thwart his designs, that one day when he was talking with Count Peter Schouvaloff—at that time Russian Ambassador in London—he allowed the latter to perceive that such was the case to such an extent that Schouvaloff told him, as he thought, in jest: " You have a coalition nightmare." To which remark Bismarck gravely replied, " Of course I have." Schouvaloff then proceeded to say that the only remedy he could see to the evils which the Chancellor was dreading would be a strong and firm alliance with Russia, as that would effectually prevent the possibility of any other coalition against Germany.   Bismarck, however, observed that, owing to the geographical situation and the autocratic constitution of the Russian Empire, it would be far easier for it to renounce its engagements than for Germany, and that, after all, the whole traditional Russo-Prussian friendship was based only on the disposition of the reigning Emperor.   Moreover, Germany, by sacrificing for the sake of Russia its relations with all the other Great Powers, would put herself in a state of most dangerous dependence on the Muscovite Empire, because she could not afford to lose sight of the grave incidents and complications that might arise from any French or Austrian aggression, and, further, it was impossible to rely upon a policy for which Prince Gortschakov was responsible.   Schouvaloff retorted that the latter was such an old man that he could be ignored in any matters relative to the future, and that it was only out of consideration for his past merits that the Emperor still kept him at the head of foreign affairs; that, besides, there was really no point of a serious character upon which Prussia and Russia could find themselves drawn into a conflict with each other.   Bismarck conceded this point, but, nevertheless, declined the " option " between Austria and Russia, and only recommended to Schouvaloff the maintenance of the alliance between the three Emperors, or, at least, of peace between them.   More he would not yield, and he carefully concealed from his interlocutor that already—it was during the Berlin Congress that this conversation took place—he had begun to give hints to Count Andrassy, in his conversations with the latter, of the possibility of the conclusion of a Prusso-Austrian agreement in the form of a military convention if not of a regular treaty. He had perfectly well realised that the whole attitude of Germany in regard to Russia during the deliberations of the Berlin Congress was bound to provoke feelings of disgust and animosity on the part of the latter Power, and that these might easily induce it in time to give its attention to the possibility of that *rapprochement* with France foreshadowed by Vicomte de Gontaut in his letters to the Duc Decazes.

Bismarck tried to explain the origin of the strained relations which, after the Congress, had established themselves between the Petersburg and the Berlin Cabinets by the fact that Germany had felt hurt at not having been informed by Russia of the text of the Convention in regard to Bosnia and Herzegovina which had been concluded at Reichstadt, in Bohemia, on July 8th, 1876, between the Tsar and Francis Joseph. This explanation, however, hardly bears examination, because it applies equally against Austria, who also had not thought it worth while to inform Germany of the nature of the engagements she had entered upon. But Bismarck was already pursuing the tactics which became so acute later on towards isolating both Russia and France, which ultimately had the unlooked-for result of helping to throw them into each other's arms. When this happened, however, he was no longer at the head of affairs.

Bismarck's whole attitude before, during, and after the Berlin Congress betrays the irritation that affected his mind and his temper. When, in 1876, the German military attaché in Petersburg, General von Werder, was requested by Prince Gortschakov to ask the German

Government whether, in the event of a war between Russia and Austria on account of the Eastern Question, it would remain neutral, Bismarck was exceedingly angry because this communication had not passed through the German Ambassador, General von Schweinitz, and he asked the Emperor William to forbid Werder for the future to accept any diplomatic mission. He also ordered General von Schweinitz to come and see him at Varzin, where he was nursing another of his periodical fits of bad temper, and he told him to declare to the Tsar that it was the intention of Germany to oppose the possibility of either Austria or Russia losing its position as a great independent state. This led to the conclusion of the Reichstadt Convention, in which Austria, in return for the cession of Bosnia and Herzegovina, promised its neutrality to Russia in the event of a conflict with Turkey.

After the fall of Plevna and the conclusion of the Treaty of San Stefano England, together with Austria, stopped the triumphant march of the Russian army at the very doors of Constantinople. Bismarck then offered his mediation, or rather imposed it on Europe. Though he maintained that during the whole of the deliberations of the Berlin Congress he had only fufilled the part of "the honest broker," he did very much more than that. It was at his instigation that the independence of Roumania was recognised, and that Bulgaria and Roumelia were divided instead of remaining united under one elected Prince, as arranged by the Treaty of San Stefano. In general, most of the advantages conceded to Russia by the terms of this Treaty were taken away from her, and it is no wonder that a profound irritation should have arisen in that country in consequence of this evident breach of faith on the part of Germany, who had thus ignored all the promises which her Emperor had made to the Tsar in return for Russian neutrality in 1870.

The result of all this was that finally Alexander II. wrote to the Emperor William complaining of the hostility which his Government was exhibiting towards him. The old Emperor, who attached great value to his good relations with Russia, then decided to meet his nephew at Alexandrovo, on the Prussian frontier. This interview was arranged by Marshal von Manteuffel, a personal friend of both the Sovereigns, *without* the knowledge of Bismarck, who, as may be imagined, was absolutely furious when he heard of it. Its effects were not altogether what the promoters of it had imagined, because its most immediate consequence was the Austro-German Treaty, followed by the Triple Alliance.

I may perhaps be forgiven if I venture to recount here a personal incident that has some importance, if only as an illustration of the methods employed by Prince von Bismarck and his *alter ego*, Baron von Holstein.

On the creation of the Bulgarian principality in 1878, the question of the Prince who was to assume its government became, of course, a most important one. I do not remember now how the candidature of Prince Alexander of Battenberg originated, but so far as my memory serves me it sprang from the desire to conciliate the Tsar, of whose Consort the Prince was a nephew, morganatically it is true, but a nephew all the same, and one of whom she was extremely fond into the bargain. However that may be, he was elected, and in due course started for the distant country which was to prove so fatal to him later on. Before he left Germany he went, in duty bound, to pay his respects to Prince von Bismarck, and it was generally supposed that the latter had more or less turned the whole enterprise into ridicule, and treated it as something absolutely without any consequences as to the future. No one, however, heard anything concerning another visit paid by the Prince to Baron von Holstein, who just about that time was transferred to Berlin as director of the political section of the Foreign Office after acting as one of the secretaries at the Berlin Congress.

Prince Alexander of Battenberg was by no means the stupid man he has been represented in Russia. On the contrary, he was keenly perceptive in his appreciation of men and events, was possessed of considerable ambition, and a sincere desire not only to make himself useful in Bulgaria, but also of playing a part in the history of the Balkan Peninsula. He certainly looked forward to the day when he would be independent of the Turkish suzerainty, and perhaps even in time to become a King, just as the rulers of Servia and Roumania had done. Considering the family ties which bound him to the Russian Imperial house, there was nothing unreasonable in this ambition. Events, however, did not occur quite as he expected, and the relations of the Prince with his Petersburg relatives soon became strained owing to his persistence in discarding the advice given to him in that quarter. After the murder of Tsar Alexander II. the situation became even more acute. The new Emperor had always disliked the Bulgarian ruler ever since the distant days when, as children, they had played together in the gardens of Tsarskoye Selo or at the Castle of Jugenheim, near Darmstadt, the favourite residence of the Empress Marie of Russia, who had left it in her will to her brother, Prince Alexander of Hesse, the father of the Prince of Bulgaria. The Tsar lost no opportunity of acquainting Alexander with his views on the subject of his activity at Sofia, which he considered in the highest degree injurious to Russian interests.

Matters had reached this unsatisfactory condition when the coronation of the Tsar took place in Moscow, in May of 1883. The Prince of Bulgaria thought he ought to be present at the ceremony, and duly appeared in the old Russian capital, together with the Prince of Montenegro. The presence of the two Eastern Princes gave Alexander III. an opportunity to manifest his feelings in no unmistakable manner. Whilst he loaded Prince Nicholas with amiabilities, he ignored or snubbed Prince Alexander. The latter, of course, was keenly hurt, and one evening, after he had endured a particularly unpleasant rebuff in one of the numerous attempts which he had made to obtain a hearing from the Emperor, he happened to meet me at a ball given by General von Schweinitz, the German Ambassador, and his outraged sentiments urged him to unburden his sorrows. He forthwith invited me to dance the cotillon with him, and whilst it was proceeding he related to me all the misfortunes with which he had met since his arrival in Moscow.

What struck me, apart from the indignation and irritation he expressed, was the assurance with which he spoke of the possibility of paying back the Tsar for the slight to which he had been subjected. In view of the circumstances, and the relative position of the two, this struck me as absolutely foolish, and I could not help telling the Prince that if he were mad enough to start an anti-Russian policy in Bulgaria he would promptly be sent out of the country, as no one would sympathise

with him in that attempt. What was my surprise when he replied to me that I was absolutely mistaken in my surmises, because he would have the support of Germany in any enterprise he undertook against Russia.

I was aghast, and asked him how this could be in view of the general belief that Prince Bismarck had openly discouraged him.

"That is what you and other people think," replied the Prince; "but, as a matter of fact, our conversation was entirely different from what was reported at the time."

"But what did Prince Bismarck tell you," I inquired, "to make your Highness so sure of obtaining the support of Germany against Russia?"

"What he told me," was the unexpected reply, "was that I could, if I worked according to certain directions which would be given me later on, *usefully counterbalance* in the interests of Germany Russian influence in the whole of the Balkans."

I will spare my readers the rest of the conversation of which this was the most salient point, but the whole trend of it convinced me that Bismarck had had in view the eventuality of using Bulgaria, and perhaps Turkey, against Russia in the event of certain European complications which he must have had in his mind. I became very uneasy, and in my turn confided the gist of my talk with Prince Alexander in a letter to my friend Donald Mackenzie Wallace, who at the time was on the staff of the *Times*, asking him, however, not to mention anything about it to anyone. To my surprise, very soon afterwards, I saw an article in the *Times*, based on this letter of mine, with the annoying remark that the contents of it had been divulged to the writer by a

Russian lady. Of course, I was very angry, and the results of this indiscretion of mine were very soon to make themselves felt by all parties concerned. First, Prince Alexander never forgave me; then I became the pet aversion of Baron von Holstein in Berlin; and at last was honoured—for I cannot call it anything else— by the recommendation of Count Herbert Bismarck to the then German Minister in Cairo, Count Arco Valley, to beware of me as a very dangerous woman. We were at the time spending the winter in Egypt, but it was only afterwards that I learned these facts, Arco having in his turn confided this timely, or untimely, warning to Chevalier Rosty, the then Austrian Minister at the Court of the Khedive. The Chevalier, who was one of my dearest friends, wrote me the amusing story, which, I must confess, I had forgotten until I chanced to come across it the other day in sorting and re-reading some old letters. Much later another friend of mine confided to me that the belief that I had instigated the publication of the article in the *Times*, with the purpose of upsetting Bismarck, was firmly established in the Wilhelmstrasse, and that it was useless to try to alter that feeling. I did not try, and after a time had the consolation of knowing that it was Bismarck who came to grief. But this whole incident made me most curious to learn what amount of truth there had been in the confession which wounded pride had induced Prince Alexander of Battenberg to make to me; so I asked the person whom I thought to be the most capable of helping me to try to " draw " Holstein on the subject. Here is what he wrote to me in reply :

" As you may imagine, it was not easy to get Holstein to say anything concerning the Eastern Question. He considers Battenberg a fool, and with his usual brutality said so quite plainly. · At the same time, he owned that the fellow might, had he only known how to do it, have come in time to play an important part in the world. He considers that it is dangerous to European peace in general if Russia becomes too strong, and that it would be far more advantageous for everyone if some hindrances were put in her way in regard to Constantinople, the possession of which she aspires to—a perfectly inadmissible thing in the opinion of Holstein. On the other hand, he quite admits that circumstances may arise which will drive the Turks out of it, a contingency which seems to make him most unhappy, because he spoke about it with a melancholy that was really most amusing. In that case, one must have at hand someone who could be put in their place, and what would be more natural than for the Prince of Bulgaria to become Eastern Emperor? I objected that Greece or Roumania might feel affronted if this honour was not left to them, but this argument did not seem to make any impression on the mind of our friend. What he is driving at, and what the all-mighty Manitou who decides all such questions is driving at, is, of course, beyond my imagination to guess."

It must not be forgotten that this letter was written in 1886, and since then many things have happened which have partly justified the forebodings contained in it. For one thing, Prince Ferdinand of Bulgaria stepped into the shoes of poor Prince Alexander of Battenberg, and he, at all events, did not show himself a fool, but resolutely led his people into the inner circle of German politics, with the consequences which we have seen.

CHAPTER XIX

Fears of Isolation

BISMARCK acknowledged that the remark made to him by Count Schouvaloff, that he had "coalition nightmare," was true. The thought of such a contingency as Germany becoming isolated in her newly acquired grandeur was continually with him. The fact that both Austria and France had the same religious faith contributed more than any other factor to his apprehensions. He relied on the possibility of maintaining on a satisfactory footing the old family relations which for so many years had linked together the Hohenzollerns and the Romanoffs, and thus to inveigle Russia into an alliance. After the Berlin Congress, however, he realised that this was entirely out of the question, and that the moment the old Emperor William I. closed his eyes Russo-German relations would undergo a sudden change.

It was on this contingency that all his future policy was based. To provide against the dangers which it implied he elaborated a plan which, carried out fully by his successors, would ensure the safety of this German Empire. In these plans he found a willing and able instrument in Baron von Holstein, who gradually acquired a great influence over his formidable chief, and ended by being his evil genius. His devotion to Bismarck, though very real, was not so much to the man as to the power possessed by him. It was Holstein who, by repeating to the latter every criticism directed against his person or his policy, developed in him that almost morbid hatred of certain people which at last obscured his powerful intelligence and made him take everything from the personal point of view.

Holstein held in his hands all the threads of Bismarck's complicated intrigues, and at last revealed them to the present German Emperor, thus influencing him against the Chancellor and inducing him at length to dismiss him in the ruthless manner that we know. Without Holstein it is still a question whether Bismarck would have fallen under the wrath of his Sovereign, and it is largely due to this unscrupulous lieutenant of his that the greatest statesman Germany has ever known ended his career in a retirement of which he had often spoken, but never believed he would be allowed to enjoy. On the accession of William II. Holstein realised very quickly that he had to make his choice between the favour of the young Sovereign and the friendship of the Minister to whom he owed his career. He betrayed Bismarck with absolute unconcern. He remained in possession of the autocratic authority he had exercised at the Foreign Office for many years after the fall of his early protector, and it was only in 1905, or about that time, that the then Prussian Foreign Secretary, Baron von Tschirsky, had more courage than either Caprivi or Prince von Hohenlohe. He took Holstein at his word on one of the many occasions when the latter threatened to resign, and coolly accepted his resignation and got it signed by the Emperor before the old fox had recovered his scared wits. Thus was ended the reign of this " Grey Eminence " who for so long had ruled the affairs of the German Empire.

WILLIAM II. IN 1884

It was with Holstein that Bismarck discussed the various complications likely to accrue from an estrangement with the Cabinet of Petersburg, which he saw looming in the distance. The active brain of his lieutenant immediately grasped the idea in the Chancellor's mind, and laid before him a plan for an Austro-German Alliance into which Italy might eventually be drawn.

Bismarck had not given a thought to the latter Power, but he saw the immense advantages which her adherence to the German Government might procure.

At that time, in autumn, 1879, Bismarck was aware of a fact which no one else yet suspected—the imminent retirement of Count Andrassy. The Hungarian statesman, who had been one of the most prominent figures at the Berlin Congress, was tired of political life, and his health, which had never been of the best, was beginning seriously to fail him. Then differences—of which he never liked to speak later on—had arisen between him and the Emperor of Austria, who always saw in Andrassy the Hungarian rebel who once had been condemned to death, and who had been one of the most active enemies of the ancient House of Habsburg. Complete as was his confidence in Holstein, Bismarck never told him anything about it, having promised his Austrian colleague to reveal to no one the secrets which had been confided to his discretion, a promise which he faithfully kept. But this knowledge made him more anxious to assure himself of the co-operation of Austria before the advent of another Prime Minister in Vienna less likely to fall in with his views than Count Andrassy. He had contrived to establish excellent relations with Andrassy during the Berlin Congress, when he had hinted at the possibility of the enemies of the past becoming stanch friends in the future. Of course, he had spoken only in vague terms, but the Hungarian statesman had understood very well what was meant and had eagerly caught at the idea. He saw at once in the common action of Germany and Austria in the Near East a possibility of revenge for the part taken by Russia in the crushing of that Hungarian rebellion which had nearly cost him his life, as well as that of securing for the Empire of which he was the Prime Minister the eventual probability of playing a leading part in the settlement of the everlasting Eastern Question. Andrassy, indeed, had entered so thoroughly into the suggestion made by Bismarck that the latter had felt somewhat alarmed at this too easy acquiescence, and prudently let the overtures he had made on the spur of the moment remain in abeyance. But when Bismarck failed in his endeavours to prevent the Emperor William I. from meeting the Tsar at Alexandrovo, he saw that the hour had struck for the development of his nebulous plan, and then it was that he consulted Holstein, of whose capacities he was forming a high opinion.

Holstein suggested forestalling consequences by previously contracting an engagement with Austria which it would be impossible for the German Emperor to disavow, but it was essential that the initiative of any such arrangement should rest with the Austrian Government. Prince Bismarck was about to repair to Gastein for his annual cure, and Holstein proposed to go to Vienna before the departure of his chief for the little wateringplace in the mountains, and to suggest that Count Andrassy should " find himself " also in Gastein at the same time as the German Chancellor. This explains the admission made by the latter in his Reminiscences that he had arranged an interview with the Austrian Prime Minister long before his Sovereign had officially signified his consent to meet the Tsar.

Andrassy arrived at Gastein on August 27th, and was at once taken by Baron von Holstein into the presence of Bismarck, who received him most cordially. The Chancellor immediately began to discuss the general political situation of Europe, and confessed his fears as to the possibility of a Franco-Russian alliance.

Count Andrassy quite well understood what was implied under the disguise of polite words, and told the German Chancellor plainly that the only counteractive step which could be taken would be to conclude an Austro-German alliance. Bismarck immediately retorted that Andrassy had given expression to the idea that he had had in his mind the whole time. The two statesmen then started to discuss the question of a purely defensive alliance against a possible attack on the part of Russia, directed against either Germany or Austria; but the suggestion of Bismarck to extend this alliance against attacks from any other Power than Russia did not meet with approval from Andrassy, who had no intention of lending himself to any plans of aggression of his colleague in regard to France, for whom he entertained very wide sympathie

After discussions which lasted two days the principal lines of a treaty were drawn up, and in order to ensure absolute secrecy against any possible indiscretion the minutes of the engagements it was proposed to enter upon were written down by Holstein, who alone with Bismarck was aware of what was going on. Andrassy left for Vienna, and Bismarck promised to bring there the authorisation of the Emperor.

Bismarck, however, in spite of his assurance before Andrassy, was by no means certain that his plans would meet with approval on the part of the old Emperor. He therefore bethought himself of securing allies who might, if necessary, lend him their aid in breaking down the stubbornness of his aged master, and addressed himself to the King of Bavaria. He wrote a long letter in which he stated the condition of affairs in Russia, and sought to persuade Ludwig that the Russian Government, notwithstanding its pacific assurances to the contrary, was steadily preparing itself for a war with Austria and Prussia at the very first opportunity after their strength had been made sufficiently secure.

After having laid stress on the fact that, according to information which had reached him from Petersburg, Count Schouvaloff had fallen under the disfavour of his Sovereign owing to his conduct during the Berlin Congress, and that the most powerful among other Ministers in Russia was now General Milioutine, the head of the War Office, Bismarck proceeded to say :

" It is at the request of Milioutine that now, immediately after the conclusion of peace, Russia, whom no one threatens, is preparing terrible armaments, and this notwithstanding the immense financial sacrifices which the recent war has occasioned. They propose to add something like 56,000 men to the effective strength of the Russian army in times of peace, and 400,000 to the battalions it would send down to its Western frontiers in case of a mobilisation. It is quite evident that these preparations can only be directed against Austria or against Germany, and this is further corroborated by the accumulation of troops which has recently taken place in the Kingdom of Poland. The Minister of War has also declared, without reservation, that Russia ought to organise herself in view of a European war.

"Under these circumstances I cannot get rid of the idea that in future peace can only be threatened by Russia, and by Russia alone. The information which I have succeeded in gathering concerning the attitude likely to be taken by France and by Italy in case of Russia declaring war against one of her Western neighbours, gives me reason to conclude that both these Powers would abstain from taking any part in the conflict. Italy is far too weak to do so, and France has declared that for the present she is not thinking of going to war, and that she did not feel strong enough, with Russia as her only ally, to attack Germany.

"As a complement to this situation Russia has asked us, in the course of the last few weeks,[1] to make a definite choice between her and Austria, and to give instructions to the German members of the various Eastern Commissions to vote for Russia in every case that appeared to be doubtful. According to my opinion this would not be interpreting in the right sense the decisions taken at the Congress. . . .

"Though for the most part they were only small and insignificant questions upon which a difference of opinion arose between the delegates, this desire of Russia to see Germany vote with her against Austria has been accompanied with threats as to the consequences of a refusal. This fact, coupled with the retirement of Count Andrassy, of which it seems the Russian Government had become aware, was of a nature to make me fear that a secret understanding had been arranged between Austria and Russia to the detriment of Germany. This fear,

[1] A lie; Russia had never asked Germany anything of the kind.—C. R.

however, was not justified, and Austria feels just as uneasy as we do ourselves concerning the unsettled policy of Russia. She seems disposed to come to an understanding with a view to a common defence of our interests in the case of Russia proceeding to attack either of us. Personally, I would consider some convention of that kind as an essential guarantee for the security of Germany, as well as for the continuance of European peace. This convention would have for one of its aims the maintenance of good relations with Russia hereafter, but would also contain a clause compelling the contracting parties to help each other in the case of one of them being attacked. Once they had this reciprocal guarantee the two Empires could then proceed to renew the alliance between the three Emperors, and as an ally of Austria the German Empire would be able to command the protection of England, so that by the pacific policy of the two great Central Powers the peace of Europe would be guaranteed by two millions of bayonets. The exclusively defensive character of the help which the two German States would engage themselves to give each other could not be considered in the light of a provocation by anyone, because a contract of the same kind is contained in the old Confederation between them of 1815, which has existed for fifty years without being the cause of trouble to anyone.

" Should it be impossible to conclude such a convention, we could not take it in bad part if Austria, under the pressure of Russian threats and in the uncertainty as to what she could expect from Germany, tried to come to an understanding with France, and perhaps even with Russia. Should this contingency arise Germany, in view of the position in which she stands in regard to France, would find herself completely isolated on the European Continent; and in the event of Austria allying herself to France and England, as she has done once before—in 1854—Germany would find herself compelled to fall back upon Russia and to enter into the views of Russian policy both in regard to Home and Foreign Affairs, and I very much fear that these are unsatisfactory and even dangerous.

" Should Russia compel us to choose between her and Austria, I believe that an alliance with Austria would give our policy a conservative and peaceful dircetion, whilst Russia would only make us follow an uncertain and unsatisfactory one. . . . I hope to be able to return home about, or soon after, the 20th of the present month, and to stop at Vienna on my way. If by that time we have not come to an understanding of some kind, at least in principle, I fear that we shall have lost the favourable opportunity to do so, because after the retirement of Andrassy, it is difficult to foresee when such a one may return.

" I have considered it my duty most respectfully to acquaint your Majesty with the present policy of the German Empire, and I must beg of your Majesty to take a note that both Count Andrassy and myself have reciprocally engaged ourselves to keep this matter an absolute secret for the present. Until to-day it is only their Majesties the two Emperors who are aware of the intention of their Prime Ministers to bring about an understanding between the two Powers."

This last phrase contained at least one untruth, because William I. had never been made acquainted with Bismarck's new plan, and was only told of it when it was too late for him to draw back without creating a

scandal, or bringing on his head the wrath of the whole
of Germany which, by means of a virulent Press campaign against Russia, engineered with consummate skill
by von Holstein, had become as much persuaded of the
existence of a " Russian danger " as she is persuaded
to-day that in the present war it is she who has been
attacked by the Allies. The approval of the King of
Bavaria was most essential to Bismarck's object, because
it would place him in the position to state that the
Austro-German alliance was viewed with sympathy even
by those German Sovereigns who had clung to that
intimate understanding with Russia which had become
a tradition not only in Prussia, but everywhere else in
Germany. King Ludwig II., of course, could do nothing
against the determination of Bismarck, but in the reply
which he wrote to the communication, from which I have
just given extracts, he inserted the following sentence,
which is most significant from more than one point of
view :

" If, owing to unforeseen complications, a war were
to break out between the German Empire and Russia,
this most regrettable change in the relations of the two
Empires would affect me in a most painful manner, and
I will not give up the hope that it will be possible to
avoid such a sad solution by bringing our pacific intentions directly to the notice of his Majesty the Emperor
of Russia."

To this remark the Chancellor hastened to reply by
another long explanation of what he knew to be the
affirmation of an arrant untruth.

" In regard to our relations with Russia," he wrote,
" I will allow myself to remark, with all due humility
to your Majesty, that the danger of complications likely

to lead to the outbreak of a war which I should most deeply deplore not only from the political point of view, but also from a personal one, is not, in my opinion, an imminent one. It could only become serious if France were ready to go hand in hand with Russia. Up to the present this is not the case, and in conformity with the intentions of the Emperor our policy will neglect nothing in order to keep up and strengthen the present peaceful relations prevailing between the Empire and Russia, and also to try and influence in the same sense the mind of his Majesty the Emperor Alexander. The negotiations concerning a closer union with Austria have only a peaceful and purely defensive aim in view."

Baron von Holstein, when relating later on the incidents connected with this curious episode in modern history, told a personal friend of mine that one of the principal arguments which he had used in the conversations with Count Andrassy had been that Bismarck knew from an absolutely reliable source that Russia meant to attack Austria in order to wrench from her Bosnia and Herzegovina, and to give up these two provinces to Servia or Montenegro. There was also to be considered the fact that the Austrian mobilisation was always a very slow one, and the advantage it would be to Austria to have at her side an ally whose military organisation was so perfect that it could within one week throw all the bulk of its immense forces into the Kingdom of Poland, and thus produce a diversion which would give to the Austrian staff sufficient time to take measures of defence in regard to Galicia, which, it was well known, would be the first point of attack on the part of Russia. Holstein quite certainly convinced Andrassy that such an aggression was planned, and he did it so cleverly that it appeared as if the Emperor William had become aware of it through an indiscretion of one of his Russian relatives. Of course, this was never said in so many words, but the impression was left on the mind of the Hungarian statesman that such was the case, and, naturally, it could not but influence him and lead him to seek the help of Germany.

It is of curious interest to note how often Germany has made use of the words "absolutely reliable source" whenever she has tried to excuse some black deed she has been planning. If my readers will remember, they occur in the ultimatum which the German Government presented to Belgium at the outbreak of the Great War, in which it is said that Germany had learnt from "an absolutely reliable source" that the French were about to invade Belgium. It is unnecessary to add that neither France, in 1914, nor Russia, in 1879, had the intentions which Germany so generously ascribed to them, but in both cases the words constituted an excuse which, if it convinced no one abroad, satisfied the German nation and gave it a pretext for adding another crime to her long calendar.

Whether Andrassy really believed all that Baron von Holstein related to him is another matter. But there were reasons why he would have liked to gather a few more laurels before bidding good-bye to political life, among which was the desire to prove to the Emperor Francis Joseph that he was above any feelings of rancour, and that the first, and indeed the only object he had in view was the welfare of the Empire whose policy had been for so many years in his hands. He had told no one but Bismarck why he was retiring, and, as we have seen, the latter had faithfully kept the secret, even in regard to Holstein, which had been confided to his discretion.

Now that many years have passed since this incident, and that the grave has closed on all who were concerned in it, it can briefly be said that Francis Joseph, among other grievances against Andrassy, had an objection to the friendship which existed between the latter and the Empress Elisabeth—a friendship which, despite all efforts, he could not end. Painful scenes had consequently arisen which had largely influenced the Count's decision to bid farewell to political life, his honour, as he expressed it a little while before his death, preventing him from continuing to serve a Monarch who had insulted him so far as to suspect him of having had stronger than the most respectful feelings for the Sovereign Lady whom all Hungary worshipped, and the brilliant qualities of whom had been appreciated everywhere and by everyone save by the husband who had outraged her at every step.

In retiring from the political stage Andrassy wished it to be established that he had always tried to promote the interests of the Austrian Empire, and this was one of the reasons which had made him respond so eagerly to the overtures made to him by the confidential servant of Prince von Bismarck, and to acquiesce in the propositions which the latter had made to him, if not officially, at least in such a manner that he could not doubt but that it had been done with the approval of the all-powerful German Chancellor. Altogether the ground had been well prepared by von Holstein. Nothing remained, therefore, after Andrassy's visit to Gastein, but to proceed with the drafting of the Treaty. It was essential, however, for Bismarck to obtain the full consent of the Emperor William to his scheme, and, as it happened, this did not prove quite the easy matter he had assured his friend it would be. The aged Sovereign was far too chivalrous to agree forthwith with what appeared to him to be an act of treachery towards his kinsman the Emperor of Russia. His all-powerful Minister had to resort to all kinds of expedients to persuade him that he was not breaking any of the engagements he had personally contracted in other directions. When the terms of the Treaty were first submitted to him William I. declared that he would rather abdicate than put his hand to a document the signing of which would dishonour him in his own eyes if not in those of the world.

CHAPTER XX

The Dual Alliance

AS I have hinted, it was in connection with this fatal Treaty of alliance with Austria that Bismarck met for the first time with anything approaching a real and serious opposition on the part of the old Emperor. In the eyes of William I. Bismarck was a great historical figure; he appreciated his genius; he admired his energy; but it is an open question whether at heart he really liked him. There were certain traits in Bismarck's character which were absolutely repugnant to his Royal master, among others his unscrupulousness. The King believed that treaties were made to be observed, a pledge kept. He may have accepted out of necessity, but certainly he had never endorsed, the principles which the first Chancellor of the new German Empire embodied in the famous phrase in his Reminiscences, and which has ever since inspired Prussian statecraft : "The observation of the treaties which bind together great States can only be conditional when the struggle for life threatens its solidity. There exists no great nation which would ever consent to sacrifice its existence to fidelity in regard to a treaty if left free choice in the matter."

When Bismarck expounded to William I. the reasons which had led him to respond to the "overtures" made by Count Andrassy, the Emperor exclaimed that he would never consent to the Treaty. Bismarck declared that he would resign, upon which the Sovereign in his turn threatened to abdicate.

This did not suit Prince Bismarck at all, who, for once in his life, was nonplussed. Holstein came to the rescue, and suggested that he should call to his assistance two men whom he thought might represent matters to the Emperor in such a way that the latter might change his mind—the German Ambassadors in London and in Paris, Count Münster and Prince von Hohenlohe Schillingsfürst.

The latter has left us in his Memoirs a record of the incident, and the story affords an apt illustration of Bismarckian methods. The Prince writes:

" *Gastein, September* 14*th,* 1879.

"Last night" [the Prince was then staying at his villa at Aussee] "I received a telegram from Holstein saying that the Chancellor wanted to speak with me this evening. There was nothing to do but to obey. I therefore started for Gastein, where Holstein received me and told me that the Chancellor wished to confer with me on a most important and serious matter.

"The situation is as follows: Bismarck, who has no confidence in Russia, has come here in order to arrange outside of the Alliance of the three Emperors another of a defensive character with Austria. Andrassy, who was on a visit to Gastein on August 28th, would not at first believe that Bismarck was in earnest, but when he had convinced himself that such was the case, jumped up to the ceiling, because it is impossible for Austria to stand alone, and she must look about her for alliances of some kind. But before the Emperor had received a report on the matter from the Chancellor his interview with the Emperor of Russia had taken place at Alexandrovo, and he does not now want to hear anything more about it. Bismarck, on his side, threatens to resign if the Emperor continues to withhold his consent. Holstein has proposed that I should be asked to see the Sovereign and try to induce him to give in, a suggestion to which the Chancellor has agreed. I have talked over the matter with Holstein this evening, and I have told him that I am not in favour of this new scheme. For one thing, I do not trust Austria, and for another, I do not consider that Russia has any serious plans for aggression. Then again, I think that an alliance with Austria would have for its immediate consequence an alliance between Russia and France, which would most certainly lead to war, whilst it seems that Bismarck believes that his scheme would ensure a permanent peace. I shall see what I can learn later on, after I have talked the matter over with the Chancellor."

"*September* 16*th*.

" I read yesterday all the documents concerning the matter, and also talked for a long time with Bismarck. The Prince has, after all, convinced me of the necessity of an alliance with Austria. He says that it is impossible for Austria to stand quite alone in view of the continual threats of Russia. She must seek an alliance with that same Russia or with France. In both cases we are running in danger of being left quite isolated in any crisis which might unexpectedly arise. The telegram which I had sent from Paris to the Chancellor concerning certain Russian overtures there had been of great use to him. The Emperor, however, on account of that fatal interview at Alexandrovo, will not hear anything

of an understanding with Austria, which he considers a perfidy against his nephew. In consequence of our conversation of to-day I shall go on Sunday to Strasburg and see what I can do there."

William I. was attending some manœuvres in Alsace-Lorraine from September 18th to the 25th, and thither repaired, in accordance with the instruction which he had received from Bismarck, Prince von Hohenlohe, who relates in the following words what occurred:

" *September 22nd.*

" The Emperor received me in his study at eight o'clock in the evening. He asked me first from where I had arrived, and then he asked me whether I had seen the Chancellor. I said, 'Yes, in Gastein.' The Emperor asked, 'Is he very greatly irritated?' I replied, 'No, only anxious.' The Emperor then related to me the whole story, told me about the letter which he had received from the Emperor Alexander, his reply, the interview at Alexandrovo, his conversations with the Tsar, with Milioutine and with Giers. Suddenly, he continued, after the most friendly promises had been exchanged between him and his nephew, the Chancellor —probably out of a feeling of revenge for the Emperor Alexander's letter—had proposed to him to conclude an alliance with Austria against Russia. This he could not do. He had the impression that Bismarck had a coalition of Austria, Germany, France and England in view, as a new scheme. I contradicted this, and said that if now, whilst Andrassy was still at the head of affairs, the alliance proposed was not concluded the Conservative party in Austria would, at our expense, come to an understanding with Russia. France would then, as a matter of course, join in it. In regard to the latter, Waddington was in favour of England against Russia, but he could be driven out of office in three months, and it would be quite possible then that creatures of Gambetta would come into power, and these would find means to get into touch with the Russian revolutionary elements and, together with them, bring about a war in order to plunge the whole of Europe in the horrors of a general revolution. An alliance with Austria would thus render Russia a double service. It would, first of all, keep in check a possible revolution, and, secondly, prevent Austria from entering into a coalition against Germany and Russia. This seemed to put matters in a new light before the Emperor. But he did not make any remark on the subject. From the whole tone of my conversation with him I have come to the conclusion that he is rather inclined to take into consideration the arguments put forward by the Chancellor, but that he fears to appear before his nephew and friend as disloyal to him. I could not arrive at any positive result in spite of all that I told him, but I accomplished the mission with which I had been entrusted, and I have told the Emperor all that I thought on this all-important subject."

Prince Hohenlohe adds to this passage of his Memoirs a memorandum, dated September 22nd, 1879, which might appear to the reader to have been written by himself. As a matter of fact, it was given to him at Gastein by Holstein, as we shall presently see. It runs thus:

"Russia is embittered against Austria. Austria prevents the execution of her various schemes in regard to the Near East. Russia will and must declare war against Austria if she wants to push these schemes through. She will then ask us what we mean to do. If we stand by Russia and remain neutral, Austria will immediately ally herself with France and England. We shall then stand together with Russia against France, Austria and England. If we do nothing at present, then Austria can arrive at an understanding with Russia. In that case, as soon as France feels it is strong enough it will start a war with us, during which it will have at its side, as unfriendly neutrals in regard to us, Russia and Austria. We should thus find ourselves in a state of complete isolation, and we might even find ourselves faced by a coalition of Austria, Russia and France. On the contrary, if we have contrived to bind Austria to us by the help of a treaty, then England will always be on our side, and then we can consider without the slightest uneasiness the enmity of Russia and France.

"In Russia the Revolutionary movement is so powerful that it is impossible to guess to what extremities the Government might not find itself driven. It is quite possible that the Constitution Reform party in Russia wishes for war in order to be able to obtain in that way the reforms which it requires. At all events, it is impossible to put any confidence in the friendship of a country which finds itself in such a state of disorder.

"The Panslavist party will suffer an ' échec '[1] through the German-Austrian alliance, and this will afford an opportunity to the Russian Conservative party to assert itself once more."

I have written at length on this Austro-German incident, because if the reader will follow it in all its details he will find that it was but the inauguration of the

[1] The word is written in French in the text.

political methods which Prussia has followed with such perseverance until the breaking out of the present war, to which it was not only the preface, but, in a certain sense, the first chapter. Bismarck, who realised that sooner or later the Empire he had founded would find itself faced by a combination of the whole of Europe against the militarism of which it was the incarnation, had had in his mind, from the very first day of its foundation, the consolidation of it through alliances which might, to a certain extent, shield it from demolition and ruin. He would have liked to induce France to forget the past—the loss of Alsace-Lorraine and the milliards it had been compelled to pay—and to consent to shake the hand which Germany extended to it. But he soon realised that this was a forlorn hope, and he understood just as quickly that the natural consequence of the war which had brought such laurels to Prussia would be a Franco-Russian alliance, which the Panslavist and Slavophil parties in Petersburg would do their best to bring about. For reasons best known to himself he had not sided with Russia during the Berlin Congress, but had tried to favour both England and Austria, especially the latter, in whom he saw a possible rival to Russia for that preponderance in the Balkans which the Muscovite claimed, and which he did not want to see her obtain. If one could have read his heart it is probable that the whole secret of his attitude would have been found in a conviction that whilst he would always find in Austria a tool ready to lend itself to all his schemes, he could not hope for the same thing from Russia, where, even at this time, there existed a strong anti-German party. Bismarck had made up his mind to keep open for German trade the road to Constantinople and Asia Minor, and this, of course, would have been rendered impossible if Petersburg and not Vienna ruled in the Balkans. All these considerations had induced him to summon Count Andrassy to his side at Gastein, and to elaborate with him this formidable conception of an Austro-German alliance. We have seen the manner in which Bismarck had called to his help Prince von Hohenlohe, in whose independence and conscientiousness the aged monarch believed implicitly, to forward his scheme. In reality the Prince was neither independent nor conscientious, and it was, indeed, in connection with him that the German Chancellor gave utterance to Walpole's famous axiom, " Every man has his price.'' Hohenlohe, in spite of his position, was ambitious both in respect to power and money. It did not take long for Prince von Hohenlohe to find his reward ; a few weeks after his visit to Gastein and his trip to Strasburg he was asked to take up for a few months the office of Foreign Secretary at Berlin, which the death of Herr von Bülow had left free. During its tenure he was allowed, as a special favour, to retain his salary as German Ambassador in Paris, together with the one appertaining to the post he was requested to fill provisionally, a combination which allowed the Prince to pay off a certain number of pressing debts.

The Austro-German Treaty was one of Holstein's pet conceptions. He knew very well that it constituted one of the blackest acts of treachery in regard to Russia and to its Sovereign that Prussia had ever been guilty of. But this man had a clear vision of the developments which the political situation in Europe was bound to undergo. He did not underrate the strength of France, and he knew very well that the next war which

Prussia would have to fight with her would be a much more formidable affair, in which France might easily find allies and friends among all those who had become weary of the growing insolence of Germany. It was to provide against this contingency that he had been working with Bismarck, to assure that they would not stand alone when the next outbreak should occur. Both the German Foreign Office and the German General Staff had decided that the country ought to prepare itself for another war, without which it would be impossible for it to proceed to the consolidation of the power it had acquired. The only question was as to the time when this war would be brought about. It remained an open one the whole time Bismarck was in power, and for long years after he had disappeared from the political scene; but the intention to provoke it has always been the leading thought in Prussian politics. If we compare what we know of the activity and the designs of Baron von Holstein and of his great chief with what has recently taken place under our eyes, we find that the events of to-day had been foreseen and prepared for by them. These designs have been carried out with a thoroughness, though, perhaps, not with the cleverness which they themselves would have exercised, but executed all the same on the very lines they had conceived.

My friend, when discussing with Holstein the circumstances I have just related, asked him why, after all, he had preferred an alliance with Austria, the insufficiency of whose army was so well known to him, to one with Russia, because, as he had added, "You surely never seriously believed, whatever you tried to persuade the old Emperor, that Russia had aggressive designs in regard to Germany?" "Of course I did not," answered Holstein. " What decided the question was the knowledge that Russia would not allow herself to be used as we might consider necessary and useful to our interests at a given moment, and that the Slavophil and Panslavist parties might, after all, turn towards France, with whom many more sympathies bound them than with Germany, to whom they had never forgiven the part she played at the time of the Berlin Congress. You see, the next war is bound to be for us a question of existence. If we fight it successfully, then we shall be able to proceed to a general disarmament of Europe, together with a restriction of our own military forces. Therefore, we ought to watch carefully for the moment when this war can be brought about with the minimum of risk to ourselves and the maximum to our foes. When we consider this moment to have arrived we must begin it, whether we like it or not; and what neither Bismarck nor myself was sure of was, whether Russia would allow us to seize it, whereas with Austria no such complication could be feared. Austria would always follow the impulse we chose to give her. This was the reason which finally decided us and which carried the day. Austria marching to war at our side, Austrian regiments led by Prussian officers. With Austria beside us, and—who knows?—perhaps one or two small Balkan States, we can crush both France and Russia and neutralise England. With Russia as an ally we might crush Austria, but we would never destroy France, and it is France which must be destroyed before the German Empire can develop itself, as it is essential it should do, in the future."

I will ask my readers to notice that the conversation here recorded took place in 1887 or 1888—that is, after the defensive alliance which Bismarck had succeeded in concluding with Count Andrassy had been renewed for a further term of six years by his successor, Count Kalnoky. Nothing then could point towards the catastrophe which was to occur in 1914, and yet how clearly Holstein exposed the Prussian programme, and with what a terrible exactitude it has been fulfilled! And this notwithstanding the fact that in Austria itself, and even among her diplomats and statesmen, there were people who saw quite clearly through the Bismarckian game and intrigues, and who deplored the facility with which these had been allowed to work their way among the public, through the medium and influence of a subsidised Press, the headquarters of which were situated in the Wilhelmstrasse in Berlin, and the leading spirit of which was Baron von Holstein.

An Austrian diplomat of Hungarian birth, who therefore ought rather to have been an enemy of Russia than one of her friends—the Chevalier Rosty, who died a good many years ago—in writing to me in August, 1896, about the famous alliance, used the following terms :

" Ainsi la fameuse triple alliance est renouvelée pour six ans. C'est un court espace dans la vie des peuples, et ne peut endiguer les courants irrésistibles qui poussent d'un côté la France à la reprise de ses provinces, et d'autre côté la Russie à la marche vers le Bosphore. Nos hommes d'état pensent que la Russie établie à Constantinople ne saurait tolérer à ses flancs une Autriche puissante. L'Allemagne profite de cette peur pour nous attirer dans une alliance appelée à lui garantir sa proie. Mais l'historien dans l'avenir aura de la peine à expliquer ce que l'Italie est venue faire là dedans. J'étais à Rome lors de la conclusion des traités, et je connais les dessous des cartes. Je vous avoue, cependant, que j'étais étonné de voir Rudini suivre les errements de ses prédécesseurs.''[1]

And a little later the same diplomat, in writing to me, made the following pregnant remarks :

'' Chez nous on commence à s'apercevoir que la triple alliance est au fond une duperie, et les articles du Lloyd sont de moins en moins appréciés. Cependant, une crise financière deviendra inévitable si nous jetons les millions par la fenêtre pour des concentrations de troupes *faites sur des conseils venus de Berlin.*''[2]

The man who penned these words died in 1892, and the letters which contain them are to-day as testimony from another world to add force to the knowledge which we already possess of the intentions of Germany, both in regard to France and to Russia, and of the determination with which she proceeded to the execution of the ruthless scheme which she hoped would establish her power and supremacy not only in Europe, but over the whole world.

---

[1] '' So the famous Triple Alliance has been renewed for six years. It is but a short space in the life of nations, and it cannot be sufficient to stop the irresistible currents which push on the one side France to try and recover her lost provinces, and on the other Russia to her march forward towards the Bosphorus. Our statesmen think that once Russia is established at Constantinople she would not tolerate at her side a powerful Austria. Germany takes advantage of this fear to try and entangle us in an alliance the aim of which is to guarantee to her the possession of the prey which she has seized. But the historian will have in the future much trouble to explain what Italy had to do in all this. I was in Rome at the time of the conclusion of the treaties, and I know well all that existed behind the cards. I will own, however, that I was surprised to see Rudini fall into the errors of his predecessors.''

[2] '' Here one begins to see that the Triple Alliance is but a ' dupery,' and the articles of the Lloyd are every day less and less appreciated. Nevertheless, a financial crisis will be inevitable in the long run if we go on squandering millions for concentration of troops on the advice of Berlin.''

CHAPTER XXI

Some Missing Documents

THE family of Prince von Bismarck published a great part of his correspondence with the old Emperor William, but it is curious that in this big volume one cannot find a single letter which really tells anything concerning the Austro-German Treaty which, after all, was one of the most important transactions that took place during the Chancellor's administration. Most certainly letters concerning it must have been exchanged between the monarch and his trusted adviser, and with various politicians and diplomats. This is the more likely in regard to the Emperor, in that at the time the negotiations were taking place with Count Andrassy the German Chancellor was far away from his Sovereign. Such an absence voluntarily suggests the probability that the exchange of notes between the Chancellor and the aged monarch would not bear the light of the day or the criticisms of the world. Bismarck had no proof that Russia nursed any aggressive designs against Germany; he had no proof that the Russian Government was about to attack Austria, and he knew nothing at all about the aspirations of either the Panslavist or the Conservative parties in the Tsar's Empire; whilst his assertion that it would be to the advantage of the latter to see concluded against itself an Austro-German defensive and offensive alliance had something absolutely childish about it.

After the fatal month of August, 1879, Germany did everything that lay in its power to spoil the relations between Vienna and Petersburg, and the Press subsidised by the Wilhelmstrasse was always trying to excite public opinion in Austria, and especially in Hungary, against Russia and its successive Sovereigns; and when Italy had joined the alliance of the two Empires the same methods were tried in Rome, where to an extent they succeeded, especially at the time when the vanity of Crispi led him to submit to the directions which he received from Friedrichsruhe   This was after the famous visit which he had paid to the Prussian Richelieu, whose disciple he proclaimed himself to be with such emphasis.   All through the years in which he remained in office Bismarck persistently worked with the one aim of sowing dissension between Austria and Russia, and representing France to Russia as a country in the throes of anarchy and revolution.

Holstein, who perhaps was more brutally frank even than Bismarck, made no secret of the uneasiness which the latter experienced in regard to this possible understanding between Paris and Petersburg.   He openly avowed that it was on that account the Berlin Cabinet had shown itself so opposed to a monarchical restoration in France, because it hoped that the aversion to the Republic which existed in Russian higher spheres might prevent the Tsar from accepting the idea of an alliance with a Government that was so entirely the opposite of his own.

Had Bismarck been left alone he would most certainly, in spite of all his assertions to the contrary, have welcomed a war with France, though he might not have provoked it for some time until he was tolerably

sure that Germany stood in no danger of being entangled
thereby in complications with Russia. Infinitely he
preferred that Germany should look on whilst Russia
fought with Austria, with the utter weakening of both
belligerents as an inevitable result. His rôle would
then have been that of mediator, and one of his conditions would have been their acquiescence in Saxony
and Bavaria becoming, if not vassals, at least the submissive allies of the German Empire—which achievement
accomplished he would have no further cause to fear
France.

Such, at any rate, were his views at the time of
which I am writing, though they changed to a considerable extent later on. Not so Holstein, who was eager
for the destruction both of France and of Russia. His
desire to hurry on the crisis which Bismarck would have
preferred to see delayed shortened his vision, and without recognising consequences he took up with the
energy which never failed him the task of creating
annoyances to the Russian Government in the Near
East, in the hope that these might bring on complications while Bismarck was still at the head of affairs. Both
men wished to keep in their own hands the direction
of the political affairs of Europe, and both were determined to leave no initiative to their subordinates, a fact
to which must be attributed the utter lack of a worthy
successor to Bismarck and the general absence of clever
diplomats in the Prussian service. Whenever one proved
capable of some initiative, some pretext or other was
discovered to induce him to send in his resignation.
The two leading minds at the Wilhelmstrasse required
only servants and did not admit collaborators, the reper-
cussion of which mistake can be found in all the negotia-

tions which preceded the outbreak of the present war. Even Prince von Bülow failed to be appreciated either by Bismarck or by Holstein, and might have fared badly at their hands if he had not taken care to efface himself as much as possible, and not to allow either of them to suspect that he was a man of individuality and not merely a machine incapable of independence of action.

The Foreign Office, in fact, under the rule of Baron von Holstein was more a *bureau d'espionnage* than anything else, and its whole policy was built on a foundation of reports which reached it from the army of secret agents sent all over Europe with injunctions to relate all the gossip they overheard. Every morning Holstein used to go to Bismarck with a bundle of reports similar to those which were brought to Louis XV. in France by his faithful *lieutenant de police*, and in which were recorded the sayings and doings not only of politicians, but of prominent members of society all over Europe. These reports allowed him sometimes to exercise a pressure on certain people whose services he required for the moment, and to become possessed of information concerning them which gave him the opportunity to discredit them if need be.

This reminds me of an incident that was related to me, and which is amusing in regard to the personality of one, at least, of the persons implicated in it. At the time that Prince von Bülow, then quite a young man, was secretary of the German Embassy in Petersburg, he had a flirtation with a lady who, for some reason or other, Holstein wanted to have in his power. The flirtation had been a very discreet one, and both the people concerned in it had hoped that the rumour of it had not got abroad. As a matter of fact it had not, but somehow Holstein contrived to become acquainted with it. The lady did not live in Petersburg, but belonged to Berlin society, and had only been in Russia on a short visit during the winter season. What was her surprise when she returned to the German capital to find herself the object of the attentions of Holstein who, as a rule, never troubled about women. She was not a particularly clever woman, but, nevertheless, she became suspicious as to the motives of this sudden friendliness on the part of Holstein. At last the shell burst, and she was given to understand very plainly that she was expected to find out certain matters concerning Bülow, upon which, for reasons best known to himself, Holstein wanted information. When she protested she was instantly reminded that her reputation was at the mercy of the people who wished to avail themselves of her services, and that it was all that her life, or rather its peace, was worth to disobey the injunctions given her. The lady became so alarmed that, placed as she was between her liking for Herr—as he was at the time—von Bülow, the necessity to safeguard her own existence at home, and the alternative to commit what in her eyes was the meanest of actions, she decided to break off her relations with the young man. She indignantly told Holstein that it was most impudent to accuse her of an intrigue of which she was innocent, and though she had arranged to meet Bülow in the near future she never kept the appointment, and carefully avoided either giving him an explanation of her conduct or having anything to do with him beyond meeting him in society when it was inevitable, and then trying not to be drawn into conversation with him. The marriage of Herr von Bülow took place a short time after this incident, and the heroine of the adventure confessed to a person who was in her confidence, and who after her death told the story to me, that she had never in all her life felt more grateful to Providence than for the news that the lovely Countess Donhoff had become Madame von Bülow, this event putting definitely an end to the possibility of any persecution of her on the part of Baron von Holstein.

This little example of the methods employed by the faithful lieutenant of Prince Bismarck is an excellent illustration of the devious means by which he obtained information of which he wished to become possessed. He had spies and counter-spies, innocent spies and unwilling spies, and spies of every possible kind who, either for money or out of fear, or simply out of idleness and desire to make themselves important, brought to his most willing ears the information which they had gathered or which he had ordered them to collect. Holstein, therefore, who never went anywhere, who scarcely saw anyone outside his circle of immediate acquaintances and the political personages with whom his duties brought him into contact, was the best informed individual in Europe.

There was not a prominent man or woman on the Continent of whose private life and general opinions Holstein did not possess the most complete and accurate knowledge. He made spying an art, and without him the famous Intelligence Department, which has contributed so much to the military and civil organisation of the German Empire, and raised it to such a high state of perfection, would never have attained the celebrity which it has reached, or proved of such use both then and now to German plans for world-dominion. Holstein made blackmailing a permanent institution, and resorted to it with the most complete unconcern whenever it suited him to do so, or whenever he saw an advantage to any scheme he might have in view. He made the lives of his victims as uncomfortable as he could, smiling serenely all the while, and allowing them to see that he was thoroughly enjoying the pangs of agony in which they were writhing.

This man, so quiet and so civil outwardly, was absolutely inexorable, and contrived to give all around him the impression that whatever happened he must not be interfered with. Not only Bismarck, but all the grave and important Ambassadors, Secretaries of State, and Ministers who ever had anything to do with him, showed themselves most careful in their relations with him and took extreme trouble to conciliate him. The only man who treated him as an equal, perhaps because he had worked with him in a way no one else had done, was the great Jewish banker, Baron von Bleichröder, who was one of his principal agents, and whose agent he had also sometimes been, *à titre de révanche.*

The Baron, by his financial connections in Paris and in Petersburg—the House of Rothschild in the one place and M. Sachs, the director of the Discount Bank, in the other—kept him supplied with news it would have been impossible for him to procure otherwise, made it his special care to take to the Chancellor all kinds of useful information, and to distribute where it was needed—this especially in Russia—a certain amount of baksheesh which Bismarck never grudged when he thought it might be advantageous to him. It was Bleichröder who generally subsidised the foreign Press, apparently for financial, but in reality for political, purposes. It was Bleichröder who often, in his discussions with Ambassadors and other influential personages who came to seek inspiration in the small study where he received such, suggested to them certain things that they ought to do or say which Holstein had previously told him would be well to mention to them.

Bleichröder had charge of the money matters, so at least it was said, of Count Herbert von Bismarck, and advised him in his Stock Exchange operations. This fact, which was very well known to Baron von Holstein, gave to the latter great facilities for exercising a certain influence both on the shrewd banker who appreciated him so well, and on the Chancellor who in many things followed the inspirations given to him by his eldest son, who again would not have cared for his father to learn that he required more money than the very generous allowance which was made to him, and which, coupled with his own salary, provided him with a nice little income that should have satisfied him in every way.

All these things were common talk in Berlin, though no one dared mention them aloud. Everyone felt more or less afraid of Baron von Holstein, and even those who had nothing to do with him, and who called him in derision "the Grey Eminence," were very careful never to cross his path.

Without Holstein Bismarck would not have done half the mean things for which he became responsible. For instance, in regard to that Austro-German Treaty, to which I may be forgiven for recurring so often in that it was one of the foundation-stones of the whole Bismarckian policy, it was Holstein who had not only urged the Prince to conclude it, but who had advised him to carry through the business without referring at all to the Emperor.

Just to emphasise the extent to which Bismarck deceived his Sovereign in regard to this question, and the impudence with which he lied to Count Andrassy, we have only to compare official dates as they appear in documents we have at our disposal. We have seen the diary of Prince von Hohenlohe, dated September 14th and 16th, in which he relates how the Chancellor called him to Gastein and asked him to go to Strassburg to see the Emperor. We had read further that the Prince only saw William I. on September 22nd, at eight o'clock in the evening, and that when he left the presence of the Monarch he had not obtained any positive results in regard to the mission which he had accepted. Now, in the official correspondence of Bismarck which his son, Prince Herbert, published after his father's death, there is a letter addressed to Count Andrassy, dated Gastein, September 20th, 1879—that is, two days before the audience given by the Emperor William I. to Prince Hohenlohe—which contains the following passage:

"I have presented full and detailed reports on the situation as discussed by us during our recent conversations, and the acquiescence of the colleagues who represent me in my absence has allowed me to surmount the various difficulties which have arisen through the distance at which I find myself from them, together with opposing influences directed against our common work, to the extent that I have obtained, in principle, the agreement of the Emperor with the views that have influenced me during our recent conversations. According to the communications which I have received from my representative, Count von Stolberg-Wernigerode, the Emperor is ready to consent to a convention in which the two Powers bind themselves to do everything

they can to maintain peace, and especially to maintain
good relations with Russia; but also, in the event of
one of them being attacked by one or several other
Powers, to resist such an attack with all the strength
which they both can muster.

"I am therefore *authorised* by my august Master
to conclude a defensive alliance between Austro-Hungary and the German Empire unconditionally, and for
either a fixed period of time or indefinitely. I entreat
your Excellency to be kind enough to enter into personal negotiations with me on the subject of this offer.
I shall have, of course, to lay before my august
Master the result of these negotiations, but I *have no
doubt as to his agreeing to what we shall decide* in the
event of your Excellency being able to accept, in the
name of his Majesty the Emperor Francis Joseph, the
propositions which I shall make to you."

People have gone to great trouble to explain the
iniquity of which Bismarck made himself guilty in changing the terms of the Ems dispatch; but it seems to
me that, bad as it was, that was but a small matter
compared with the audacious lies contained in the letter
which I have just quoted. And what can one think
of the moral character of a man capable of writing so
to the Prime Minister of a foreign Power on a matter
the importance of which was of so tremendous a nature
when he had every reason to fear his Sovereign would
not consider it even, and when he was using all the
means in his power, and all the influences of which he
could dispose, to try to win over this Sovereign to his
point of view? Again, there is the impudence of the
reference to Count Stolberg, who did not know one
word concerning the alliance until it had become an

accomplished fact! Further commentary is unnecessary in face of the eloquence of these two dates.

And now what were really the terms of this famous Treaty in which Italy was to join a few months later, and which was definitely signed on October 7th, 1879? In view of what has developed from it, it is just as well to recall its stipulations. These consisted of three principal points:

1. In the event of one of the two Empires being attacked by Russia the other was bound to come to its help with all the resources of which it was capable.

2. In the event of one of the two Empires being attacked by any other Power than Russia the second was to adhere to an attitude of friendly neutrality.

3. In the event of the attacking Power being helped by Russia the obligation mentioned in Article 1 operated on the two contracting parties.

The official object of the Treaty was to assure the security of the two Empires; its real purpose was an offensive alliance against Russia, and eventually against France.

The specious arguments put forward by Bismarck, coupled with his threats of resignation, finally induced the Emperor to do what was required of him by all the people in whom he had confidence—his Prime Minister, his son and his wife, and Prince von Hohenlohe—but with touching *naïveté* William I. insisted on informing the Tsar as to what had been done. This, of course, was entirely against the wishes of Bismarck, who would have preferred that the latter heard nothing at all about it. This frankness of the aged Monarch compelled the Chancellor somewhat to change his tactics, and induced him, immediately after his arrival in Vienna, to seek the French Ambassador at the Austrian Court, and to assure him that his presence there did not mean anything hostile to France. It was adding insult to injury, but this was nothing new to Bismarck.

This journey of the great Minister to Austria was, perhaps, one of the greatest triumphs which he achieved in the course of his triumphant career. The Austrians are a good-natured people, and they seemed to have forgotten Sadowa in the ovations with which they received the man who, after having humiliated them in every possible way, now came to offer them his friendship. The population of Vienna cheered him as it did not often cheer their Kaiser. The Emperor Francis Joseph received him with great pomp at the Hofburg, assured him of his everlasting friendship, shed tears of joy over the Treaty which Andrassy had signed in his name, and declared effusively to the successful and lucky Chancellor that he would always think of him as a dear brother! Nothing in the way of compliments, expressions of gratitude and of admiration were omitted, and, secure in the future, Bismarck returned to the solitudes of Varzin in order to contemplate the great work which he had brought to a close. Little did he think that this Treaty, which he considered as a shield against any possible danger of Franco-Russian aggression against the German Empire, would, by a strange irony of destiny, be the direct cause of the establishment of the Triple Entente.

CHAPTER XXII

Bulgarian Matters

IT is a common saying in Russia that old men forget what they thought or did in their youth. In like manner one might say the same of a statesman when out of power. We find in the Reminiscences of Prince Bismarck a curious chapter treating of the future policy of Germany and of Russia, in which he says, among other things, that the absence of every immediate interest in all questions concerning the Near East is of great advantage to German policy, and that it is in Germany's interests to remain at peace with all her neighbours. This may have been the Chancellor's opinion after he had been dismissed by William II., but he certainly did not hold it during his long years of intrigue in order to thrust Russia into difficulties in the Balkans or to sow dissension between her, Austria, France, England and all the other countries in Europe. Even if we could believe that it was his innocent desire to draw the Tsar into an intimate alliance with Germany, we have seen how he secretly encouraged Prince Alexander of Battenberg, and the ominous manner in which he told him that Bulgaria might become a useful counterbalance to Russian influence in the Balkans, a statement which certainly was not uttered without intent, for Bismarck always thought twice before saying anything. But even if, for the sake of argument, we admit that the Prince of Battenberg did not understand the

Chancellor, we find confirmation of the latter's sympathies with the cause of the enemies of Russia in the Near East in the Memoirs of Hohenlohe, who, on September 6th, 1883, writes from Gastein :

" Bismarck spoke to me about the Russian armaments, and added, ' they always say nice things, but they continue to arm, and have already got their troops ready and equipped on the frontier. Of what use to me are fine words when at the same time one keeps holding a loaded pistol at my breast? This kind of thing cannot go on. They may protest that these armaments concern Austria only, but we cannot allow Austria to be destroyed or even weakened. If we looked on without interfering or rendering assistance we should find ourselves after the war confronted with a triple alliance against us of Austria, France and Russia.' It seems to me," continues Hohenlohe, "that Bismarck wants to extend our alliances still further. The presence of Bratiano, whom he has summoned to Gastein, seems to indicate that he is thinking about an alliance with Roumania. He is very much occupied with Bulgarian affairs, and it appears that Prince Alexander is now very much set against Russia, in which Bismarck encourages him. The Prince of Montenegro wants to take Herzegoyina, and undertakes in that case to keep Albania in order and submissive to the Turks. Karageorgevitch wishes to become Prince of Bulgaria so as to get hold of Servia later on. That is the drift of Russian intrigue in the Balkans."

Prince Hohenlohe certainly cannot be accused of inventing these things. This admission of his confirms absolutely the confidences which poor Prince Alexander of Battenberg poured into my ear in Moscow in 1883, and is another proof of the interference of the German

EMPEROR WILLIAM I
IN 1884

Government in the various complications which made the Near East the scene of so many untoward and serious events all through the years which followed upon the Berlin Congress down to the breaking out of the present war. But it does not agree in the very least with Bismarck's assertions. Even at that time the various schemes which culminated in the building of the Bagdad Railway were on foot, and Baron von Holstein for one was working with all the energy of which he was possessed towards the supplanting of Russian influence with that of Austria-Germany in the Balkan Peninsula.

Undoubtedly it was in view of the various complications which he determined to bring about in the event of their not developing unhelped that Germany, in the years which followed upon the conclusion of the Triple Alliance, did everything possible to strengthen her armaments. Bismarck well knew the security of the Empire depended upon the victorious issue of another war which he was determined should occur. After that he hoped to come forward as the apostle of a general disarmament of Europe. With Austria installed in the Balkans, a great Bulgaria ruled by a prince devoted to Germany, France deprived of a few more provinces, and Russia thrown back behind the Vistula, with her line of fortresses in Prussian hands—he never ceased working to make sure of victory—it would be relatively easy to talk about peace. Europe would then be entirely German, or, at least, under German influence, and German Kultur would rule the world. The scheme was a magnificent one, and perhaps had Bismarck lived long enough, and remained long enough in power, he might have accomplished it.

It is just as well at this point to recall the remark of Bismarck after he had forced through the years from 1871 to 1888 a series of enormous credits for increased armaments. More than once the Reichstag opposed the war-burden, but, as I attempt to show, Bismarck triumphed.

The legend which Bismarck's worshippers have always tried to spread is that he was a partisan of peace all through the last years of his life and administration. But was he? In 1871 the military Budget of the German Empire was voted by the Reichstag for three years. In 1874 and 1880 it was done for a far longer time, namely for seven years. The nation as well as the Reichstag was of opinion that this Budget represented a burden far too heavy for the financial resources of the country, and did not want to engage themselves again for such a considerable period. This was in 1887. Bismarck was advised that the parliamentary opposition to the proposals of the Government was very strong, and that it was just possible these might be rejected by the Reichstag. This electrified him and urged him to make one of the most famous speeches of his life, in which he publicly declared, for the first time—until then he had avoided expressing an opinion on the subject—that France was always thinking of her lost provinces, and preparing for a desperate effort to regain their possession.

But for once his eloquence failed to convince his listeners, and the Budget was only voted for a space of three years. A dissolution followed upon this attempt at independence on the part of the Imperial Parliament, and strong measures had to be resorted to in order to influence the elections and secure a majority willing to consent to the series of measures which the Government declared to be indispensable to the military security of the country.

Just before the death of the Emperor William I. the Prussian War Office again applied for increased credits. The opposition of the Reichstag was crushed by Bismarck in the famous speech which contains the phrase, "We Germans fear God, but nothing else in the world." And then added scornful words that shook perhaps for the first time the complacency of the Tsar Alexander III. as to the pacific intentions of the Berlin Cabinet, "We are no longer anxious to be liked either in Russia or in France." This occurred on February 8th, 1888. Exactly one month after that date the reign of William I. came to an end, and three months later there occurred in Petersburg an apparently trivial incident which proved more important than the people concerned in it could have imagined, and which had much to do with the conclusion of the Franco-Russian Alliance.

Before relating it, however, I must return once more to the subject of the Bismarckian intrigues in the Balkan Peninsula. The story of poor Prince Alexander of Battenberg had come to a sad ending. Bismarck declared that he deserved his fate and abandoned him, posing as the champion of Russian interests at Sofia and as the adversary of Battenberg, whose fault had been that he had obeyed Bismarck too well. But Alexander of Battenberg's disappearance from the political scene was, in a certain sense, a check to German plans. The Tsar had seen through Germany's scheme, or at least looked upon it with suspicion, and considerable prudence was required in order to establish on a firm footing a Germanophile Sovereign at Sofia.

The idea of placing Prince Ferdinand of Saxe-Coburg

on the throne which Alexander of Battenberg had been
compelled to abandon had not been at all agreeable to
Bismarck. He did not care for the Coburg dynasty,
whom he suspected of being too much under English
influence; he hated the Orleans family on account of
their claims to the French throne, and the thought of
a grandson of Louis Philippe becoming a Sovereign in
his own right was extremely distasteful to him at first,
and caused him to dispatch instructions to General von
Schweinitz, the German Ambassador in Petersburg, in
which he enjoined him to declare to M. de Giers, then
Russian Minister of Foreign Affairs, that Germany
would go hand in hand with Russia and support the
latter in regard to the Bulgarian question. This
became known to Prince Ferdinand, but it did
not impress him in the very least. He knew perfectly well what he had to do, and also that his
greatest difficulty consisted in conveying to the German
Chancellor several things which he was perfectly well
aware would considerably modify the latter's ideas as
to his (Prince Ferdinand's) individuality, and it is
likely that but for a lucky chance he would not have
contrived to do so, at least not immediately. The lucky
chance came with a journey which Princess Clementine
of Coburg, the clever mother of the newly elected Prince
of Bulgaria, made to Italy about that time, where, as
fate would have it, she met Baron von Holstein at
Bologna. He was enjoying one of his rare holidays.

He did not as a rule like to go away, because his experience had taught him that the proverb, *"Les absents
ont toujours tort,"* is an exceedingly true one, and he
hated to trust the secrets in which he dabbled to a subordinate, whom, of course, it was impossible to initiate

entirely into the details of the various intrigues without which he could not live. It happened, however, that at times his overwrought nervous system imperatively claimed a rest, and then he would go away for a while without letting anyone know whither he was repairing; and sometimes these holidays, so grudgingly and sparingly taken, gave him opportunities to learn many different things he could not have discovered at home.

Holstein never allowed an opportunity to slip by. He therefore hastened to ask for an introduction to the Princess Clementine. In her way the old lady was as clever as the Baron, and she also managed to keep herself very well informed as to the social status of the people whom she admitted into her presence. She had heard a great deal about Holstein, and she did not attempt to hide from him the great pleasure it gave to her to meet him "at last." They had several interviews, after which Holstein returned to Berlin with very different opinions from when he had left it.

Prince Ferdinand was elected, and, duly provided with the considerable sums of money which his mother put at his disposal, he embarked upon what the generality of his friends believed would be an adventure without a morrow. The Tsar had declared that he would never recognise him as Prince of Bulgaria, and the other Great Powers had also repudiated him. People wondered how he had plucked up sufficient courage to start for Sofia with such immense confidence in his own powers. Some suggested that most probably he had "strong protections" somewhere, but the "where" remained shrouded in impenetrable darkness.

On his arrival in his new dominions the present King of Bulgaria proved himself far shrewder and cleverer than anyone had imagined. Ferdinand did not attempt to conciliate conflicting interests. He meant all along to snatch Bulgaria from Russian influence, but he proceeded to do so in quite a different manner from that of Alexander of Battenberg, perhaps because that whereas the latter had simply been given hints as to what would be profitable for him to do, his successor had received complete instructions as to the course of conduct likely to prove advantageous to him.

The underground policy which Ferdinand of Coburg inaugurated from the very first day he set foot on Bulgarian soil had not escaped the notice of the Russian Government, and the Tsar Alexander III. conceived suspicions that the action of the Berlin Cabinet in regard to the Bulgarian question was not free from double dealing.

He had, indeed, allowed some of his suspicions to become known, to the surprise of Prince Bismarck, who, so far, had not been informed by Holstein of the details of the latter's conversations at Bologna with the Princess Clementine of Orleans-Coburg. The Chancellor protested his good faith, and became very angry when he perceived that this was doubted. At that time he had not realised the formidable trump card which Ferdinand I. would prove in the difficult game which he was playing. Or rather which Holstein was playing together with him, as, for reasons of his own, the latter had thought it advisable to let matters take their course a little longer in order to bring them to a climax, after which there would be no drawing back for anyone.

The first thing for Germany to do, in view of this distrust of the Tsar, was to lull his suspicions by proving to him that Germany was an innocent lamb, unjustly calumniated by its enemies in general, and by France in particular. Holstein calculated that if once Alexander III. became convinced that someone had wanted to make him quarrel with the German Government, by false representations to the latter's intentions, he would no longer be easily led to fear that his plans in regard to the Near East might meet with a check or a rebuff.

It was known that the Russian Sovereign had set his heart on the reinstatement of the regime in Bulgaria prior to the reign of Prince Alexander, and that he considered the election of Prince Ferdinand in the light of a personal affront. Any intriguer, therefore, who designed to spoil the good relations between Russia and Germany would at once turn his attention to that Bulgarian question, which was in all respects like a barrel of gunpowder in the midst of the general European situation. If persuaded that he had been led astray by misrepresentations the Tsar would be the first to take in a friendly clasp the hand of the people who had been calumniated to him. Baron von Holstein therefore embarked upon another complicated intrigue, the development of which was to provoke a nine days' wonder all over Europe.

He had agents scattered everywhere, especially in France, where Baron Mohrenheim, who at that time was Russian Ambassador in Paris, was working with great perseverance towards the conclusion of a Franco-Russian alliance. Mohrenheim, most unfortunately, had been accused of dabbling in financial speculations which he would have done better to avoid, considering his official position. It is not for me to say whether the accusations were justified or not. The fact remains that they had been common talk not only in the Paris Press and in Parisian political circles, but also abroad. It may be that he was not sufficiently prudent in his relations with financial personages, who afterwards boasted quite openly of having advised him in regard to certain Stock Exchange operations, absolutely honest and correct in themselves, but which, of course, were supposed to have been based on information which he had been enabled to obtain through his official position.

The Baron was a diplomat of the old school, with most polite manners and a considerable experience of Foreign Office routine. He was a *persona grata* at the Russian Court owing to a long sojourn at Copenhagen, where he had been admitted into the inner circle of the Royal family, and had known the present Dowager Empress of Russia when she was still a girl.

Mohrenheim relied far too much on the secret police service which the Russian Government had established in Paris. Certain of these agents were afterwards discovered to be in the pay of the German Government, a fact of which the Russian authorities were blissfully ignorant, and which had a great deal to do with many of the complications that subsequently arose when the Franco-Russian alliance came to be seriously discussed. One of these agents one day brought to Baron Mohrenheim certain documents relating to the Bulgarian question, among others the copy of a so-called dispatch of Prince Reuss, the German Ambassador at Vienna, to Prince Ferdinand of Coburg, which, if it had been a genuine document, would have established beyond doubt the complicity of the Berlin Cabinet in the anti-Russian movement which was becoming every day more and more pronounced.

The very style of composition should have put the

Russian Ambassador upon his guard against this document, for his diplomatic experience ought to have made him detect certain expressions in it of which no *homme de métier* would have made use. In his delight, however, at having at length in his hands proof of the German intrigues at Sofia, about which he had more than once spoken with his chiefs, and which, as he hoped and believed, would definitely incline the Tsar towards adopting this plan of an understanding with the French Government, he failed to do so. He dispatched the precious documents for which, needless to say, he had paid a very handsome price, by special messenger to the Princess Waldemar of Denmark (née Princess Marie of Orleans), the sister-in-law of Alexander III., with whom she was a great favourite, with the request that she would find a favourable moment to lay them before the Tsar.

The Princess was completely deceived by the communication of Baron Mohrenheim, and she took the first opportunity that presented itself to execute the commission he had begged her to undertake. The famous letters were shown to the Russian Sovereign, and aroused his ire to such a degree that the interview which had been arranged between him and the old Emperor William I. at Stettin was immediately cancelled. This caused an enormous sensation in Germany and considerably surprised Prince Bismarck, who had given himself a great deal of trouble to bring it about, the more so that he considered it in the light of a great event, the importance of which was further enhanced by the peculiar circumstances of the hour. The Crown Prince Frederick William was already suffering from the cancer to which he succumbed a few months later, whilst his father's age pointed to the probability of a change that would soon bring about drastic modifications in German political life. It was essential that cordial relations should be established between Alexander III. and the future German Emperor, and Bismarck was doing all he could think likely to secure them. It was, therefore, a matter of great mortification to him to find that at the eleventh hour all his work had come to nothing, and that the Tsar for some flimsy reason had excused himself from meeting his great-uncle. Strenuous efforts were made to clear the horizon, in which it is said that the then Prince of Wales took part, Bismarck having appealed to him to try to put an end to the evident misunderstanding which had arisen. At last the Tsar was persuaded to take Berlin on his way home from Copenhagen, where he had stayed rather longer than usual owing to illness in the family circle. It was not an easy matter; indeed, it was only upon the representations of the then Queen of Denmark that, if he evaded staying for a few hours in Berlin, it would create a sort of scandal which would be doubly regrettable in presence of the misfortunes that had fallen on the German Imperial family through the hopeless illness of the Crown Prince. This personal argument decided him at last to pay his respects to his aged grand-uncle.

When the matter had been settled, and then only, did Baron von Holstein seek the Chancellor and tell him what he had done. The first feeling of Bismarck was one of intense rage, then he very quickly saw the capital which could be made out of the devilish invention of his confederate, and quietly, and even with a certain satisfaction, awaited the arrival of Alexander III. in Berlin.

The latter, of course, received the formidable Minister

a few hours after he had reached the German capital. The interview took place at the Russian Embassy, and the first thing which the Tsar did was to take out of his pocket the famous letters that Mohrenheim had sent to him and to show them to his visitor with the quiet request for an explanation. Bismarck glanced at the papers, and then just as quietly declared them to be forgeries, perpetrated for the evident purpose of disturbing the long friendship which had united the Romanoffs and the Hohenzollerns. The explanation which followed completely justified the anticipations of Baron von Holstein, and the Emperor of Russia was convinced that he had been fooled by a handful of intriguers. When he left Berlin he was not, perhaps, quite convinced of the sincerity of the assurances of friendship which had been lavished upon him, but he had been effectively persuaded that Prince Reuss had never written the incriminating letter supposed to have been addressed to Prince Ferdinand of Coburg.

Once more matters seemed to readjust themselves between Berlin and Petersburg. There were some people, however, who, though they were convinced that Baron Mohrenheim had fallen a victim of a clumsy though successful plot, did not believe in the denials which Bismarck had made with such pathos, and remained certain that he was continuing at Sofia, with more caution, perhaps, and also with more luck, the game he had been playing when Prince Alexander of Battenberg was there. It was quite evident to those who knew him that he would continue to foment anti-Russian intrigues in Bulgaria, if only because it was in his interest always to keep an open door in the emergency of some new complication in regard to the Balkan

Peninsula. He had not concluded in vain the Treaty of alliance which bound his country with Austria, and it was more than likely that, sooner or later, he would seize an opportunity of provoking a conflict between the latter Power and Russia, of which the Eastern Question would furnish the excuse.

In view of this inevitable solution to the ever-increasing Balkan difficulties it was necessary for Russia that she also should have some strong allies on whom she could rely for help at a given moment. Therefore a closer union between her and France became absolutely indispensable. The great difficulty was to bring it about, in view of the fact that M. de Giers, then in charge of the Foreign Office in Petersburg, had decidedly strong pro-German leanings, and had been working sedulously towards the establishment of better relations between the Russian and the German Courts, whilst everything relative to the French Republic was decidedly taboo to him, his strong monarchical convictions making him hate everything connected with demagogy, no matter in what shape or form.

Now I come to the incident to which I referred at the beginning of this chapter, asking indulgence for introducing the personal element in it which, unfortunately, I cannot avoid.

Among those in France who had been most ardently predisposed in favour of a Franco-Russian alliance was the famous Madame Juliette Adam, whose salon in Paris was such a great political centre during the years which followed immediately upon the establishment of the Republic. Madame Adam was a woman of genius, whose conceptions were always sound and earnest, and whose views were far wider and far broader than those of

many of the reputed statesmen of her time. She was
a great friend of mine, and we had often discussed this
question of an alliance between our two countries as
the only means to check Teuton ambitions. Madame
Adam had acquaintances among the Orleanist party,
and in particular among the small circle of people who
lived in the intimacy of the Princess Clementine of
Coburg, the mother of Prince Ferdinand of Bulgaria,
and she had learned through them several things which
had corroborated my suspicions engendered by my conversation with Prince Alexander of Battenberg, and on
the confidences which Baron von Holstein had made to
my friend, and which the latter had repeated to me.
We would both have liked to prove that the famous
forged dispatches had been sent by an agent of the Baron
to Mohrenheim, but this, of course, was not possible
on the information we possessed. At length, however,
Madame Adam became possessed of certain papers, not
forgeries this time, which established clearly the double
game played by Bismarck all through the years which
had elapsed since the Congress of Berlin. The almost
insurmountable difficulty then presented itself of bringing them under the eyes of the Tsar. It was most
essential, in view of the changes about to take place in
Germany, and of the well known aggressive feelings of
the young man who would take his grandfather's place
on the throne of the Hohenzollerns, to put Alexander III.
upon his guard by making him acquainted with the
papers which had come into the possession of Madame
Adam. At that time—it was in April, 1888—I was
staying in Petersburg, whither I had been called by my
father's last illness. Madame Adam wrote to me asking
whether I could find a way of getting the papers to the

Tsar. I discussed the matter with my old friend Count Ignatieff, but he was not in favour with his Sovereign, and any attempt he might have made in that direction would certainly not have been well received. In the meanwhile Madame Adam had sent the papers to Petersburg through a lady whose name is rather well known, the beautiful Miss Maud Gonne. She brought part of them to me, whilst others were sent by a French Deputy, M. Lucien Millevoye, who, unfortunately, did not display in this affair the tact he might have done, as will presently be shown. I read the papers, and found them conclusive in their evidence. They consisted mostly of correspondence exchanged between Prince Ferdinand of Coburg and German agents. But the difficulty remained as to what could be done with them. I at last had the inspiration of taking them to M. Pobedonostseff, at that time Procurator of the Holy Synod, and perhaps the most influential man in Russia, and of asking him what he thought about them, and whether he would be disposed to help us in the matter. M. Pobedonostseff read the documents, and immediately told me that he would himself lay them before the Emperor.

The awkward part of the story was to follow. Pobedonostseff wished to see M. Lucien Millevoye. I did not know at the time that he was an active partisan of General Boulanger, then at the height of his glory and fame, and that, in accepting the mission with which Madame Adam had entrusted him, he had pursued another aim about which he had told her nothing, because if he had she would certainly have chosen another messenger. He had come to Petersburg with certain propositions emanating from the General himself, which he developed to M. Pobedonostseff, thereby raising the latter's suspicions and fears of becoming entangled in an intrigue which was hopeless from the very outset. It was this fact which prevented M. Millevoye from seeing the Emperor, which he would surely have done under different circumstances. Later on M. de Giers came to see me at the Hôtel d'Europe where I was staying, and we had a long conversation concerning the papers which had been transmitted to the Tsar, about which he was very interested, whilst wondering how they had reached the hands of Madame Adam.

I have related the story exactly as it occurred, and would not have done so had it not been that almost all the personages concerned in it are alive, and that Juliette Adam, Miss Maud Gonne, and Lucien Millevoye can all three of them testify that the incident took place exactly as I have narrated it. Whether it had anything to do with the sending of the Russian fleet to Toulon, the visit of the French fleet to Cronstadt, and the subsequent understanding between the Republic and the Tsar's Government it is impossible for me to say or to express an opinion upon, but it is a fact that after the documents sent to me by Madame Adam were placed in the possession of the Procurator, the Franco-Russian relations improved until they ripened into the alliance which Great Britain joined for the general benefit of all the parties concerned.

Looking back upon the only political intrigue in which I have ever taken part, I cannot regret the share I had in it, feeling convinced that I rendered a service to my country and to the cause of civilisation in general by helping to denounce the undercurrent of German politics.

The curious side to this story can be found in the

Memoirs of Hohenlohe (which always help one to understand the complicated political system followed by, Bismarck and the secret service machinery organised by Baron von Holstein). On May 25th, 1888, during the last days of the life of the Emperor Frederick, and a few weeks after Madame Adam had sent the letters to Petersburg, the Prince refers to a conversation which he had on that same day with the then Crown Prince and present German Emperor, during which the latter mentioned the forged documents sent to Alexander III. at Copenhagen, and added that they had been fabricated by Mohrenheim and Ignatieff. The latter, who disliked Mohrenheim, had most certainly nothing to do with the papers that Baron von Holstein had caused to be transmitted to the Russian Ambassador in Paris, but, as I have related, he had been involved through my having consulted him in the matter of the papers brought to Russia by the friends of Madame Adam. It is probable that one or other of the innumerable secret agents of the Intelligence Bureau of the Wilhelmstrasse had an inkling that something had been going on in which Ignatieff had been concerned, and in the reports which had been made to the then Crown Prince by Bismarck the names of the two statesmen had been mixed up intentionally, probably in order to represent as a Panslavist intrigue the two distinct incidents of the false and genuine documents which had reached Alexander III.

CHAPTER XXIII

Behind the Veil of Intrigue

IT was in the course of the year 1887, when Prince Ferdinand of Coburg was elected to the Bulgarian throne, that German intrigues in the Balkans began to assume a more active form. By that time the old Emperor William, whose ninetieth year had struck, had ceased to be more than a figurehead in the government of the German Empire. His son and successor was struggling against the attacks of the disease to which he was to succumb a few months after his father's death. Prince William of Prussia, the Kaiser of to-day, was not yet able to assert himself as he would have liked to do. The eyes of Europe turned, therefore, to Germany in anxiety as to what would be its course in the near future. Bismarck was directing affairs, but no longer the Bismarck of 1866 and 1870. The ponderous, clever politician had given place to an irritable, nervous old man, with an autocratic temper which he did not even attempt to restrain, and a tyrannical disposition from which not only his immediate subordinates, but also perfect strangers who displeased him suffered. He had fallen under the influence of Baron von Holstein, who was now the real master of the situation. People abroad were so obsessed with the great central figure of Bismarck that they failed to observe that this redoubtable personage had, in the course of time, reduced politics to a personal equation. It is an undeniable fact that towards the end of his career the German Chancellor became a tyrant; that the only matter which engrossed his attention was the success of his own schemes, independent of everything else. At times, it is true, he still showed himself interested in big questions of State, and to the end he was concerned over the possible danger of a Franco-Russian alliance; but the great thing which absorbed his attention, to the detriment of everything else, was the continuance of his own tyrannical sway, not only on the politics of Germany, but also on German society, on the Press, and even on the members of the reigning dynasty. For many years he had at regular intervals played with the weapon of his resignation, with which he had threatened the old Emperor whenever he was crossed or some objection raised to something which he had proposed, certain that this would bring his aged Master to what he called " reason," and make him yield to his Minister even at the expense of his personal feelings and opinions. But after the illness of the heir to the throne had assumed a threatening aspect Bismarck no longer spoke of retiring from the position he had occupied for so long a time; but, on the contrary, he applied himself to win the good graces of the young Prince who, in all probability, would soon occupy the throne of his grandfather, and thus secure for himself a longer tenure of power. He feared more than ever any adverse influences that might represent him as having outlived his time.

It was this dread of having to resign that, more than anything else, induced him to foment trouble abroad, which he imagined and expected would require his presence at the head of affairs so imperatively that even a new Sovereign anxious to rule alone would not find courage to dispense with his services. He professed to be nervous in regard to French "intrigues" in Alsace-Lorraine. They only existed in his imagination, but he persisted in representing them as fraught with terrible peril for the security of the German Empire. His irritability, too, increased in a remarkable degree, and to this Holstein contributed by the continual tales which he used to bring him of the sayings and doings of people whom he considered, rightly or wrongly, as his enemies, and who on their part were imprudent enough not to hide their feelings towards him. Such, for instance, was the case with the Empress Augusta, who, generally so dignified in all her actions, lost her equanimity wherever the Chancellor was concerned, and showed her want of tact by speaking openly of his many peculiarities. This, of course, was immediately reported to Bismarck, very often by the people with whom she had conversed. A case in point was when she received the then French Minister for Foreign Affairs, M. Waddington, and asked him, when he went to Berlin in 1878 as a member of the Congress, whether Bismarck had been in a good temper, adding that when he had "nerves" he was simply impossible. The Chancellor immediately became acquainted with these remarks of the Empress and was infuriated, this time it must be confessed not without reason, for Augusta certainly would have done better not to have spoken about her husband's Prime Minister with a member of the French Cabinet. She always called Bismarck "*le grand homme*" when she had occasion to mention him.

An interesting incident relative to this once occurred in my presence. It was on one of the rare occasions when the Chancellor had condescended to attend a festivity of some kind or other at the Imperial Palace. A lady, who was rather well known for her sharp tongue, was talking with a foreign diplomat when the Chancellor suddenly entered the room by a door which was close to the spot where they stood. The diplomat, who, it must be remarked, was a *persona grata* with the Empress, observed to his companion *sotto voce*, "Here comes the great man." Bismarck overheard the remark and walked furiously up to the culprit and asked him, "Of whom are you speaking? Are the words 'great man' to be considered as applying to myself? If so, I must tell you that I think it most unseemly for a foreign diplomat to make fun of the Foreign Minister of the Court to which he is accredited." The unfortunate young man on being thus snubbed in public nearly collapsed. The lady, however, did not in the least lose her presence of mind, but, turning to Bismarck, coolly said, "The words which you have overheard, Prince, could not by any possibility apply to yourself, because no really great man could have behaved as you have just done." For once the Chancellor was nonplussed, but if he could have killed the woman who had administered this well-deserved rebuff there is no doubt that he would have done so with the greatest of pleasure.

Women in general were braver than men with Prince Bismarck, perhaps because they felt safer from punishment, in which they were vastly mistaken, for the Chancellor could be just as ferocious with the fair sex as he invariably was with men. He was far too much of a Prussian ever to be merciful, and in his adversaries he saw only the enemy to be destroyed and not spared, even occasionally as a matter of policy, such as after Sadowa had led him to oppose the General Staff and

King William I. when they insisted on marching upon
Vienna.

Baron von Holstein, who was more closely acquainted
with the temperament of the Chancellor than anyone
else, played upon this side of it with all the skill of which
he was capable, and often, indeed, took advantage of it
when he had a personal score to wipe off. Holstein was a
perfect artist in all matters of revenge, and the manner
in which he handled the Press, for instance, was absolutely marvellous. It was not in vain that this Press—
the principal organs of which were the semi-Govern-
mental *Post*, the *Gazette* of Cologne, and a few other
papers entirely devoted to the interests of the Government, from whom they received most generous sub-
ventions—was called the " Reptile Press," because
anything more venomous than the articles which Holstein inspired has never been known in the annals of
journalism. His manner of working in this direction was
in this wise. The editors of most of the principal organs
of the German Press, or their representatives in Berlin,
generally visited the Foreign Office every morning in
search of news. The Baron always received them in the
most amiable manner possible. He would talk with
them about the weather and then proceed to refer to
politics, in general touching upon different subjects
which, he remarked, might be considered from different
points of view. Whenever any political complication
was looming on the horizon, he generally represented it
as being of no importance, but added that there might
be some patriotic men who would judge them in such
and such a manner, which, of course, might or might
not be the correct one. This, as a rule, was sufficient,
and the people to whom he addressed himself took the

hint, and the next morning, or a few days later, one could read a virulent attack on the political party or the foreign country whose doings had been thus brought to the attention of the Press by Holstein. In the rare cases when they had not understood what he had meant to convey to them a swift punishment overtook the papers to which they belonged by a loss of advertisements which threatened their very existence, for, as a rule, these were covered by the secret funds at the disposal of the Baron, who was far too shrewd to pay in cash or an official subvention the services he demanded from the Press. He was essentially *un homme de façade,* and wanted to be able to deny with an apparently clear conscience any accusation of inspiring the Bismarckian newspapers. When these did their duty they were overwhelmed with advertisements from all kinds of small trading concerns, who seemed to have an unlimited amount of money at their disposal wherewith to announce the excellence of their wares, which, nevertheless, they sold but scantily. This stream of prosperity flowed steadily until transgression occurred of certain unwritten laws as severe and unbending as those of the Medes and Persians, when it suddenly ran dry, and was cut off until such time as it pleased the great Manitou of the Wilhelmstrasse, Baron von Holstein, to renew it.

Now this Press had become more and more aggressive in tone as time had passed, encouraged doubtless by Bismarck's rabid anti-French and anti-Russian attitude. The Chancellor propounded a series of measures, totally unjustified, destined to add to the already unenviable lot of the inhabitants of Alsace-Lorraine, among the principal of which was the question of passports, which he contrived to make the unfortunate Emperor Frederick

EMPEROR FREDERICK III

III. endorse, much against the latter's will, and which
Prince Hohenlohe tried in vain to oppose. The Chancellor seemed determined to excite the anger of France
by every means in his power, and to sow distrust in its
mind against Germany. The rapidly approaching end
of the Emperor, and the grave condition of Frederick,
were but minor considerations to which his mind gave
no attention. His sole desire was to bring matters to a
climax in regard to foreign politics, so as to be enabled
to strike a blow strong enough to shatter for ever that
troublesome fear of a coalition of Europe against the
German Empire.

It is curious and very significant of the state of moral
unscrupulousness which the efforts of the Chancellor had
succeeded in imposing not only upon his country, but
in a certain sense upon the whole of Europe, that the
people in whom he had the greatest confidence, such as
the Baron von Holstein and the banker Bleichroder, were
those whom he had made the most impatient, and who
judged him the most severely The latter—who was
supposed to be more than anyone else in Berlin in " the
secret of the gods "—after the death of William I. and
during the short reign of his unfortunate successor, spoke
quite openly of Bismarck's political vagaries, and owned to
Hohenlohe during a conversation on May 26th, 1888,
that he no longer understood the policy that was being
carried on at the Wilhelmstrasse. He could not see why
France was continually being threatened when she had
the unanimous desire to live on good terms with Germany. The same remark could be applied to Russia.
There the continual unpleasantnesses had the result of
depreciating the value of the rouble, thus allowing Russia
to send her goods to Germany with considerable profit.

U

As soon as the rouble increased in value, then Russia would have no advantage whatever in exporting her produce.

Bleichroder was of opinion that Bismarck wished at all costs to remain in power and to secure himself with the future Emperor, at that time still the Crown Prince William. There had been a time when he had told the Crown Prince that he would stay at his side only on condition that war should not be declared on any nation, but at present, remarked Bleichroder, he would do so even at the cost of a European war. His continuous efforts to provoke a conflict with France were nothing but a concession to the warlike proclivities of the future Emperor and of his military advisers.

Herbert Bismarck, too, had a good deal to do with the aggressive tendencies which has father displayed. The old Prince, in spite of his mercilessness and utter unscrupulousness, had one soft spot in his iron character, and that was love for his eldest son, whose defects he never perceived, and whom he would have liked to become his successor. The Grand Duke of Baden's remark, when the Emperor William II. dismissed his grandfather's adviser and great Minister, that the question was one as to which dynasty should govern the German Empire—that of the Hohenzollerns or of the Bismarcks, was not such a paradox as it seems at first sight. It is certain that Herbert believed himself to be capable of continuing the work of his father, and that the latter, in his blind affection for his son, was convinced of it. There was a time when Herbert exercised a considerable influence over the mind of the present Emperor. This was during the last winter of the life of William I., when it was still a question as to who should die first: the aged

Sovereign bowed down with the weight of his ninety-one years, or his son smitten by a disease for which no science has so far found a remedy. Herbert Bismarck toadied to William, the heir to the Crown of United Germany, tried to ingratiate himself into his favour by appealing to his worst instincts and by flattering the most distressing defects of his character.

The Chancellor, whose experience of mankind and of the human heart ought to have rendered him more sceptical, was entirely deceived as to the real character of the young man in whom he had hoped to find a submissive instrument of his own will and schemes. William II. had seemed to be as wax in the powerful hands of Bismarck and his son Herbert, who especially had deluded himself into the firm conviction that his future Sovereign would simply place into the hands of the Bismarck family all the burden which fate had laid upon his shoulders, contenting himself with the pomp and advantages of his exalted position, not troubling as to what would happen to his realm.

This was the more surprising in view of the fact that, so far back as the year of his marriage with the Princess Augusta Victoria of Schleswig-Holstein, Prince William had acquired the reputation of being a young man absolutely devoid of scruples, and who, to quote the words of Prince von Hohenlohe, was always in conflict with his father and feared by his own mother. This might have given Bismarck good grounds for going carefully with him, but he fully believed himself capable of retaining absolute control of the youth by impressing him with the sense of his own importance, thus thinking to ensure his sway. The calculation proved an entirely erroneous one, but this was to take Bismarck some time to discover.

In the meantime the Chancellor was steadily working towards the furthering of his ambitious plans in relation to the European political situation generally. He, who had declared that he would not sacrifice the bones of a single Prussian grenadier on the altar of the Eastern Question, was beginning that interference in Turkish and Balkan affairs which Germany continued to exercise for so many years. As far back as 1880—that is, at the time when he still hoped that Prince Alexander of Battenberg would be able to maintain himself at Sofia—Bismarck had secured for Germany a predominant position at Constantinople by inducing the Sultan to entrust to German officers the education of his troops. This had intensely displeased the then Crown Prince, Frederick William, who feared that their presence in Turkey might lead to their services being employed against the signatory Powers of the Treaty of Berlin in the Balkan Peninsula, and he had requested Hohenlohe, then Ambassador in Paris, who was about to go to Varzin on one of his periodic visits to Bismarck, to acquaint the latter with his apprehensions on the subject. The Prince immediately replied that he could not share them in the very least, and, on the contrary, that he considered the dispatch of this military mission as likely to prove of great advantage to the interests of the German Empire. For one thing, it would give the officers sent to Constantinople an opportunity to prove what they were really worth, and it would also enable the German Foreign Office to obtain trustworthy reports as to what was going on in Turkey, which it would be quite impossible to obtain otherwise. Then again, the influence Germany would thus acquire in Turkey might prove of inestimable value later on. The question as to what Turkey would do with these officers, and whether their going there would be acceptable or pleasant to the other European Powers, ought not to influence Germany in the very least, because its policy had but one aim—the furtherance of German interests. It might, one day, be of advantage to Germany to have Turkey as a friend, and while Turkey could never become dangerous for Germany, circumstances might very easily occur when her enemies would also be those of Germany, and this contingency ought never to be lost sight of in any plans one might make for the future. History, indeed, has proved the importance, in European politics, of the Near East.

My friend once asked Holstein why he did not try to smooth down the difficulties in regard to Bismarck, and induce him to look at things and people with less antagonism and more indulgence. "Why should I do so?" retorted the Baron. "Things cannot go on as they are. So long as the Emperor is alive it is easy for Bismarck to do what he likes; but do you really suppose that a young man impatient to reign and to have his own way in everything will resign himself to be a mere puppet in the hands of his Prime Minister? And do you seriously think that Bismarck will ever agree to consult someone else after twenty-five years of uninterrupted power, especially when that one is a mere child in experience? No! a rupture is almost unavoidable, and Bismarck will not triumph. It is therefore far better to make the inevitable more acceptable to public opinion than it would be otherwise, by allowing the world to see that Bismarck has become unbearable. The more general this knowledge, the easier it will be for the Emperor to dispense with his services. It will have to come to that, whether he likes it or not; I always submit to inevitable facts, and only try to tone down as much as possible their unpleasantness."

"But *you* mean to stick to your guns, no matter what happens?" inquired my friend.

"Most certainly," was Holstein's emphatic reply, given with that enigmatical smile of his that meant so much or so little.

"You see, my dear friend," he went on after a few moments' silence, "Bismarck has outlived himself. He has had the rare luck to bring to a finish the work he had set himself to perform, and it would have been infinitely better for his reputation in history if he had died immediately after the German Empire had become a reality. In the eighteen years which have passed since the French war he has made the mistake of thinking that a nation can be governed in the same way in peace as in war. He may impose his opinions on his audience ,while he is addressing them, but the convictions of his hearers fade as reason takes the place of enthusiasm. And then he clings too much to office, not on his own account, but for the sake of his son. Without Herbert the Prince would have been endurable, but Herbert has contrived to shake his father's power. Whenever he wishes to do something on his own initiative, Herbert interferes, not only because he fails to understand, but because the plans do not suit his own mercenary views. You can have no idea of the kind of buying and selling and speculation which goes on here," and Holstein waved his hand in the direction of the room sacred to the Under-Secretary of State   "He studies far more the daily quotations of the various Stock Exchanges of the world than the map of Europe. All he cares for is money, and he would not hesitate for one single instant to plunge his country in the throes of war if he could by doing so add to his ill-gotten millions. Bleichroder could tell you many a story I should not care to repeat. Only remember that the *raison d'être* of the newspaper campaign which is started now and then without any apparent cause is generally to be found in the fact that the younger Bismarck's account is overloaded with some stock or other which he desires to get rid of. Bleichroder himself has been making too much money owing to the close touch in which he stood to our Foreign Office to say anything, but he is beginning to get tired of this kind of thing, besides being far too shrewd not to know that the moment the old Emperor closes his eyes there will be found plenty of people to acquaint his successor with what is going on in the Bismarck family circle. And then . . . then . . . there will be the devil to pay. For the present Prince William requires the help of Bismarck because he is frightened at the thought of what his position will be when his father ascends the throne, even if he occupies it but for a short time. But when he is the master I doubt whether he will consent to be treated like a child by his Prime Minister, or rather by the latter's son, because this is what it amounts to. The Chancellor thinks that he can make his place hereditary in his family," added Holstein, who thus anticipated the words which the Grand Duke of Baden was to use later on—"and you surely cannot think that an enterprising and energetic Sovereign will ever consent to such a dynasty rivalling his own?"

My friend listened aghast to this declaration of a man whom he had always known to be unscrupulous, but whom he had believed to be at least grateful to the statesman to whom he owed his career. Holstein,

however, in his own way, was just as eager for power as Bismarck, but in justice to him it must be said he was not greedy from the monetary point of view. He loved intrigue far better than money, and the only thing which might have affected him would have been the thought of having to retire into private life with his chief. His efforts were therefore directed to the task of impressing all those on whose good will he directly or indirectly depended that he had nothing to do with certain actions of his great chief.

The death of William I. would sound the knell of the omnipotence exercised by his Chancellor. This outburst on the part of Holstein explains the aggressiveness of the German Press, and why the widespread opinion that another war was imminent was not denied by the Secretary of State. In 1887 war was in the thoughts of everybody, and was even wished for by a good many. The military party clamoured for it because it believed that the spirit of the German Army required to be maintained, and that could only be done by active service. The nation was in favour of it because it was beginning to feel the burden of the terrific and ever-increasing armaments. The Socialists looked upon it as a sad necessity, but hoped that certain reforms which they claimed would have a better chance afterwards. The Emperor's grandson was most eager for it, as his ambitions led him to envy the reputation and the laurels of Frederick the Great, to whom some of his flatterers and admirers had compared him. Financial people saw in a war the means to extend their influence. Herbert Bismarck looked forward to it as the possibility to make milliards of the millions which he had already amassed. The only persons who were against it, and who would never have allowed it to break out had they been spared, were the aged Sovereign and his son. Both of them were about to die, and in disappearing to leave a free field to the activity of their successor. Unfortunately for the peace of the world, William II. was to take up anew the sword which he had snatched out of Bismarck's hand, and to continue the policy of lies, deceit, unscrupulousness and ruthless cruelty.

Part IV

William II. in Power

CHAPTER XXIV

Last Days and First Days

JANUARY 1st, 1888, was the first day of a year which was to bring about a complete change not only in the history of Germany, but also in that of Prince Bismarck. Had circumstances been different, and the Emperor Frederick III. still been a strong and healthy man, the Chancellor would not have felt any misgivings as to what would happen after the death of William I. In spite of the difference in views which had existed between the Crown Prince and his father's Minister, yet the relations of the two men had remained cordial, and the former was far too conscious of all that his dynasty owed to the latter. The heir to the German throne, like all the Hohenzollerns, was grateful by nature, and his Imperialist ideas and tendencies had been gratified by the energy with which the Chancellor had worked towards the building of this new Empire, for which he cared more, perhaps, than for the old Prussia that had been the cradle of his race, different in this from William I., who was far prouder of his title of King of the old Realm to which he had succeeded than of that of Emperor. Both Frederick and the Crown Princess were fully conscious of the fact that the small kingdom which had been looked upon with scorn by so many people had become a great and powerful monarchy, and that it was to Bismarck it had owed this transformation.

Frederick William, therefore, had quite made up his

317

mind that though he would not obey his Prime Minister
blindly he would not part from him when he ascended
the throne, and he had told Bismarck so more than
once.   The great statesman did not, in consequence,
feel any anxiety at the idea of a change of reign.   Ever
since the war of 1870 with France the future Emperor
Frederick had nursed one great idea, and that was to
try to bring about a general if not total disarmament,
or, at least, a considerable reduction in the military forces
of Europe.   Had a longer life been granted to him, it
is probable that he would have attempted it together
with Nicholas II. of Russia, who took the same initiative
during the first years of his reign, and most probably
the combined efforts of these two Sovereigns might have
brought about such a result and allowed the influence
of the Hague Conference to be something more than
it is.   Bismarck knew very well that the Crown Prince
had got an idea of the kind, but he did not view it with
such an antagonism as might have been supposed.   He
was far too clever not to realise that it would be impossible in the long run to go on increasing the armaments
of the whole of Europe on the scale that had been done
for years without its culminating one day in a catastrophe
such as the world had never yet seen, which might compromise, and perhaps even destroy, the great work it
had taken the best years of his life to accomplish.   Before
things came to such a pass an effort might well be made
to try to stem the torrent, which otherwise might sweep
everything down before it, and to do something to compel
the world to put an end to the ever-increasing spirit of
militarism which was fast becoming a formidable danger
to the whole of humanity.   Bismarck, indeed, though he
showed himself so warlike during the last years of his

administration, once told Baron von Holstein that it might have been desirable to enter into the peaceful schemes of the Emperor Frederick had the latter lived. But whilst the old Emperor had been at the head of the State the army always remained the first consideration. His grandson shared his opinions on that subject, and added to them the impetuosity and impatience of youth, on account of which Bismarck would have preferred that the course of nature should prevent William II. from ascending the throne for a few years longer. But when circumstances had shown that his inheritance was only a question of months, the Chancellor had immediately applied himself to the task of trying to assume the direction of the younger William's mind, a thing that was easier said than done, considering the character of the young Prince.

All this worried Bismarck, and, indeed, had worried him for a longer time than people had guessed or suspected. Brutal as he was, he had sometimes exclaimed that the old Emperor was outliving himself, and that it would have been better for the country if he had closed his eyes sooner than proved ultimately the case. The fact was that as Holstein told his friend and confidant, the Chancellor considered it would have been of advantage to the course of affairs in general if the Crown Prince Frederick had become Sovereign whilst his eldest son was still a boy, or at least relatively young enough to be kept in a position of complete subordination in regard to his parents. Bismarck knew that Frederick William would not interfere with him; he did not feel quite so certain as to that point in regard to the son.

The relations between Prince William of Prussia and Bismarck were not at all so intimate as people imagined.

It had been in the interest of both of them to foster among the public the opinion that they looked up to one another, and were determined always to act in perfect accord. But the Prince, who all through his life had played a double game, had only flattered Bismarck, and tried to insinuate himself into his good graces and favour, because he required to have somebody on his side on whom he could rely in the difficult months which would follow on the demise of the old Emperor. That that period would need much skill to negotiate the grandson of William I. did not doubt for an instant. But, at the same time, he fully meant to keep the independence of his own opinions, and never allow the Chancellor to forget with whom he had to deal. Bismarck, on his side, did not feel as enthusiastic concerning this pupil of his —the future William II. liked so to call himself—as he pretended was the case.

Notwithstanding these pretensions, there were some people who suspected that this great friendship, about which such fuss was being made, was nothing else but bluff. Prince Hohenlohe narrates in his Memoirs that when the news of the last illness of the old Emperor reached him at Strasburg he went to tell his secretary, Herr Heuduck. " I was sure until now that Prince William is entirely in accord with Bismarck," writes Hohenlohe, " but Heuduck, though he agreed with me in a general way, told me that there were some signs which pointed to the likelihood that the Prince, when once he became Emperor, would not be able long to bear with Bismarck. It seems that there exist some Conservative elements at enmity with Bismarck which might easily overturn him. This would be most unpleasant. Prince William, as it is, is not popular in Germany, and will have to be very careful if he wants to win public opinion to his side.''

According to Holstein, who differed in this from the generally accepted version, there occurred far fewer complications in the relations between the Emperor Frederick III. and Bismarck than is commonly supposed. In spite of the callousness of the latter, he felt sorry for the Sovereign stricken in the full strength of his manhood, and enduring with a patient and silent heroism the tortures of a lingering and most painful death, the inevitability of which he was fully aware. The most serious conflict of his short reign with the Chancellor occurred on the occasion of the prolongation of the term of the legislature in the Reichstag, as well as in the Prussian Landtag, from three years to five, that had already been decided before the death of William I.

Frederick did not care for it, but after his attention had been drawn by his Minister to the particular circumstances inherent to the German Constitution, which did not allow the Emperor the privilege of vetoing the decisions of the Reichstag, when they agreed with those of the Bundesrath, where he only possessed one voice as King of Prussia, he immediately granted the signature which was required from him. But in regard to the Prussian Landtag he inquired from Bismarck what was the point of view of the Prussian Constitution concerning his rights, and upon hearing that the King as well as each of the two Chambers was at liberty to accept or to refuse his sanction to any legislative Bill, he reserved his decision. A few days later, on May 27th, he sent back of his own accord to Bismarck the definite text of the Bill duly signed as well as approved by him.

The other cause of conflict, which, however, never

assumed the proportions accredited to it by the public, arose in consequence of the proposed betrothal of the Princess Victoria of Prussia with Prince Alexander of Battenberg after his relinquishment of the Bulgarian throne. The engagement had met with the sympathies of the Empress Frederick, who always favoured marriages of affection, and who was anxious for her daughter to make one. For years the young Princess had been in love with the handsome Prince Alexander, but so long as her grandfather had been alive the thing had been out of the question, as William I. was violently opposed to the idea. After his death, however, the Empress Victoria brought forward the question once more, and tried to push it through against her husband's better judgment. The Emperor Frederick was antagonistic to the scheme, first, because in his heart he did not think the Battenbergs good enough to marry a Princess of Prussia, and, secondly, he feared complications with Russia as a consequence of the marriage. His daughter's tears, however, shook his resolution, and he might even in time have been induced to consent if Bismarck had not appeared upon the scene. He tried to enlist on his side the sympathies of Queen Victoria, to whom he explained during the audience which she granted to him at Charlottenburg the various reasons which rendered such a marriage highly unacceptable for all concerned. Finally the thing fell through, after having caused much stir among the public.

It is an interesting and remarkable psychological sidelight upon the sentiments of Frederick III. that this incident did not affect the dying Emperor half so much as did the Puttkamer incident, which threw such a shade of trouble on the last days of his short reign.

This Puttkamer affair arose out of the interference of the Minister of that name in the elections, where he was over-zealous in pushing forward, by all kinds of devices, the governmental candidates, and to defeat those belonging to the Opposition parties. The Emperor was incensed, and wrote personally to von Puttkamer requesting him to hand over his resignation, which was done. Prince Bismarck, though he had provoked the conflict, as he had long wished to get rid of a colleague he had more than once found in his way, yet contrived, as the Empress Victoria reproached him with later on, to throw upon the dying Frederick all the odium of this dismissal, and he invited in a demonstrative manner the fallen Minister to dine with him a few days after the latter's resignation had become an accomplished fact.

This, however, did not affect the personal relations of Bismarck with Frederick III., though it is not to be disputed that it caused friction between him and the Empress Victoria. The two men remained friendly towards each other until the end, and perhaps Frederick was not sorry to know that he would leave after him, to moderate the ambitions and aggressiveness of his son, so experienced a politician and statesman.

The fact was that no one trusted the impetuous young man; but, at the same time, no one cared for Bismarck, who was fast making himself odious to everybody. His insolence, his overbearingness surpassed everything. And his son Herbert behaved, if possible, more outrageously than his father. He actually had the impertinence to say to the Prince of Wales (afterwards Edward VII.), who had come over to Potsdam for the funeral of his brother-in-law, that an Emperor deprived of speech ought never to have reigned. The Prince,

justly incensed at this remark, declared later on that if
it had not been for the circumstances that he did not
care to add to the difficulties of his sister's position, and
that he cared a good deal for the maintenance of good
relations between Great Britain and Germany, he
would have thrown the younger Bismarck out of the
window. As it was, Albert Edward added, it had only
been with great difficulty that he had restrained himself
from doing so.

One wonders sometimes whether, without his son,
Bismarck would have contrived to keep his position until
his death. Perhaps yes, perhaps no. It is, of course,
impossible to say; but it is quite certain that at the time
of the accession of William II. all those people who
were aware of the under-currents that were shaking the
equanimity of the Berlin Court were looking forward to
the day when the old giant would fall under the blows
dealt out to him by the hand of that much loved son.

A growing cause for European anxiety was the influence that the military party was gaining upon the
mind of the new Emperor William, and especially concerning the power that General von Waldersee was
exercising in that way through his wife. This lady was
related to the young Empress Augusta Victoria, who
was extremely fond of her and always ready to listen to
her advice. The astute Bleichröder was one of those who
followed with the most interest the events which were
going on around the young Monarch. He said to Hohenlohe that Waldersee was a personal enemy of Bismarck,
and that he had proved himself as being able to do anything in the world, no matter what, in order to obtain
what he wanted. He was quite capable of telling the
unexperienced and passionate Sovereign that he was

but a puppet in the hands of Bismarck, who alone governed Germany. With William I. such tales had had no effect, and he had merely smiled both at them and the people who had carried them to him, but with a young man this might be different. For this reason the Chancellor heartily wished Waldersee elsewhere. He added that the new Emperor would not begin a war of his own accord, but that if it broke out it would not be unwelcome to him.

The latter fact explains, perhaps, why Bismarck, in spite of all that one could tell to him, had adopted such a quarrelsome policy with his neighbours, and especially why he had suddenly inaugurated, against the better sense of everybody, including Prince Hohenlohe, the aggressive measures already referred to in regard to Alsace-Lorraine. Hohenlohe—who was Governor-General of the annexed provinces—consulted the Grand Duke of Baden on the subject, who advised him to yield rather than resign. The Grand Duke explained that it was necessary to react against the new Franco-Russian intrigue that, according to the information which he declared he had received from trustworthy sources, was being actively pushed forward, and the object of which was to induce France to occupy the Italian military harbour of Spezzia. This would naturally result in a Franco-Italian war, during which Germany would be prevented by Russia from interfering, and one of the aims of which was to bring about a restoration of the Pope's temporal power. This would hold Austria back and prevent her from marching to the help of Germany, and it would also considerably damp the enthusiasm of the German Catholics for their home government, a fact which caused much speculation both in Russia and in

France. According to Bismarck's knowledge things had
proceeded so far that the English Cabinet had become
alarmed, and instructed the Duke of Edinburgh to
bombard Toulon in case the French squadron occupied
Spezzia. When one reads to-day these stories, worthy
of Rinaldo Rinaldini, one wonders only how a serious
man like Hohenlohe could ever repeat or Bismarck
relate them, so absurd do they seem. Nevertheless,
Bismarck had recourse to tales of the same kind whenever
he had occasion to sow distrust in Germany against France
and Russia, not because he objected to them individually,
but because he was absolutely determined to prevent their
ever becoming allied with each other.

It is curious to watch the indecisions of the great
Bismarck during the first twelve months that followed
upon the demise of the Emperor Frederick. His splendid
assurance seemed to fail him, and he allowed himself to
be carried away by passion in political matters. Above
all things, he wanted to assume and keep control over
the young Emperor. Yet he did not hesitate to rebuke
him. Thus, for instance, when, after the death of
Frederick III., his son and successor had caused the
approaches of the New Palace in Potsdam, where the
unfortunate Sovereign had breathed his last, to be surrounded by troops and had prevented the widowed
Empress from coming out of her room into the garden
where she had wanted to gather roses to put on the bed
of her deceased husband, it had been Bismarck who had
protested against this gross insult offered to the unhappy
and broken-hearted Victoria. He reminded William II.
that it was not with impunity one ventured to offend a
Princess of Great Britain. His intervention proved
successful, because the guard was withdrawn, but the

manner in which it had been installed was calculated yet further to embitter the relations of the young Kaiser with his mother.

Personally, I do not believe for one moment the truth of the story related by Prince Radolin when he said that Bismarck had replied that he had no time to go and see the widowed Empress when the latter had asked to speak with him. Hard as he was, he would not have done such a thing, if only on account of the reason that he would have hoped by a personal interview with her to learn a few things which still were not quite clear to him concerning certain incidents that had taken place at San Remo.

Talking about San Remo reminds me of the scenes which were reported to have occurred there between the then German Crown Princess and her first-born son. Neither of them ever referred to them, but that scenes of some kind had taken place was pretty well known. Holstein, always on the look out for news, even tried the Princess's lady-in-waiting, the Countess Hedwig Bruhl, and paid her a long visit, under some pretext or other, to try to discover of what nature had been the painful explanations, the distressing sounds of which had shook the walls of the Villa Zirio. He, as well as Bismarck, would have liked to learn the exact truth, in which they both hoped to find weapons against the young Emperor in case he felt tempted to show the same independence of character in regard to his Prime Minister as he had manifested in questions where his father and mother were concerned. But Countess Bruhl either knew nothing or did not wish to say anything, and so Baron Holstein for once in his life was baffled in his curiosity.

Holstein was playing a curious double game at that period I am referring to. Whilst to all appearances he seemed to identify himself more than ever with the policy of his great chief, he tried in an underhand way to insinuate himself into the good graces of William II., to whom more than once he secretly communicated papers of importance before the Chancellor did so, thus allowing the Sovereign to form an idea as to their contents before being asked to give his decisions in regard to the proposals which they contained. He explained his conduct by the fear of irritating Bismarck, but the Emperor, not being a fool, understood very well what lay behind this excuse, and felt grateful to the Baron for his attention. Thus private relations established themselves between the Monarch and the astute director of the political department of the German Foreign Office. These relations, however, never became public, and did not survive the dismissal of Bismarck, as Holstein fondly believed they would.

Almost as soon as William II. ascended the throne the Chancellor wrote a private letter to the Tsar Alexander III. in which he referred to the dying words of the old Kaiser, and expressed the hope that the relations between Germany and Russia would remain as cordial in the future as they had been in the past. He added the significant remark that so far as he was concerned he would far rather retire from office than ever lend his hand to any estrangements between them, and in concluding, referred to the so-called French intrigues, the influence of which, he freely owned, might become dangerous. The excitable brain of his young Sovereign might conceivably lead him into rash actions which he would be the first to repent later on. The letter had remained unanswered, and Bismarck was particularly irritated at being passed over as a man whose communications were not of sufficient importance to merit acknowledgment.

At the same time the attention of the Prussian Foreign Office became more absorbed than it had ever been with everything that concerned the Near East. Bismarck declared that the next great European crisis would begin in that corner of the world, and perhaps also . . . end. A strong desire to develop German trade and industry in Bulgaria suddenly sprang into existence, and relations between the Berlin Cabinet and the Government of Prince Ferdinand became, somehow, an established thing, notwithstanding the fact that Germany had not then recognised him as Prince of Bulgaria. German capitalists also made themselves much at home at Constantinople, where Russia was losing ground every day.

Altogether the whole course of German policy was being diverted into an entirely new channel, one of its most curious features being that whilst the Emperor was becoming every day more rabidly Austrian in his sympathies, Bismarck, on the contrary, affected to have lost his trust in Austria after Andrassy's retirement, and made no secret of the fact that he hoped that when she would attack Russia it would be upon her own initiative, so that the *casus foederis* could not be applied by her to Germany. The Grand Duke of Baden even went so far as to say one day that Bismarck, after having preached war for so many years, suddenly affected to be all in favour of peace, and was making all kinds of advances to Russia, simultaneously with the appearance in the inspired Press of venomous articles against Austria,

Thus, the Grand Duke asserted, had Bismarck tried to bring confusion into the public mind in regard to foreign relations with Germany merely to satisfy his personal antipathies. There was a good deal of truth in the sarcasm of this comment. But, then, the Grand Duke had never cared for Bismarck, though in many things he had been one of the strongest supporters of his policy, partly out of necessity, and partly out of conviction. He had known too much of the secret intrigues of the Chancellor, and he had despised them with all the loftiness of a mind which, while not great by any means, had always remained honest and above undignified compromises. His opinion may be accepted as being that of all sincere German patriots who, whilst admiring the colossal work of the great statesman to whom they owed so much, yet regretted the many errors into which he had been led, and especially the double game which seemed more and more, as time went on, to be the only one that he cared to play.

Holstein, who, perhaps, knew better than anyone else the mind of his chief, had come to the conclusion that his days were numbered, a conclusion that had made him at once adopt a line of conduct calculated to prevent himself from being engulfed when Bismarck's downfall occurred.

A few months after the death of the Emperor Frederick III. the situation of Bismarck could be summed up in a few words. The Titan was aware that a final and decisive blow was about to be struck at him, and he was throwing himself from one side to another in the vain hope of escape. But—and this is what few people have realised because so very few have paid any attention to the domestic side of Bismarck's life, it was not for himself that he was fearing the executioner's axe, but for that much-beloved son who, unknown to his father, had been the principal cause of his ruin, and whom, in his fond blindness, he had hoped would succeed him one day as heirs to a throne succeed to their father's crown.

CHAPTER XXV

William II. and Bismarck

SMALL disagreements occurred between William II. and Bismarck from the very first hours of the new Monarch's reign. The young Emperor had been in the habit as Crown Prince of visiting the Chancellor almost daily at the latter's own house, and several times also after his accession he went to consult Bismarck at his own house. Then, one morning, he summoned him at Potsdam, a proceeding which surprised the old man considerably. Bismarck excused himself from complying with his Sovereign's wishes on the plea of ill-health. When this was reported to him William II. drily remarked that it was regrettable that a Prime Minister should be so sickly as not to be able to fulfil the duties of his position, and this was the great hindrance in the management of public affairs. Of course, the words were repeated, even in an aggravated form, to the person whom they concerned, and that did not please him, as may be easily imagined.

William II. objected from the first to what he called the "hesitating and unsettled" policy of Bismarck. The expressions sounded surprising when one remembered the ferocious determination and inflexibility of the Prince's administration; but in reality the words were a nearer appreciation of the whole European situation than the man in the street could suppose. The Bismarck of 1888 was no longer the Bismarck of 1870. He had tried to

the best of his immense intellectual powers to consolidate
the great work he had achieved, but he had at the same
time made that effort administer to his personal, or rather
to his paternal ambitions, and sought to prepare an easy
future for his son as his successor as the head of the
Government of the German Empire.   Others had seen
through this ambition, and very quickly made capital out
of it by sowing distrust against the old Chancellor in the
mind of the general public as well as in that of the young
and energetic Prince who was about to take into his own
hands the conduct of affairs in the German Empire, and
whose ardent nature and temperament refused to accept
anything which savoured of a compromise.

William II. had most decided views in regard to the
foreign policy he meant to maintain.   He had made up
his mind to hold fast to the alliance with Austria, in
opposition to any understanding with Russia.   It is a
curious fact that though, in preference to that of his
own parents, he had chosen his grandfather as the example
to follow, he had inherited none of the Russian sympathies which William I. possessed to such a high degree,
but nursed many of the prejudices held by the Emperor
Frederick in regard to the Empire of the Tsars.   He
believed that one could not trust to Russian promises;
he considered that it was indispensable for the maintenance of the European equilibrium to prevent Constantinople from falling into the power of the Muscovites;
and, thirdly, he felt a personal antipathy for the person
of Alexander III., who had not taken sufficiently *au
sérieux* his young and impetuous Prussian relative.

The Russian Emperor was far too strong in his personality not to have perceived the shallowness of many
of the theatrical performances so dear to the heart of

William II., and his earnest, straightforward nature considered them with an indulgent, but by no means patient, contempt. This the young German Monarch had very quickly perceived, because he was a shrewd observer, and resented it accordingly. His feeling, therefore, was sympathetic to the voices of those who sought to antagonise Russia, and he determined that he ought to prepare against the contingency of a conflict with Russia. Some observers go farther than this and assert that Wilham II. was determined to provoke war at the earliest moment he thought opportune, and in which he reckoned that Austria would not only help him, but also give him the occasion for. Bismarck objected most absolutely to any such scheme, and told his young master so. He knew very well that a war with Russia would make sure of a Russian alliance with France which would constitute a formidable danger for the security of the German Empire. On the other hand Bismarck believed that if—according to his own pet theory—a war were fought single-handed by Germany against France, and with the French as the instigators, Russia would remain neutral, as she had done in 1870. About the issue of such a war with his Southern neighbours Bismarck had no misgivings, and it infuriated him to find that the young man who had neither the experience nor the authority of either his father or grandfather showed himself so stubborn, refusing to accept his views and opinions with the same deference his predecessors on the throne had done.

This state of things, however, conspired to lead Germany at a faster pace than ever along the path of militarism. Out of different motives it is true, but the effect was the same. Bismarck wished to crush France as soon as possible; the Emperor wanted to destroy the power of Russia, with the help of Austria, and then to come to terms with France, extending to her a hand of friendship filled with many gifts, among which he even admitted in his mind as a possibility the autonomy of Alsace-Lorraine.

Between the two men the military party was becoming a paramount factor, and persistently and openly spoke about the coming war. In June, 1889, the then German military attaché in Paris, Captain von Huene, arrived in Berlin on leave, and whilst there spoke quite openly about the necessity of increasing the German armaments in view of an approaching conflict. He said that the French army was fast becoming superior in many respects to the German force; that its armaments and its powder were excellent, and that the infantry was quite wonderfully well disciplined and equipped. He assured his superiors that the French generals and officers were eager for another war, in which they fully believed they would this time be victorious. On the other hand, he lamented that, according to what he had seen and heard, it would take at least another six months before the new modifications introduced in the training of the Prussian troops could be sufficiently well advanced to allow the risks of a campaign to be run. He added that he felt absolutely certain that a war between Germany and France could not be avoided, and that most likely it would break out immediately after the Exhibition about to take place in Paris.

As a contrast to these utterances we find in the Memoirs of Hohenlohe mention of a conversation which he had in August of that same year of 1889 with General von Waldersee, who was then head of the German General Staff. The latter advised him not to be in a hurry to sell the estates which the Princess Hohenlohe had just inherited in Russia from her brother, Prince Peter of Sayn-Wittgenstein. According to the Russian law she had to part with them in the course of the next three years, but in that time many things could occur. " This," adds the shrewd Prince Clovis, " seems as if Waldersee wanted to hint at the probability of a war with Russia in the immediate future."

This was also the opinion prevailing among the military party, while the German Press invariably represented Russia as the one great enemy of Germany and of its famous Kultur and civilisation. Bismarck was pursuing quite a different aim. He wished to get rid of the Austrian alliance, to arrange a close union and understanding between Germany and Russia, and to abandon Austria to its fate. He soon convinced himself that Russia did not wish to change her attitude in regard to Germany, and so sought to revive his flirtation with Austria. These hesitations on the part of a man who had never known before what hesitation meant had made the Emperor distrustful, and inspired him with a great deal more confidence in his own strength than he had ever felt before. Conflicts, at first small, had arisen between him and Bismarck, and these led to complaints by the Emperor against the authoritative manner and the impatience at contradiction which Bismarck was displaying. " He thinks that I am a boy," declared William II. more than once to several people, and he forgets that at any moment I could remind him that I am his Sovereign."

The Grand Duke of Baden related these incidents to Prince Hohenlohe one day when he was in an expansive mood, and told him that William II. had of

late often spoken in this strain. The eventuality of
Bismarck having to retire, therefore, should be thought
of, was the hint the Grand Duke added. To this
remark the Prince retorted by asking what, then, would
happen, because, though the Emperor probably believed himself quite capable of managing alone the foreign
affairs of the Empire, this might become very dangerous.
The Grand Duke replied that the Emperor had had
enough of Bismarck, and added that Herbert Bismarck, too, had made himself unbearable to his
Sovereign. William II., indeed, only intended to keep
his Chancellor in office until the new military credits
had been accepted by the Reichstag, after which he
should immediately dismiss him.

This kind of thing went on for some months, when
it became evident that a crisis of some kind was bound
to happen. Here I must relate an incident which so
far I know has not yet been revealed. It came to me
through a friend of Holstein, who had it from Baron
Bleichroder. Though Bismarck himself did not even
admit in imagination the possibility of being curtly dismissed by his Sovereign, his son Herbert believed in
the eventuality, and toward the end of February, 1889,
when no one outside a very small circle of people thought
of the possibility of the fall of the Chancellor, he sold
secretly funds to a considerable amount in expectation
of their fall on the news becoming public, and thus
realised a handsome profit out of his father's disgrace.

The crisis, as generally happens, was provoked by
an incident which in other circumstances would have
been easily passed over. William II., who had ever
since his accession given a great deal of his attention
to the social and economical questions of his Empire,

W

caused to be published without the counter-signature of the Chancellor a circular calling together an international conference of representatives of the working classes to discuss different questions concerning their position in regard to capitalism. Bismarck blamed severely the terms of this circular, and told the Emperor that it would have a detrimental influence upon the elections then impending. He complained that the Emperor was communicating without the intervention of his Prime Minister with the other members of the Cabinet, and reminded William II. that a Royal Order issued by Frederick William IV. on April 8th, 1852, gave to the President of the Council the sole responsibility of every official measure, and forbade any step being taken that had not been previously submitted to the Prime Minister for approval. Upon this William II. declared he should issue a decree abolishing that statute. This was the immediate cause of the conflict, and the one which the public was asked to accept. It would not have been wise, nor in the interests of the Sovereign, to allow the public to guess that the real reason lay in Bismarck's conduct of foreign affairs. A suspicion had taken firm hold of the mind of the young Emperor that Bismarck was leading them, according to plans he had not thought it necessary to lay before his Imperial master, towards the abandoning of the Triple Alliance and the conclusion of a treaty with Russia, which the Emperor absolutely refused himself to sanction. It must here be added that in Vienna strenuous efforts had been made to shake William II.'s confidence in his Prime Minister, to which even the Emperor Francis Joseph himself had lent himself.

That the German Emperor was entirely given up

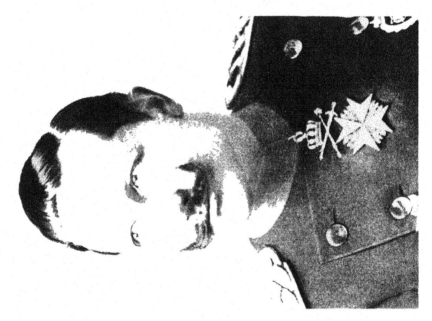

to the cause of Austria at the moment when he was parting from Bismarck can be seen out of the very imprudent confidences which he made to the Generals in command of the different army corps whom he summoned to Berlin at this juncture, and to whom he related the reasons which had induced him to dismiss the Chancellor. He told them that Russia had wished to occupy Bulgaria, and had asked for Germany's neutrality in case she should send troops to Varna. With this demand Bismarck would have been ready to comply, but he, the Emperor, could not do so, because he had promised to be a true ally to the Emperor of Austria, and was in honour bound to stand by Francis Joseph. The occupation of Bulgaria by Russian troops would mean an Austro-Russian war, and he would not abandon Austria. He then solemnly declared that he would throw in the fate of Germany with Austria even if this involved the risk of becoming entangled in war with Russia and with France at the same time. Most enthusiastic cheers greeted this oration. But when Bismarck was informed of its purport he merely raised his shoulders, with the remark that the Emperor understood politics after the manner of Frederick William IV., one of the most bitter sarcasms that he could possibly have uttered.

On February 20th and on March 1st the elections for the Reichstag had taken place, and, as Bismarck had foreseen, they had been held on the issue of the working class question, based on the circular which the Emperor had caused to be published. Their result had been a considerable majority against the Chancellor. The latter wished to come to an understanding with the leaders of the different Parliamentary groups, and he invited Wind-

horst, the chief of the Catholic party, to an interview.
This put the climax to the affected irritation of the Emperor—in reality it was only " affected "—and he sent von
Lucanus, the chief of his private officers, to Bismarck
to demand an explanation and to command him to ask
for the Imperial assent whenever he thought it necessary
to hold communications with deputies belonging to the
Opposition groups. The Chancellor, justly incensed this
time, replied that he would allow no one the right to
say whom he was or was not to receive in his house.
The next day was March 15th. The Emperor had had
an interview with Holstein in the early morning, after
which he had told the Grand Duke of Baden that he
had heard Bismarck had written to the Tsar to inform
him that, against his advice, his Sovereign was going
to inaugurate an anti-Russian policy. He did not say
from whom he had received this information, but had
himself at once driven to the house of the Chancellor.
It was ten o'clock in the morning, and the latter, who
kept very late hours, was still in bed; he had to get up
and to dress in a hurry to receive his Monarch. William II. began the conversation by asking him what his
negotiations with Windhorst meant. Bismarck answered
that he had not negotiated anything with him, only received him privately. " I must again request you to
keep me informed when you think it necessary to confer
with Parliamentary leaders," insisted the Emperor. " I
cannot admit any interference concerning my relations
with anyone," retorted Bismarck, " and the commands
of my Sovereign do not concern the Princess Bismarck,
who alone has the right to say whom she will or will
not receive in her drawing-room. It is only in compliance with a promise which the Emperor William I.

asked me to give to him upon his death-bed that I have consented to remain in the service of his grandson, and if I have ceased to please your Majesty I am quite ready to retire.''

'' I accept your resignation,'' said the enraged Sovereign, who left the room banging the door behind him, whilst Bismarck did not even attempt to accompany him to the door, as etiquette would have required him to do. Two days later, on March 17th, William II., finding that the threatened resignation had not yet reached him officially, sent his aide-de-camp, General von Hahnke, to ask the Chancellor to forward it to him without any further delay.

Holstein, in the version which he gave of the circumstances that accompanied this historical event, declared that the first idea of Bismarck had been to throw his resignation into the face of the Emperor and to leave the same night for Friedrichsruhe, leaving his family behind to pack up their belongings. But here Herbert interfered. He clung to office far more than his father had ever done, and he feared that his own chances of remaining secretary for Foreign Affairs would suffer if the latter irritated the Sovereign more than was already the case.

Whether this was true or not it is, of course, difficult to say, but things certainly looked as if the Chancellor was clinging to power and hoping for something impossible to happen that would allow him to retain his post and his dignities. He replied quite coolly to General von Hahnke that, in presence of the gravity of the general situation and circumstances, he would consider it a want of conscience on his part, both in regard to his Sovereign and to his Fatherland, if he voluntarily deserted the post which he occupied. If he sent in his resignation, as he was requested to do, it would give to the public an entirely false impression of what had occurred. His Majesty had the right to dismiss him whenever it pleased him to do so, but he could not of his own accord put an end to his political career by an act which he considered likely to have fatal consequences for the German Empire.

Hahnke had to retire without the resignation he had been ordered to bring back with him. The Grand Dukes of Hesse, Baden and Saxe-Coburg tried to interfere in the conflict, but William II. would not listen to the advice they attempted to give him. He sent a second messenger to Bismarck, this time von Lucanus, with instructions to request once more his resignation, adding that he was surprised not to be earlier in possession of it. The message was that William II. could only give him a few hours' longer grace.

Bismarck then replied that he was quite ready to sign his retirement, but that, as the document in which he would express his reasons for resigning the offices he had held for so many years, and would be the last official one emanating from the pen of a Minister who had figured more or less conspicuously in the history of Germany and of Prussia, he required a certain time in which to write it. He owed it both to himself and to history, he added, to explain why he had been dismissed.

There was nothing to do but to wait, and at last, on March 18th, Bismarck signed the letter in which he fully related the differences between him and the Emperor which, according to his opinion, had brought about his retirement. In it he declared that for some time William II. had put restrictions on the authority with which he was invested that prevented him from conducting the affairs of the State in a way worthy of him, and of the services which he had rendered to his country. He added that, in regard to the foreign relations of the Empire, the policy which the Sovereign wanted to follow appeared to him to be of a nature likely to compromise all the important results which he had obtained in that direction during the two preceding reigns. And he ended his letter with the following remark, the deep irony of which could not help striking in a most unpleasant manner the Monarch to whom it was addressed: "I would have already, one year ago, presented to your Majesty the request to be allowed to give up my functions if I had not had the impression that your Majesty desired to make use for some time longer of the experience and of the faculties of a faithful servant of your ancestors. But now that I am quite certain that your Majesty does not need them any more I can retire from political life without having to fear that this decision will be condemned as premature by public opinion."

And a few hours before having dispatched this document, the last official paper which was to bear his signature, Bismarck declared to one of his confidants, Moritz Busch, that he "did not wish to take upon his shoulders at the close of his career the stupidities and the mistakes of a presumptuous and inexperienced mind." He wished still, in short, to keep up before the world of his day the fiction that his retreat had not been a compulsory one.

Holstein's version is probably nearer the truth because it is the more human. He saw Bismarck immediately after the visit of General von Hahnke. From the window of his study he had watched the General take his departure, and feeling sure of its purport he had sought the presence of Bismarck in the endeavour to learn some particulars of the interview. He found the Chancellor in his arm-chair, his arms hanging listlessly at his side, and his face suddenly aged by ten years and pathetic in its deep despondency. When Holstein had asked him what had occurred, and whether he was to call anyone to his help, his chief had merely shaken his head and then called him by a sign to his side. "It is all over," he had said in a stifled voice, "and destiny wants me to look upon the destruction of my own work."

And then after a time he had added: "Can you understand what it is to feel that one has become nothing after having been everything?"

At this moment someone knocked at the door. Bismarck straightened himself up, and after having passed his hand over his eyes, as if to shake off a bad dream, turned round to his stupefied subordinate and in his usual voice asked him what he had come for and what was the current business of the day, settling to it in his usual manner as if nothing out of the way had occurred. It was only after lunch that he had acquainted the Princess Bismarck and Herbert with what had happened, and in concert with them decided what was to be done.

Later on he unburdened his soul to Holstein, and confided to him his apprehensions as to what the future held in store for Germany. He was very well aware of the desire of the Emperor to come to some kind of arrangement with France, to the detriment of Russia, and he held the idea as absolutely disastrous. It was madness, Holstein reported that Bismarck said to him, to try to provoke a conflict with Russia before one had assured oneself of the alliance and co-operation of Turkey and of other Balkan States, and this he thought the Emperor William rendered impossible. "It is curious," Bismarck added, "how, after declaring that he wanted in everything to follow the example of his grandfather, this rash youth does precisely what this grandfather would have particularly objected to—pick a quarrel with Russia, with whom we ought always to remain upon good terms." One might have reminded Bismarck that there had been a time when he had himself done everything possible to thwart Russian policy not only in the Near East, but everywhere else.

Holstein is credited with the best definition of the great Chancellor's character and intelligence. He declared that Bismarck's was a mind "that would inevitably come to grief when it found it was unable any longer to perform extraordinary and wonderful things." This was so most absolutely, because nothing in Bismarck's policy, apart from the raising of the German Empire, testifies to what is called in French "*l'esprit de suite*." We see him perpetually wandering from one thing to another, attacking in turns the Roman Catholic Church and trying immediately afterwards to make friends with it; rushing into the arms of Austria and then embracing Russia; allying himself in matters of home interests to all the different parties in the Reichstag; proposing one social reform after the other, and in the midst of all these things remaining absolutely personal and forgetting that politics cannot be conducted in accord with one's feelings of aversion or of attachment to this or to that person, to this or to that nation. With another Sovereign than old William I. Bismarck would have been compelled to retire almost immediately after the French war, or at least as soon as it had become evident that for him governing meant the extension of his own despotism over everything and everybody with whom he came into contact. He only maintained himself in power because he happened to be standing beside a Monarch who was so really great that it did not matter to him whether others should be considered or should think themselves so. With an undoubtedly intelligent but at the same time vain and self-reliant man like the present Kaiser it is only to be wondered how two years could pass by without matters having been brought to the supreme climax, after which there remained nothing for Bismarck to do but to bid good-bye to the responsibilities and to the cares of political life either of his own accord or because it had been imposed upon him by a will for once stronger than his own.

The days which elapsed between the visit of General von Hahnke and the official publication of the Chancellor's retirement were perhaps the most terrible in his whole life. He used to sit for hours in his chair, looking into space with eyes that seemed to pierce the future, to seek there for the revenge on those personal wrongs of his which he considered far more important than the gravest interests of the German Empire. At times he used to fall into fits of rage, during which he broke whatever happened to be within his reach, then he would relapse into a silence whence it was almost impossible to rouse him. Had he been allowed to follow his first impulse, to leave Berlin for Friedrichsruhe immediately after the request of the Emperor for his resignation, there would have been at least some dignity in his departure, but this did not suit the designs of Herbert, and Herbert sacrificed his father to his own selfish and greedy purposes.

Hohenlohe, whose relations with the Chancellor had become rather strained, had arrived in Berlin on the very day that the newspapers had published the astounding news of the dismissal of the man with whom were associated some of the most glorious pages in German history. He thought it polite to pay him a visit, and to tell him how much he had been surprised at the events that had just taken place, and how little he had expected them. " You could not have been more surprised than myself," replied Bismarck, " because three weeks ago I did not think it could be possible I would have to go away, although I ought to have been prepared for it, because the Emperor wants now to govern alone." And he forthwith began pouring into the ear of his visitor the whole long story of his real and supposed wrongs. It was evident that he could not forgive William II. for his ingratitude, but his irritation was most violent against the Grand Duke of Baden, whom Bismarck charged with indirectly bringing about his dismissal by the manner in which he had encouraged the Emperor in his ideas of independence.

All these recriminations took away from the dignity of the fallen Minister, and, had circumstances been different, would have harmed him in public opinion to a considerable degree had not the nation resented his departure. The Emperor's conduct was considered to have been ungrateful, and Bismarck consoled himself for his misfortunes and disappointment by noticing the expressions of disapproval to the address of the Sovereign that one could hear everywhere in Berlin.

The Chancellor had one more interview with Holstein before handing over the direction of affairs to his successor, General Caprivi. The first thing that he asked this lieutenant who for so many years had worked beside him, and helped him in so many of his vast schemes, was when he meant to resign. Holstein replied that he had no intention of doing so. This surprised the Prince so much that he exclaimed, " But how will you be able to work without me? " The Baron smiled and remarked that he would work towards the day when he would see his former chief return to the place which he had been compelled to abandon. " I shall never do so," said Bismarck, " unless—unless "—here he made a long pause—" unless the nation calls upon me to repair some of the stupidities which he is sure to perpetrate."

He then gave instructions to Holstein as to what was to be done in order to avoid a rupture with Russia. The latter promised everything, but meant the whole time to conduct affairs along quite a different course to the one in which they had been led so long while Bismarck presided over matters. Holstein was already busily engaged looking out for his successor as Foreign Minister, and had submitted several names for the Sovereign's approval, foremost among them that of Herr von Marschall, one of the cleverest diplomats that the Prussian State had ever possessed.

As the hour for his departure was drawing nigh the former Chancellor recovered some of his lost dignity. He asked to see the Empress Frederick to take leave of her. She immediately received him. He had been her enemy for many years, but the noble woman felt some pity for him in her kind heart, and, apart from this, she resented the manner in which he had been dismissed.

On March 29th, 1890, Bismarck left for ever the house where he had spent so many eventful years. A few hours before he had been at Charlottenburg, carrying a bunch of roses which he laid on the coffin of the old Emperor with whose help he had been able to perform so many great things. It was his last and his only sincere good-bye. A huge crowd accompanied him to the railway station, and when he got out from his carriage at the door, tall and erect in his cuirassier uniform with its yellow collar, he appeared more like the gigantic ghost of a gigantic past than like a Titan fallen. The multitude cheered him vociferously and covered him with flowers. He looked grave but peaceful. For one brief moment he was again master of himself, as of old, and the only sign of emotion which he gave were the words, "The Emperor shall see me again," which, from his railway carriage, he threw as a farewell to the crowds that had gathered to see him depart.

There was something so solemn in this leave-taking that even Holstein felt awed. It is not every day that we see something really great disappear into space, and many on that eventful evening had the feeling that a new leaf had been turned in the book of German history. In future days more than one sad thing was to be inscribed upon the blank page which that day lay extended before the eyes of the nation.

CHAPTER XXVI

After the Crash

BISMARCK gave to the world as the reason of his dismissal that, after having thirty years of almost unlimited power, with his Sovereign, his country and the Reichstag deferring to his advice, it had been impossible for him to become a docile servant. And as if to accentuate this fact he had given directions to have written on his funeral monument the significant words: "Prince von Bismarck, a faithful German servant of the Emperor William I.," which desire was executed by his family.

The fact, however, was that Bismarck might have maintained himself in his position had he only succeeded in converting to his point of view the new Sovereign, and had he not had his son Herbert at his side, to whom he had gradually come to report all his actions, and whose future had become his first consideration. It is incontestable that it was a great deal due to the conduct of that much-loved son that Bismarck's political career had come to such an abrupt end.

It seems that the whole Foreign Office was tired of the domineering ways of Herbert Bismarck, who was far more its master than even his father. Those belonging to the inner official circle, too, had discovered the unscrupulous way in which Herbert used for the advantage of his various financial speculations the knowledge which his official position allowed him to obtain. This gave his enemies a strong weapon against him, which they used mercilessly as soon as they found that they could do so with impunity. The elder Bismarck they accused of having suddenly become strongly pro-Russian, and Russia, ever since the accession of William II., had fallen into strange discredit, especially among the military party. The people knew that all along the Emperor had nursed the dream of a reconciliation with France, and they who were in his confidence were aware that his greatest ambition was to visit Paris in his official capacity and to arrange some kind of *modus vivendi* between the German Empire and the country he declared he esteemed beyond all others. Whether these assurances were sincere it is better not to inquire into too closely, but the fact remained that at the beginning of his reign William II. refused himself to endorse the aggressive policy of his Prime Minister in regard to France, and felt inclined to make some concession to the feelings of the French nation.

Whoever had the opportunity to see the former Chancellor in Friedrichsruhe after his dismissal realised the tragedy it was to him. His was not a nature capable of appreciating any rest from his colossal labours; he missed this same work to such an extent that his inactivity became for him a real obsession. What especially infuriated him was to see all that he had been working for turned topsy-turvy, and his most cherished political and diplomatic complications crumbled to pieces. For instance, Caprivi refused to renew a secret convention with the Russian Government, in which Bismarck had engaged himself to guarantee to it the liberty of its movements in Bulgaria and at Constantinople if it consented in its turn to promise Germany its neutrality in

case of another war with France. When Bismarck was
asked a few days later by a visitor to Friedrichsruhe how
he could reconcile such a convention with those which
existed already between the Berlin Cabinet and Turkey,
the former Chancellor exclaimed, "Conventions are
made to be broken, and I should not have worried over
that one at all after it had done its duty and helped me
to get rid of the nightmare of a Franco-Russian
alliance."

Not one single person found grace in Bismarck's
eyes—neither Hohenlohe, neither Marschall, neither
Bülow, neither Caprivi, nor the Emperor. The last two
were the special objects of his sarcasms, and he openly
declared that, according to what he heard, it seemed to
him that the Government of the German Empire was
drifting away towards the unknown under the guidance
of a capricious leader. He laughed at the new German
Colonial policy so dear to the heart of William II., and
he did not spare from his raillery either the philanthropic
ideas of the Emperor, as shown in the new social legis-
lation which was being introduced, or the commercial
policy inaugurated by Caprivi, to whose administration
he prophesied the greatest disasters.

Unfortunately, all his rage and invective only added
to the number of his enemies. At the same time his
conduct exasperated the Emperor and caused considerable uneasiness to the Government. Soon the quarrel
between Bismarck and William II. assumed such considerable proportions that one began to speak about the
possibility of the Emperor instituting a criminal prosecu-
tion against his grandfather's great Minister and adviser.
Patience did not belong to the qualities with which the
Kaiser was endowed, and though he did not have the

courage to proceed to any extreme measures against Bismarck he took another course which was perhaps even more mortifying, and he caused a circular to be sent to Germany's representatives abroad, in which they were advised not to attach any importance to whatever the former Chancellor might say or write. But the situation reached its climax when the latter wished to go to Vienna to be present at the marriage of his son Count Herbert with an Austrian lady, the Countess Margaret Hoyos.

Some of the very few friends left to Bismarck tried to persuade him to have this marriage celebrated somewhere in the country quietly, but he had refused to listen to reason; he fully intended to make this occasion an opportunity to prove to the world that he had not become so unimportant as his Sovereign seemed to think. He had written to the Great Master of the Emperor of Austria's household to ask for the favour of an audience with that Monarch, and he meant to tell him many things that he himself admitted it would be unadvisable to publish in the newspapers for the moment. Francis Joseph had signified his consent, and everything seemed to be going on quite well when one fine morning the German *Reichsanzeiger* published two Imperial communications, one of which was an order forbidding the German Ambassador in Vienna to be present at the marriage ceremony of Count Herbert Bismarck, whilst the other one was a severe censure of the old Prince for his free use of the Press. William II. did not rest there; he also wrote to the Emperor Francis Joseph asking him not to receive Bismarck, and to cause no official recognition of his presence to be made in the Austrian capital.

Francis Joseph had held friendly relations with

x

Bismarck for something like forty years. But Francis Joseph had never been one of those who could be trusted either by his friends or by his foes, and when Bismarck arrived in Vienna on June 19, 1892, he was met by the news that the audience which already had been promised was refused. At the same time was communicated to him the contents of a note addressed by Caprivi to the German Ambassador in Vienna, in which was said among other things that the Emperor William made a difference between the Bismarck of former days and the present one, and that he wished it to be understood that the latter would never have in the future any influence on the affairs of the German State. The note added that it was the Sovereign's desire its contents should be communicated to Count Kalnoky, who was at that time Austrian Minister for Foreign Affairs. Nothing more offensive nor more insulting could have been imagined, and it is but natural that Bismarck should have become enraged at finding himself treated in such a manner after all that he done for the welfare and for the greatness of the German Empire and the German Fatherland. He immediately summoned to his side a correspondent of the Vienna paper, the *Neue Freie Presse*, and to him he unburdened his soul, criticising without mercy the administration of Count Caprivi, and openly declaring that henceforward it would be war to the knife between them. For once he felt he had got the German nation at his side, and, indeed, what had taken place at Vienna, instead of harming him in public opinion, had given a new life to Bismarck's popularity. On his leaving Vienna he was made the object of great manifestations of sympathy, and all along his way to Kissingen, whither he repaired after the wedding of his son, he

was received with ovations and expressions of enthusiasm
for his person that must have consoled him for many
a rebuff.

When he had returned to Friedrichsruhe, both
Bleichroder, the banker, and Holstein visited him there.
The former had been one of those who had tried to persuade him not to go to Vienna. Now he wished to hear
from him his impressions upon all that had taken place
there. Bismarck did not hide his feelings from his old
friend and financial adviser, and he told him among other
things that, whatever might be the opinion of the
Emperor William, the nation would like to see him once
more at the head of affairs, and that he meant to take
possession of his seat in the Reichstag, whither he had
been elected by the town of Hanau, in order to start
a campaign against the Government, in which he was
convinced that he would be followed by the country.

This made Bleichroder uneasy. The shrewd financier
knew very well that in some points Bismarck was right,
and he also understood that if the latter took up to lead
an opposition in Parliament the Government of the day
would have but a poor chance of holding its own against
him and his ever-increasing popularity. When he returned to Berlin he asked Holstein to call upon him, and
they discussed the situation together, with the result
that the Baron in his turn started for Friedrichsruhe.

His account of his visit is most interesting. He came
at once to the point, and told his former chief that he
had come as an ambassador to learn what were his conditions for the conclusion of a peace which no one, he
affirmed, wished for more than the Emperor himself.
To his surprise Bismarck replied that he had no conditions to make; he did not care for the Emperor nor

for what the latter thought about him. Germany was being led to its ruin, and he owed it to the memory of his old master and to his own reputation in history to protest against it.

Holstein allowed the old Prince to have his say, and then suddenly asked him what he would do if, exasperated by opposition, the Sovereign had him imprisoned. Bismarck instantly replied: "I wish he would; that would be the end of the Hohenzollern dynasty, and there are others that could take its place."

Holstein then inquired if he meant by that his own line.

"I am not a fool," answered the former Chancellor, "and you must not take me for one; but any dynasty I should support would have a fair chance to maintain itself on the Imperial throne. I am not thinking of Prussia, of course."

The Baron was not a man to be taken aback by anything. He dropped the mildness and aimed with his big batteries. What he really told Bismarck he never confided to anyone, but the result of his conversation was that the Prince convinced himself that, unless he desisted from his provocative attitude, the misdeeds of his beloved son Herbert would be made public, and that the proofs of the latter's speculations on the Stock Exchange were in the Emperor's hands, who would not hesitate to use them in case of need.

The news came like a thunderbolt on the aged man, who had never expected anything of the kind. He did not even ask Holstein to promise him secrecy—he knew very well the Baron would not speak unless compelled to do so—but after his conversation with him he modified much of his conduct. At the same time he contrived to convey to the knowledge of William II., by Holstein, that he, too, possessed certain papers, the publication of which might prove highly embarrassing to the young Monarch, among which figured a number of private letters of the latter written during his father's last illness. This was sufficient to prevent the possibility of violent measures either in regard to Bismarck himself or in the direction of Count Herbert.

The health of the old Prince received a serious shock from all these emotions and worries, and at last he fell seriously ill. This was in autumn of the year 1893. The Emperor, in the meanwhile, had also allowed his reason to take the upper hand on his impetuousness, and he seized upon the former Chancellor's illness to send him an olive branch in the shape of a bottle of rare old wine out of the Imperial cellars. He had already offered him the use of one of his castles on the Rhine as a residence during his convalescence. Bismarck had refused, of course, but in terms of politeness, and the ice had thus been broken after four years of continual strife. The Sovereign also invited his grandfather's adviser to visit him in Berlin on the occasion of his jubilee of twenty-five years' military service, and this invitation the aged Prince did not decline.

On January 26, 1894, Bismarck returned to Berlin. Everything was arranged to give this visit an appearance of triumph. The Emperor's brother, Prince Henry of Prussia, had met him at the station, and it was in his company that, escorted by two squadrons of cuirassiers, in a Royal carriage with outriders, Prince Bismarck had reached the Imperial castle, where rooms had been prepared for him, and where the Emperor and Empress, surrounded by their sons, had received him in state. Crowds without number had waited for him in the streets and had given him the warmest of welcomes.

The country was glad to see that at last a reconciliation had been effected between the old and great statesman whose gigantic work was to leave such deep traces in the history of the world and the Sovereign from whom differences had parted him. Bismarck was perhaps the least moved of the two when they met again at last in the presence of the guard of honour who presented arms before the rehabilitated Minister. He understood very well the meaning of all this : after one had not succeeded in reducing him to silence by threats one wanted to shut his mouth and to bury his resentment under the flowers with which one covered him.

A family luncheon took place almost immediately after Bismarck's arrival, a luncheon at which he was the only guest, then he called on the Empress Frederick, and on the same evening, at seven o'clock, he took the train back to Friedrichsruhe. His visit, short as it had been, had, nevertheless, caused a considerable sensation, and some fears were expressed in some quarters that the Emperor might be tempted to call him back at the head of affairs. This was especially the case at the Foreign Office, where no one wished for his return, not excepting Holstein, who, finding that under the régime of Caprivi he was left far more free to do what he liked, would not have welcomed at all being put back under the control of an exacting and not always just master, and who, besides, had every reason to dread that he might be reminded of certain things he had told the Prince during his famous visit at Friedrichsruhe. So, with characteristic prudence, he presented, on the very next day after the former Chancellor's return to Berlin, a report to the Emperor, in which he emphasised several grave mistakes which his old chief had made in diplomatic and political matters, among which figured his conduct during the Berlin Congress, his intervention in China in favour of France, and his interference between Great Britain and Russia in regard to the Afghanistan conflict.

These fears, however, were quite groundless. William II. had got absolutely no intention to recall Bismarck to power. He had realised that this estrangement between them was beginning to harm his own popularity as a Sovereign, and therefore tried to take the venom out of the teeth which had already bitten him so hard, and he allowed something of what he had had in his mind to escape him during a conversation with Hohenlohe, who had congratulated him on the wisdom of the step which he had taken. Hohenlohe had remarked that the rabid Bismarckians were not yet satisfied with what had been done, but that they declared the Emperor ought to have gone first himself to Friedrichsruhe.

"I am aware of it," had replied William II., "but could have waited a long time for such a thing. *had* to come here first."

CHAPTER XXVII

The Outcome

AS time went on no change came over the opinions of the Emperor; he still clung to his favourite idea of an arrangement with France, owing to the value French neutrality would be to him in the event of an Anglo-German war that already at the time I am writing about was on his programme. Bismarck knew very well that it was an absolute illusion on the part of William II. to imagine that France could give up the hope of recovering its lost provinces. He knew, too, that Russia rather than France held the key to the general European situation.

The obduracy of William II. in this matter did not arise out of a mere spirit of antagonism to his ex-Chancellor. It lay deeper than that. He had made up his mind that sooner or later Russia had to be driven back in Asia, and he had had his eye all along on the possibility of Prussia obtaining the fortresses which defended the line of the Vistula on the Russian side, which he considered would then be in far better hands. This idea had haunted his mind ever since the day he had been sent as quite a young man by his grandfather to attend some Russian manœuvres near Brest Litovsk, and when he had been struck by the strong works of fortification that defended this part of the world against the possibility of an invasion from the West. No one then admitted the thought that Prussia and Russia would ever find themselves at war with each other, but the active brain of the present Kaiser had gone farther than his elders in this respect, and I remember very well that on his return from Brest Litovsk he gave way to some expressions which, when remembered later on in the light of subsequent events, might have meant a good deal more than could have been expected at the time they were uttered.

The young Sovereign was perhaps a remarkably clever man, but the divine spark of genius with which he thought he was richly endowed evaded him.

This illusion on the part of William II. and his vascillating nature were often the object of Bismarck's satire. Not very long after the reconciliation a man who, during the whole time Bismarck had been in power, had belonged to the Opposition, though he had known him well, happened to be in Hamburg. He thought it decent to try to see the Prince, just to show that he had not forsaken him, as so many others had done. He wrote to Friedrichsruhe, and, receiving a favourable reply, repaired to the castle by the next train.

He was very well and even warmly received by the great statesman. After luncheon Bismarck took his visitor for a walk in the beautiful park amidst which the house was built. The Prince was in a communicative mood, and freely commented on the circumstances that had accompanied his dismissal. He did not mention the Emperor with any bitterness, but with an un-measurable contempt · "He will never keep any Minister for long," he said, "because it will be impossible for any responsible adviser of the Crown to endorse the vagaries of a mind which can never settle seriously to anything and which only goes by feelings, discarding the dictates of reason. One cannot govern a country as one commands a regiment, and militarism cannot be applied to politics without producing chaos and trouble. Stability is required to lead men and to rule nations, and a politician must first of all look toward the future and any complications the latter may bring. Sentimental politics, inspired by vanity or by revenge, are never sound. It is all very well to talk about what ought to be done, but in real life the only thing which has got to be considered is what can be done. This the young man who believes himself to be able to improve upon the work of his grandfather forgets entirely. It is all very well to make war, but war, like everything else, ought to have a purpose, and without one I would never have lent myself to an attack either on Austria or France. Now, what possible purpose could a war with Russia have? We do not require Russian territory, and a campaign against it, even if it became a victorious one, would only entangle us in difficulties on account of Poland, which would become an embarrassment for everybody.

"There was a time when I advocated an alliance with Austria against Russia, but then the political constellation was very different from the present one for one thing, and for another, I was sure that with the Emperor William I., and even with his heir, the Crown Prince Frederick, Austria would never be allowed to seek a futile quarrel with anyone, and the peace of the world would not become seriously endangered.

"At present things are changed; the Sovereign is essentially an adventurous character, capable of allowing his feelings to carry him away to where his sympathies are engaged.

" This is what made me consider the advisability of our turning once more our attention toward Russia, an alliance with whom might be of great use to us against a possible French aggression and in other directions. The Emperor would not understand me. He thought that he knew best; youth often does. This was the real reason why we quarrelled. He will quarrel with other people, and I can hardly believe that he will ever bear to have a Chancellor with a private opinion of his own, unless the latter takes particular care to hide that such is the case. But, then, this will mean the return to absolute government, and an absolute government, to be carried on successfully, requires far different qualities than those of William II."

" Germany has been governed absolutely by yourself," said Bismarck's visitor. " It therefore surprises me that you use the words, ' the return to absolute government ', instead of saying the ' continuance of absolute government.' ''

" Ah! '' sighed the Prince, " that was very different. I may have been autocratic, but I do not think that I have ever boasted such was the case. There lies the difference."

He smiled and looked at his interlocutor, then went on, this time with something of excitement in his voice ·

" On the whole, I am glad that I have been turned out of office in the way it has taken place. I was, I will own, very angry at first, but at present my ideas have somewhat changed. It is a comfort to think that I have no responsibility in what is going on, that, whatever befalls Germany, my name will be left out of it; that, on the contrary, people will say that if I had been at the head of affairs such and such a thing would not have happened. It would most probably have happened all the same, because it is impossible to arrest a river in its course—and what is the temper of a young man who believes he knows better than anyone else but a river—and then the world would have said that Bismarck had grown old, and had lost that sure touch in politics he had wielded before. This would not have suited me, and might have put me before history in an entirely false light. As things have turned out, I shall be regretted more and more as time shall go by, and as new ideals will take the place of those which were fashionable in my time. Then I shall be revenged, even if I do not live to see it. It is all that I require. As for the German Empire—well, it must take its fate, as so many other things in the world have to."

"But you believe in its prosperity?" asked the Prince's visitor.

"No, I do not," was the unhesitating reply.

"What do you mean?"

"Precisely what I say. I do not believe that the Empire, such as I have made it, has got many years of existence before it. It will have to be transformed in some way or other, and it depends on exterior causes how long a time this transformation will take to become apparent to the naked eye. The German Empire, to consolidate itself, requires a different Emperor from William II. Believe me that, in saying so, I am not giving way to personal spite, but to a deep feeling of patriotism. I know that what I have done is destined to perish. I only hope that I shall not be compelled to see the catastrophe which will carry away what has taken me such trouble to create."

He paused for a few moments, then went on:

" I have made a great mistake, and I see it now—
I have not given sufficient care to the choice of men
among whom my successor had to be taken. But, then,
I never could stand human stupidity; it is one of those
capital errors for which there exists no forgiveness. I
ought to have tried to create a school of diplomats and
political men. I have not done so, and we see the result.
There is not now, with the exception of Hatzfeld, one
single man whom one could call a statesman in our
Foreign Office. Hohenlohe is too selfish to be ever anything else but personal. Bülow is clever and brilliant,
but seldom sees beyond the satisfaction of the present
triumph. No, I see no one."

Evidently the old Prince was prejudiced, but in the
remarks which I have quoted can, nevertheless, be de-
tected something above personal spite and personal
regrets. The statesman was not dead in him yet on that
day when he thus unburdened his soul to a man who
had been in the past one of his most violent adversaries,
though retaining personal friendly relations with him.
It was the statesman foreseeing what the future was
holding in reserve for the German Empire.

The last triumph which Bismarck was to know
occurred on April 1, 1895, when his eightieth birthday
was celebrated with a pomp which might have reminded
him of the ovations that so often had greeted his steps
all through his wonderful career. This eightieth birthday
was to mark the close of the career of the old Titan
upon whose shoulders had rested for so many years the
fate not only of his own country, but also of the whole
of Europe. He was to live for three years longer, with
all his remarkable intellectual faculties unimpaired, but

dissatisfied, morose, and unhappy at having, as he once pathetically exclaimed, to look into the newspapers for details as to what was going on in a world the destinies of which he had controlled for so many years.

In spite of the affection of his children, he found himself lonely and miserable in a solitude to which he never got used, but out of which he did not desire to escape. In those hours of enforced rest he had the leisure to recapitulate the past, and in this self-examination he found his punishment.

Death, however, proved more merciful to him than men had been. His last illness was a short one, and carried him off after a struggle which had only lasted a few hours. It was on July 30, 1898, that he breathed his last, just about midnight, whilst a hurricane was blowing in the North Sea, and the wind shaking the walls of the Castle of Friedrichsruhe and howling among the trees of the stately Sachsenwald. He who had roused so many tempests passed away during a storm.

The man has disappeared, but the evils of the system which he inaugurated have survived both him and his works. We feel their effects to-day; we see how bad they are, and we realise their impotency. He had trained a whole nation to believe that might was right, and a dynasty to think that its will ought to be the one supreme law that guides it. His policy, at first clear and determined, had at last dwindled into incoherency. After he had gone, those who succeeded to the place which he had filled, but which they merely occupied, tried to follow in his footsteps. They failed. He wrote a great page in the history of Prussia, but a sad one in that of Europe.

And what of William II.? The young Sovereign, who had for a time flattered Bismarck, toadied to him, and made use of him for the furtherance of his own schemes, thought himself a match for him, and believed himself capable of carrying out a conception which he had never properly understood. Thus, for instance, in regard to Alsace-Lorraine and his desire for an understanding with France which for so many years remained the Utopian dream of the Kaiser's fertile brain. It has been related to me that, during the crisis brought about by the two Balkan Wars that preceded the present great European conflict, William II., in his desire to assure himself of the neutrality of France in the case of a struggle with Russia, which he kept all the time encouraging Austria to begin, had gone so far as to take upon himself the arrangement of a plebiscite, in which the inhabitants of the annexed provinces would be called upon to declare whether they were willing to remain German or to become French once more. It was the Emperor Francis Joseph who interfered, and who prevented him from taking any steps in this direction. The plan had got a shadow of Bismarckianism about it which had appealed to the imagination of a Sovereign who had made caprice the one powerful motive directing his actions.

Bismarckianism without Bismarck! Its imitation was to bring savage ruin to the world, despair to millions of human beings, destruction everywhere. Its results have been the bankruptcy of Christianity in a nation who had substituted might for right, brutal appetites for justice and honour, and a horrified, terror-stricken Europe today anxiously awaits the dawning of the new era that will sweep away the last remnants of the detestable system. Of this system, to which we owe such incommensurable misery, Bismarck was the founder and William II. the real executor.

INDEX

ABEKEN, Herr von, a fateful telegram
from, 175
Abzac, Marquis d', 232
Adam, Madame Juliette, and the
Franco-Russian Alliance, 294
"La Société de Berlin" of, 210
Adlerberg, Herr, 40, 44
Albert, Prince Consort, 29
Albert Edward, Prince (Edward VII.,
King), attends funeral of Em-
peror Frederick III., 323
Alexander II., Tsar, a complaint to
William I., 237
a sinister report to, 228
and the Treaty of Paris, 192
murder of, 238
Alexander III., Tsar, cancels a meet-
ing with William I., 291
coronation of, 239
suspicions of Germany, 285, 288
the Holstein forged documents and,
191
Alexander of Battenberg, Prince, 237,
285, 322
confidences to author, 239, 282,
295
Alexander of Hesse, Prince, 238, 239
Alexandra Feodorovna, Empress, 38
Alexandrovo, a fateful meeting at,
246, 259
Alliances, Bismarck's view of, 60
Alsace-Lorraine, French "intrigues"
in, 301
Alvenslebem Convention, the, 82
Andrassy, Count, Bismarck and, 235
Empress Elisabeth and, 255
interview with Bismarck, 247
retirement of, 245
Angoulême, Duchess of, 171
Anspach, 110, 114
Augusta, Empress, and Crown Prince
Frederick's letter to William I.,
97

Augusta, Empress (contd.)—
and Bismarck, 32, 33, 34, 59, 65,
66, 77, 97, 173, 183, 210, 211,
218, 301
and the Kulturkampf, 218
intrigues of, 168, 171, 210
relations of William I. and, 93, 168
the captivity of Napoleon III and,
183
the Schleswig-Holstein question
and, 104
Vicomte de Gontaut Biron and, 222
von Roon's criticism of, 58
Austria and Prussia, 10, 49, 100
and the German Confederation, 5
and the Prussian conditions of
peace, 114
appeals to Napoleon III., 110
Archduke John of, 2
becomes a pawn in the hands of
Prussia, 112, 115
humiliation of, 108
mobilises against Prussia, 109
position in the new Germany, 2
Prince Felix Schwarzenberg (See
Schwarzenberg)
result of Convention of Olmutz, 14
separation from Germany, 5, 7
strained relations with Prussia, 29
war with Prussia, 109
Austro-German Alliance, the, 245, 257
a pet conception of von Holstein,
264
Austro-German Treaty, the, 237
Austro-Prussian War, an armistice,
111
peace negotiations: Prussia's demands, 113

BADEN hostility to alliance with
Prussia, 153
signs preliminary Treaty of Union,
159

Y

Baden, Grand Duke of, 140, 325
 and Bismarck's dismissal, 342
 and the Imperial title, 202
 hostile to Austria, 145
 on Bismarck, *père et fils*, 337
 on Bismarck's *volte-face*, 329, 330
Bagdad Railway, the, 283
Balkans, the, German fear of Russian
  influence in, 281
 German intrigues in, 232 *et seq.*,
  240, 285, 299
Bavaria, a secret Convention with
  Prussia, 134
 and the lesser States, 11
 complete Prussianisation of, 160
 hatred of Prussia, 195, 197
 negotiations for union with Prussia, 147
 Prussian intrigue in, 139
 sides with Prussia on Luxemburg
  question, 151
 under the heel of Prussia, 159
Bayreuth, 110, 114
Belfort remains French territory, 203,
  204
Benedek, General, a check for, 110
Benedetti, Count, 120
 and the peace recommendations, 114
 interview with William I., 172
 the "insult" at Ems, 179
Berlin, a conference upon Union at
  154
 diplomatic relations with Stuttgart
  broken, 13
 war fever in, 180
 William I. signs order for mobilisation, 180
Berlin Congress, the, 235, 236, 248, 263
Bernstorff, Count, and Queen Augusta,
  59
Bethmann-Hollweg, Dr. Maurice von,
  128
 and Polish independence, 220
Beust, Count von, 9
 Bismarck's hatred of, 191
Biron, Vicomte de Gontaut, 191, 221
 his idea of a Franco-Russian
  rapprochement, 232
Biron von Curland, Princess, 232
Bismarck, Count Herbert von, 276
 a shrewd move by, 337
 an impertinent remark to the Prince
  of Wales, 323

Bismarck, Prince (*contd.*)—
fear of war with France, 114, 119, 205
final interview with Holstein, 347
first diplomatic success of, 83
Frederick III. and, 84
friction with Empress Victoria, 323
growing unpopularity of, 101, 108
his dread of resignation, 300
his son, 306, 333, 337, 342, 350, 356, 357
Holstein and, 243
Holstein's version of his dismissal, 341, 343
Imperialism of, 85, 121
in a rage, 172, 173
in 1887, 299
increasing irritability of, 209, 235, 299
interview with Napoleon III., 24
invited to enter the Cabinet, 56, 63
isolation of, 101
Italy and, 109
Kaiser offers the olive branch, 357
keen psychological instinct of, 199
last days of, 365, 366
last official paper of, 343
memorable sayings of, 52, 60, 107, 196, 264, 285, 352
Minister in Petersburg, 32
Monarchical convictions of, 14, 46, 51, 57
nonplussed, 302
not originator of German Hohenzollern Empire, 6
on "absolute government," 363
on Prince Gortschakov, 38
on the Olmutz Convention, 22
on treaties, 257
opinion of Russia and France, 39
overhears a private conversation, 186
policy of deceit, 185
political début of, 14
presented to Queen Victoria, 29
President of Council of Ministers, 86
private letter to Alexander III, 328
proposes division of German States, 107
Prussian Minister in Paris, 60
rebuffed by Napoleon III, 185
rebukes William II., 326

Bismarck, Prince (*contd*)—
reconciliation with the Kaiser, 357
Reminiscences : a curious chapter, 281
Roman Catholicism and, 217
sarcastic criticism of William II., 339, 361, 362
scheme for welding the Southern States, 137
secret of his power, 52
sensational declaration by, 69-70
serious illness of, 357
signs the Peace Treaty, 121
strained relations with the Crown Prince, 91
suspicion in Russia against, 73
sympathy with, after dismissal, 354
threatens resignation, 258, 259
underhand intrigues of, 131
unexpected firmness of William I., 116
unpublished memoirs of, 37
unscrupulousness at Sedan, 182
unstable character of, 345
Vienna's ovation to, 280
visits Paris Exhibition, 132
von Schleinitz and, 54, 55
withdraws his predecessors' Budget, 69
Bismarck, Princess, author and, 213
Bleichroder, Baron von, 275
Bismarck's frank talk with, 355
criticism of Bismarck, 305
Bloudov, Countess, 40
Blowitz, M de, 229
his article in the *Times*, 230
Bohemia, Germany and, 5
invaded by Prussian troops, 109
Bonjean, Senator, 215
Bosnia ceded to Austria, 235, 236
Boulanger, General, 296
Brest Litovsk, Russian manœuvres at, 360
Bruhl, Countess Hedwig, 327
Buchanan, Sir Andrew, and the Alvenslebem Convention, 82
Bulgaria, candidature of Prince Alexander, 237
matters in, 281 *et seq.*
Bulow, Herr von, a flirtation in Russia, 272
Bismarck on, 365
marriage of, 273

Bunsen, Baron von, a fiery epistle from Count Pourtalès, 18
memoirs of, 5
Buol, Count, an autograph letter from, 36
Busch, Moritz, 343

CAPRIVI, General, an official note to Vienna, 354
Bismarck's sarcastic remarks on, 352
refuses to renew a secret convention with Russia, 351
succeeds Bismarck, 347
Chambord, Comte de, 171
Charlottenburg, Bismarck at, 348
Chaudet, M., 215
Christian IX., King of Denmark, and the Duchy of Schleswig, 102
Christian of Sonderburg Augusten-berg, Duke, 101
Clementine of Coburg, Princess, Holstein and, 286
Constantinople, a German military mission to, 308
Cortès, Donoso, a letter from, 6
Crimean War, the, 29
Bismarck's opinion of, 53
Crispi, Signor, 270
Cronstadt, French fleet at, 297
Customs Union. (See Zollverein)

DALWIGK, Herr, at Union conference, Berlin, 155, 156
Darboy, Archbishop, 215
Decazes, Duc, 225, 228, 232
De Guéry, Père, 215
Delbruck, Councillor, 155
Denmark, Prussia at war with, 104
De Winter, mayor of Dantzig, 88
Donhoff, Countess, marries von Bulow, 274
Dresden Congress, the, 27
Dual Alliance, the, 245, 257 et seq.
entry of Italy into, 270, 279
Duncker, Max, 86

EISENHARDT, Herr von, 200
Elisabeth, Empress, and Andrassy, 255
Ems, William I. and Benedetti's meeting at, 172

Ems dispatch, the, new light on, 166 et seq.
true story of, 174
Espionage, 232, 272 et seq.
inauguration of system, 186 et seq.
Eugénie, Empress, a letter to Alexander II., 192
an unjust accusation against, 180
loss of political influence, 179

Franco-Prussian War (*contd*)—
unscrupulous omission in armistice,
193-4
Franco-Russian Alliance, completion
of, 297
German fears of, 54, 55
inception of, 285
necessity of, 294
Frankfurt, Parliament of, 4, 5
Treaty of, 205
Fransecky, General, 111
Frederick III , Emperor, accession, 305
an audience with Prince Hohenlohe, 161
and Alsace-Lorraine, 304
and the peace proposals, 117
Bismarck and, 84, 321
hatred of war, 117, 162, 163
his father, 84 *et seq.*, 93
his ideal, 318
illness of, 291, 299, 305
Imperialism of, 99, 196, 200, 317
marches on Koniggratz, 109
strictures of, as Crown Prince, 88,
89
the Dantzig incident, 88
the Paris bombardment, 185
the Puttkamer affair, 323
the smaller German States and, 84
Frederick VII., King of Denmark,
death of, 101
Frederick, Empress, Bismarck's visit
to, after his dismissal, 358
leave-taking of Bismarck, 348
Frederick William, Crown Prince
(*See* Frederick III)
Frederick William IV., King of
Prussia, and the insurrection
in Hesse, 15
death of, 55
Frankfurt Parliament and, 1, 2
in a dilemma, 15
offer to Bismarck, 27
the army and, 3, 4
Frederick William of Brandenburg
(the Great Elector), a charge to
his descendants, 125
Freydorf, Herr, at Union Conference,
Berlin, 155, 156

Galicia, Germany and, 5
Gérard, M., Bismarck's hatred of, 211

Gerlach, General von, a letter from
Bismarck, 29
German Confederation, the, and the
Schleswig-Holstein question, 102
Austria and, 5, 7
English statesmen and, 5
reorganisation of, 104
German Empire, proclamation of, 194
Foreign Office, the, 272
German Southern States, the, conferences in Stuttgart, 140
secret treaties with Prussia, 130,
140
Germany, a significant forecast of, 7
a subsidised Press, 267, 303
Bismarck's fears of isolation, 243
Bismarck's ideal, 50
development of militarism, 324
kultur of, 38
monarchical and democratic attitudes of, 1, 2
religious troubles in. (*See Kulturkampf*)
separation of Austria, 5
strained relations with Russia, 235
the dawn of Imperialism, 1 *et seq*
Ciers, M. de, pro-German tendencies
of, 294
Goltz, Baron von, 103
Gonne, Miss Maud, 296
Gortschakov, Prince, and the Treaty
of Paris, 192
Bismarck and, 38
humiliation of, 191
suspicions of Berlin, 127
Covone, General, 109
Gramont, Duc de, 170
a tactless telegram, 174
mistrust of the Empress, 179
Gravelotte, the battlefield of, 204
Great Britain enters Triple Entente,
297
Great Flector, the (*See* Frederick
William of Brandenburg)
Great War, the, ultimatum to Bel-
gium, 254
Guelph fund, the, 198
Guibert, Archbishop, 216

Hahnke, General von, ordered to obtain Bismarck's resignation,
341

Hanover, annexation of, desired by William I., 114

Hanover, King of, denounces the Treaty, 8

Hatzfeld, Bismarck on, 365

Henry of Prussia, Prince, Royal honours to Bismarck, 357

Herzegovina, cession of, 235, 236

Hesse, a history-making insurrection in, 15

annexation of, asked for by William I., 113

Hesse-Darmstadt assents to preliminary Treaty of Union, 159

Hesse, Grand Duke of, and dismissal of Bismarck, 342

Heuduck, Herr, 320

Heydt, von der, and the Zollverein, 157

Hohenlohe, Cardinal, 133

and the *Kulturkampf*, 214

fear of the Jesuits, 217

Hohenlohe, Prince Clovis von, 133 *et seq.*, 258

a curious report to the King of Bavaria, 134

advocates union of Bavaria with Prussia, 146

and Holstein, 190

and the *Kulturkampf*, 214

Bismarck on, 365

Bismarck's ally in Bavaria, 135

concludes a military alliance with Prussia, 134, 160

converses with Waldersee, 335

convinced of necessity of Dual Alliance, 259

discusses Dual Alliance with William I., 260

Governor-General of Alsace-Lorraine, 325

on Commune victims, 215

on de Blowitz' *Times* article, 230

on Russian intrigue in the Balkans, 282

Prussian tendencies of, 134

received by Crown Prince of Prussia, 161

report of Union conference at Berlin, 154-5

resignation of, 146

signs the Treaty of Union, 159

the Luxemburg incident, 149

Ignatieff, Count, 296

Italy, an alliance with Prussia, 109

and the Jesuits, 216, 217

Bismarck and, 109

cession of Venice to, 110

joins the Dual Alliance, 245, 270, 279

Jesuits, the, abolition of the Order in Germany, 214

Jesuits, the (*contd.*)—
notable enemies of, 216
John, Archduke of Austria, 2

KALNOKY, Count, 267
Karolyi, Count, 114
Kiel harbour and canal, 104
Koloschine, M., 225
Koniggratz, battle of, 109
Kulturkampf, the, 133, 212, 214
Empress Augusta and, 212
Kutusoff, General Count, 191

LAZAREFF, Mlle. de, 232
Le Flo, General, 228
Leopold of Hohenzollern and the
Spanish throne, 166 *et seq.*
relinquishes candidature of Spanish
throne, 173
Levinstein, Mr, and Bismarck, 35, 36
Lhyys, M. Drouyn de, 127
London Conference, the, 132, 152, 192
Lucanus, von, 340, 342
Ludwig II., King of Bavaria, 134
a momentous letter from, 146
authorises negotiations for union,
147
Bismarck on a Dual Alliance, 248
hatred of Prussia, 197
refuses to meet the King of Prussia,
160
signs his own "*déchéance,*" 200
tragic death of, 135, 191
Luitpold, Prince, 200
Luxemburg, evacuation of fortress of,
127
inner meaning of the question, 153
Napoleon II's negotiations with
Holland for, 131
neutrality of. a conference in
London, 132, 152, 192
question of cession to Prussia, 24,
127, 149

MACMAHON, Marshal, 232
and the French Ambassador in
Berlin, 226
Manteuffel, Marshal von, 16, 237
Margherita of Savoy, Princess, mar-
riage of, 161
Marschall, Herr von, 348

NAPLES, the King of, and the Jesuits,
216
Napoleon I., Emperor, Bismarck on,
43
Napoleon III., Emperor, a missed opportunity, 110
a prisoner, 183
and Bismarck, 24, 60, 100
and the Franco-German War, 119
apprised of Prussia's conditions of
peace, 113
Bismarck's appreciation of, 29
compromises himself, 120
creates Rhine Confederation, 126
desires a Franco-Prussian alliance,
60
indiscretion of, 62
mistrust of Austria, 61, 62
rebuffs Bismarck, 185
regrettable weakness of, 179
the Hohenzollern candidature for
Spanish throne, 172, 174
Nesselrode, Count de, Bismarck and,
34
Neundorff, Mdlle. von, 211
Nicholas I, Tsar, interviews Emperor
Francis Joseph, 15

Nicholas II., Tsar, and disarmament, 318

Nikolsburg, a Peace Council at, 115
  Convention of, 110, 112
  the Treaty of, 21

Nordeck, Councillor von, 155

North German Confederation, a provisional arrangement, 195
  organisation of, 126
  reorganised, 131

Nothomb, Baron de, 226

Obolensky, Princess, 223

Oldenburg, Prince Peter of, 191

Olivain, Père, 215

Ollivier, Emile, 174
  and the consort of Napoleon III., 179

Olmutz, Convention of, 14
  a sequel to, 18, 21
  Bismarck's view of, 22
  Prussia's humiliation, 17

Orloff, Prince Alexis, at the Congress of Paris, 73

Orloff, Princess, 73
  criticism of Bismarck by, 74
  German sympathies of, 74

Palmerston, Lord, 5
  on the Schleswig-Holstein question, 101

Paris, Congress of, 73
  Exhibition (1867), the, William I.'s visit to, 132
  fall of, 193
  siege of, 184, 191, 193
  Treaty of, revision asked by Russia, 191

Peel, Sir Robert, 5

Perponcher, Count, and the Luxemburg Treaty, 151

Peter of Oldenburg, Prince, 191

Philipsborn, Councillor, 155

Plevna, fall of, 236

Pobedonostseff, M , 296

Podbielski, General, 186

Polish mutiny of 1863, the, 82
  question, the, 219
  the *Kulturkampf* and, 212

Posen, the Poles of, 220

Pourtalès, Count Albert, on the Olmutz Convention, 18

Reichsanzeiger, the, Imperial communications in, 353

Reichstadt Convention and the cession of Bosnia and Herzegovnia, 235, 236

Religious persecutions in Germany. (*See Kulturkampf*)

Reuss, Prince Henry of, 140, 290
  a letter to Prince Hohenlohe, 141

Rhine Confederation, the, creation of, 126

Roman Catholic Church. (*See Kulturkampf*)

Roon, General von, 186
  and Bismarck, 55, 173
  and the bombardment of Paris, 184
  displeasure at Bismarck's "witty digressions," 75

Rosty, Chevalier, 241
  on the Triple Alliance, 267

Roumania, independence of, 236

Russia and Prussia, 33 *et seq.*
  and the Berlin Congress, 266
  asks for revision of Treaty of Paris, 191
  Bismarck's fear of, 27, 248
  coronation of Tsar, 239
  German hostility towards, 236
  German influence in the Court of, 37
  strained relations with Germany, 235
  suspicion of Bismarck in, 73
  the Dual Alliance treachery to, 264

Russell, Lord John, 5

Russell, Lord Odo, 227

Rzewuski, Count, on Bismarck, 40, 44, 49
  on the Convention of Olmutz, 18

SADOWA, a sequel to the Olmutz Convention, 18, 21
  battle of, 109

Sagan, Duke and Duchess of, 222

St. Privat, the battlefield of, 204

San Remo affair, the, 327

San Stefano, Treaty of, 236

Saxe-Coburg, Grand Duke of, and Bismarck's dismissal, 342

Saxe-Weimar, Grand Duke of, 192

Saxony and the Convention of 1850, 11
  annexation of, desired by William I , 110, 114

VALLEY, Count Arco, 241

Varnbuler, Herr von, 140, 148
  at Union Conference, Berlin, 155, 156
  visits Hohenlohe, 155

Venice ceded to Italy, 110

Versailles, proclamation of German Empire at, 194
  Prussian headquarters, 184

Victor Emmanuel, King, and the Jesuits, 216
  dispatches a military mission to Berlin, 109

Victoria, Empress, a request to Bismarck, 205
  the San Remo incident, 327

Victoria of Prussia, Princess, question of betrothal of, 322

Victoria, Queen of Great Britain and Ireland, Bismarek's presentation to, 29
  Frederick III.'s consultation with, 322

Vienna, a suppressed book in, 23
  Bismarck refused audience of Francis Joseph in, 354
  Bismarck's ovation in, 280

Vienna, Congress of, question of precedence, 201

Vienna, Treaty of, and the Prussian frontiers, 70

Virchow, Herr, 102

Vitzthum of Eckstadt, Count, 127

WADDINGTON, M., Empress Augusta's query to, 301

Wagner, Richard, Ludwig II. and 238

Waldemar of Denmark, Princess, 291

Waldersee, General von, 324
  Hohenlohe's chat with, 335

Wallace, Donald Mackenzie, 240

Weber, Councillor, 155

Wellington, the Duke of, advice to Hanover and Saxony, 9

Werder, General von, and the neutrality of Germany, 236

Werthern, Baron, 141, 149, 150
  William I. irritated with, 174

William I., Emperor, a snub for Benedetti, 175
  accepts a "shameful peace," 117

"

William II., Emperor (*contd.*)—
  disagreements with Bismarck, 332
  dismisses Bismarck, 306, 340, 341
  imprudent confidences of, 339
  in power, 317 *et seq.*
  rebuked by Bismarck, 326
  reconciliation with Bismarck, 357
  unfilial letters of, 357
  unpopularity as Prince, 320
William of Hohenzollern, Prince, 55
Wimpfen, General, 183
Wincke, Herr von, 143
Windhorst, chief of Catholic party, 339

Wittgenstein, Countess Caroline, 217
Wittgenstein, Princess Leonille, 221
Wrangel, Field-Marshal, 143
Wurtemberg, hostility to alliance with Prussia, 153
  signs preliminary Treaty of Union 159
  the Convention of 1850, 11
Wurtemberg, King of, a momentous speech by, 12

ZOLLVEREIN, the, 142
  discussed at Union conference, 155

PRINTED BY
CASSELL & COMPANY, LIMITED
LA BELLE SAUVAGE, LONDON, E.C.4
F 15.617